PLA[...]

Titus Maccius Plautus (25[...]
most successful playwright [...]
influential comic author of all time.

Like Shakespeare and Molière, he began his
career as an actor in popular farces, which undoubt-
edly sharpened his unique sense of what made
audiences laugh. Plautus' achievement is particularly
remarkable since he is the earliest Roman author
extant. His rise to fame coincided almost precisely
with Rome's rise to world dominance.

Plautus transformed the sedate, sentimental drama
of Hellenistic Greece into boisterous musical farce,
tailored to please the rough-hewn Romans of his day.
In his comedies the strict, puritanical Roman social
order is temporarily turned topsy-turvy—and the lowly
slave reigns supreme.

Shakespeare's *Comedy of Errors* is an adaptation of
The Brothers Menaechmus (in this volume). Molière
imitated Plautus in *The Miser, Amphytrion,* and
elsewhere. Moreover, the huge success of *A Funny
Thing Happened on the Way to the Forum* (a combination of several comedies) proves Plautus is still very
much alive on Broadway and in Hollywood.

This trio of his best plays has been translated by a
Plautine scholar of international repute. The *American
Journal of Philology* has described Yale professor
Erich Segal as "a writer with a vivid theatrical imagination who can devise good stage directions for his
translations and turn out dialogue with the proper
lively ring."

"Excellent translations."
—J. N. Hough, *Classical World*

"Extremely successful in catching the sense and
following the meter."
—Edmund Wilson

Bantam Classics
Ask your bookseller for these other World Classics

Plautus:
Three Comedies

The Braggart Soldier,
The Brothers Menaechmus,
The Haunted House

Translated from the Latin,
with an introduction and notes, by
Erich Segal

BANTAM BOOKS

TORONTO · NEW YORK · LONDON · SYDNEY · AUCKLAND

PLAUTUS: THREE COMEDIES

A Bantam Book / published by arrangement with the Translator

PRINTING HISTORY

First published by Harper & Row 1969
Bantam Classic edition / January 1985

Cover art, "Marble Relief of a Comedy Scene," courtesy of Archeological Museum of Naples. Photographed by Fotografia Foglia, Naples.

ISBN 0-553-21169-2

Published simultaneously in the United States and Canada

PRINTED IN THE UNITED STATES OF AMERICA

O   0 9 8 7 6 5 4 3 2 1

Contents

Preface to the Bantam Edition

One evening in the summer of 1962, I saw an Italian translation of Plautus' *Casina* convulse a huge audience at the Stadio di Domiziano in Rome. Until that time, like so many academics, I had regarded Plautus as merely a name in literary history: a good man long ago, the best comic author in *ancient* Rome. That night I learned otherwise. Good old Plautus is still flourishing wherever great professional clowns do his comedy justice.

My first attempt at Plautine translation was *The Braggart Soldier*, which, to my amazement and delight, actually made people laugh when it was played at the Harvard Loeb Drama Center in 1963. Encouraged by requests from teachers and directors, I subsequently rendered two other comedies that I regarded to be among the playwright's best: his *Menaechmi* and *Mostellaria*.

When the trio of plays was ready for publication, my Yale colleagues Thomas Cole and Kenneth Cavander read and corrected the manuscript, while Hugh Lloyd-Jones, of Oxford, reassured me on what he termed "justifiable conjectures."

The occasion of this Bantam reprint enabled me to make further revisions, and I am grateful to Walter Moskalew for his many suggestions. I have also benefited from seeing these plays produced, most recently by Richard Beecham at the University of Warwick, in England.

These productions reassured me that Plautus is still alive and well and—I dare to hope—also living in the pages of this book.

E.S.

Department of Classics
Yale University
May 1984

Introduction

Late September in early Rome c. 200 B.C. It is the autumn Harvest Festival, and the natives are restless. Many thousands of rough and rowdy Romans mill about, bored by the ceremonies they have been obliged to sit (or stand) through, half of them drunk, the other half wishing they were.[1] On a crude stage which has been thrown together for the occasion, an actor appears. He shouts desperately for silence, hoping to turn the unruly mob into something resembling an audience. Then he speaks the magic words:

"I bring you Plautus!"[2]

Suddenly, sweet silence. From the thousandth row, you can hear a pun drop.

The very name of Plautus meant belly laughs, charm, wit, song—in a word, entertainment. Plautus knew what they wanted and how they liked it. He gave his public not only enough, but *too much*, which is the quintessence of all that evokes laughter.[3] To approximate Plautine musical comedy in modern terms, you would need the combined talents of Cole Porter, Rodgers and Hart, and John Lennon—with a little help from his friends. The combination sounds unlikely, if not downright impossible, and serves to explain why Rome, so prolific in other ways (viz., two Catos, two Scipios, Caesars by the dozen), could produce but one Plautus. There were attempts to reproduce his

---

1. Horace, *Ars Poetica,* line 224: *Spectator, functusque sacris et potus et exlex.*
2. *The Brothers Menaechmus,* line 3.
3. Cf. Max Eastman, *The Enjoyment of Laughter* (New York, 1936), p. 150: "It is the *too* much—always and absolutely—not the *much* which is funny."

style. Plautus was not only imitated, he was even forged: soon after his death comedies "by Plautus" began to appear in large number. Imitation may be a form of flattery, but forgery is the supreme tribute. Still, Plautus was, in every way, inimitable.

He was also the first known professional playwright. Aristophanes was an amateur in the sense that he did not have to write for a living. With Plautus, however, the notion of his next play and his next meal were inextricably intertwined. Like Shakespeare and Molière (both of whom wrote in what may be described as "the Plautine tradition"), the theater was his career, his life, and his livelihood. Terence, that other Roman playwright with whom Plautus' name is so incongruously linked,[4] simply did not stand up in the theater. But Terence's audience did. In fact, they stood up and walked out.[5]

What little we know of his biography does not help to explain how Titus Maccius Plautus rose from humble origins in Sarsina in the north of Italy[6] to become what a later Roman writer eulogized as "the glory of the Latin tongue."[7] In 254 B.C., the generally accepted date for Plautus' birth, Rome was still a relatively insignificant nation. But she was in the midst of the first of her three wars with Carthage, a powerful Phoenician colony in Africa. The prize was the Mediterranean world, and it did not take the Romans long to win it. By the time Plautus was in his teens, conquered Sicily had become the first Roman province. With Sicily's wealth and strategic position came an extra benefit: culture. From at least the sixth century B.C., it had been a highly civilized island, where all the arts had flourished, especially the drama. In Sicily, for the very first time, the Roman soldiers saw theaters.

The first Punic War ended in 241 B.C. In 240 the first play was produced in Rome at the autumn Harvest Festival (ludi Romani). It was a Latin adaptation of a Greek tragedy, done by a captured slave named Livius Andronicus.[8] The following year, Livius adapted both a comedy and a tragedy, and thus a tradition began: each year

---

4. Terence (c. 195–159 B.C.) has left us six Latin comedies more or less in the Menandrian tradition. The fact that he enjoyed popular success only once (with the Eunuchus, his most Plautine play) did not matter so much to him, since he was a protégé of the so-called Scipionic circle and did not have to write plays for a living.
5. See the prologue to Terence's Hecyra, especially lines 29ff.
6. See Mostellaria, line 770, and my note, p. 259.
7. Aulus Gellius, Noctes Atticae, 19.8.6: Plautus, linguae Latinae decus.
8. The early history of the Roman theater is sketched by Livy, 7.2.

at the Harvest Festival the holidaying Romans would see stage plays translated/adapted/debased[9] from Greek originals. Plautus wrote in this tradition—he made his debut at some unknown occasion after 215. Since Livius Andronicus survives merely in fragments, Titus Maccius Plautus also owns the distinction of being the earliest extant Latin author. We still have 20 of his comedies, more or less complete (he may have composed as many as 130, and "doctored" others). This is nearly twice as many comedies as Aristophanes left behind. In fact, no ancient author—including Euripides—bequeathed more dramas to the modern world.

What were the Greek models rendered by the Roman dramatists? As might be expected, the sources for Latin tragedy were mainly Sophocles and Euripides. But what bears some explanation is the fact that the models for Latin comedy were *not* Aristophanic. In fact, what is commonly known as Aristophanic comedy was already dead while Aristophanes himself was still living.

As we look back at Classical Greek literature, we distinguish between two very different types of comedy. First, the so-called Old Comedy, those wild, bawdy, lyrical-satirical choral extravaganzas, whose most famous (but by no means only) practitioner was Aristophanes (c. 448–c. 380 B.C.). For various and complex reasons, this genre did not survive the fall of Athens in 404 B.C. Old Comedy did not fade away; it just died. The so-called New Comedy that then took the stage was radically different: it was typical, atopical, polite, apolitical. It had neither chorus, nor songs, nor "jokes" as such. In fact "Aristotle-on-Comedy" compares the two genres by noting that Old Comedy overemphasized laughter, and New Comedy disregarded it.[10]

New Comedy presented stock characters in stock situations. Its locale was the city, its people the bourgeoisie, its plots romantic: boy meets/wants/has previously raped girl. Its whole milieu was at once realistic (no Birds or Clouds on stage), and yet removed from reality. Reading Greek New Comedy, we have no notion that during the time of its composition the Hellenistic world was torn constantly by war and strife. The tears it sheds are only those of the lover,

---

9. Check one, according to your critical bias.
10. The *Tractatus Coislinianus*, a document considered by some to epitomize Aristotle's (lost) views on comedy. See Lane Cooper, *An Aristotelian Theory of Comedy*, New York, 1922, p. 226.

sighing like a furnace. Plays may begin with an outrage—to a maiden, long ago, in the dark—but all always ends well; Jack marries Jill. The final chord is always one of apology and conciliation. A tame contrast with the Aristophanic finales, which usually conclude by celebrating the triumph of unrepentant outrage!

The only New Comedy author who has left us anything but fragments is the legendary Menander (c. 342–292 B.C.). He was made a legend by legions of ancient critics (none contemporary with him) who celebrated him as the nonpareil of civilized comedy. To the Roman scholar Quintilian, Menander was perfection itself, in speech, in character analysis, and in his portrait of life.[11] Plutarch enthusiastically lauds Menander's polish and his "salt."[12] This kind of praise has been reechoed through the ages. Menander is never acclaimed for his hilarity, and judging by extant Menandrian drama,[13] he was no laugh riot. Rather, his plays presented a series of polished, sedate character studies of the Hellenistic leisure class. They were essentially unmusical (there were some choral entr'actes) and uncomic (no gags). Perhaps some of Menander's colleagues, such as Philemon or Diphilus,[14] were funnier, but it is unlikely that their comedy remotely resembled the broad musical farce of Old Comedy. Suffice it for us to note here that when the Romans looked for Greek comedies to adapt, Aristophanes was completely out of sight.[15]

Whatever his colleagues or successors may have done, Plautus himself did not produce literal translations of New Comedy. Scholars have long debated the precise nature—and worth—of Plautus' changes, but it is fairly safe to state that he transformed what was simple metrical dialogue in the Greek to multimetrical song in the Latin; he added gags where there were none in the original; he poured on a plenitude of puns (there are virtually none at all in

11. Quintilian, *Institutio Oratoria*, 10.69.

12. Plutarch, *Moralia*, 347 E.

13. We have large fragments of several plays, as well as the *Dyskolos* ("Sour-tempered Man"), discovered entire in the mid-1950s, and first edited by Victor Martin in 1958. Hugh Lloyd-Jones's Oxford text was published in 1960.

14. See *Mostellaria*, lines 1149ff., and my note, p. 291.

15. The "influence" (if any) of Aristophanes on Plautus is a subject which needs further study. The classicist is referred to A. M. G. Little, "Plautus and Popular Drama," *Harvard Studies in Classical Philology*, 49 (1938), pp. 205ff. In "Nota Plautina," *Maia*, 6 (1953), pp. 302ff., Benedetto Marzullo argues for certain specific parallels between Aristophanes and Plautus, concluding with a plea that this aspect of Plautus be examined in more depth.

Menander). If he did not always change the plots (he sometimes did), he would at least emphasize those aspects and characters that amused him most. The prologue to his *Casina* illustrates this: the "title character," the maiden Casina, will not appear during the play. Nor, adds the prologue, will the young man who is in love with her. The reason? *Plautus noluit* (line 65), "Plautus didn't want to." In other words, there was in Plautine adaptation an exercise of some artistic volition. In the *Casina* the Roman playwright was far more interested in presenting the misadventures of the libidinous old codger, which he does hilariously. Youthful romance? *Plautus noluit.*

Where did Plautus get the impulse for the melodies and broad farce which he added to his sedate models? The most obvious answer is from his own genius, and this is quite true. But there had always been at Rome a native type of subliterary comedy, known as the *fabulae Atellanae*, or Atellan farces, named after the Campanian village of Atella, where the genre probably originated. This crude entertainment presented little skits with stock low-life characters like Bucco, the babbling fool; Pappus, the foolish old codger; Dossenus, the hunchback buffoon; and Maccus, another type of simple fool. The spirit of these lusty, mob-pleasing farces pervades Plautine comedy.

The playwright at one time may well have been an actor in one of these troupes. Certainly his *nomen,* Maccius, bears a suspicious resemblance to one of the Atellan types, and his *cognomen* has been translated by some scholars as "flatfoot,"[16] which may also suggest a previous career in baggy tunics. His ancient biography states enigmatically that early in his life Plautus made a fortune in some kind of "show business," *in operis artificum scaenicorum.*[17] It is a happy idea to imagine our author in a band of strolling players. It would certainly help to explain his unique instinct for crowd pleasing.

The two sources of Plautine style parallel the two strains which blended to become Molière's special comedy. The critic Boileau rather snobbishly criticized Molière for combining the high and low comic styles, complaining that in *Les Fourberies de Scapin* he "joined Terence and Tabarin," that is, he forced (Italian) *commedia dell' arte* to stand side by side with (Latin) classics. Without the

---

16. Originally, "Plautus" may well have been "Plotus," meaning "flatfoot," another clownish nickname.
17. Plautus' biography is preserved by Aulus Gellius, *Noctes Atticae,* 3.3.14.

depreciatory tone, we may paraphrase Boileau to state that Plautus "joined Athens and Atella." As in the case of Molière's combination, it was a good match.

Despite the Italian-Atellan touches just mentioned, Plautus' comedy still alleges to be Attic. In fact it protests—too much, of course— that it is Greek (see the absurd pronouncement by the prologue to *The Brothers Menaechmus,* lines 7ff.). Plautus' characters all pretend they are Greeks, usually living in Athens or the vicinity. The Roman playwright makes a good deal of comic hay out of this pretense. When his characters are living it up, they claim to be "Greeking it up,"[18] a notion which has special reverberations for the Roman audience. The citizens of the early Roman republic were a puritanical folk, prim, proper, abstemious and reserved, who despised the Greeks for their dissolute ways. There is, then, an extra comic dividend added when the Roman comedy hell-raisers are Hellenic. A famous example of Plautus' "Greek irony" is the moment when the slave Stichus, in the process of arranging a little dinner party, breaks the dramatic illusion to assure the Romans that slaves *could* behave this way in far-off Greece: "We're allowed to do this sort of thing at Athens" (*Stichus,* line 448). But Plautus' Athens was no farther from Rome than Beaumarchais's Seville was from Paris. Unlike Beaumarchais, or Montesquieu in the *Lettres Persanes,* where Persian means Parisian, Plautus intends no satire. His only target is the funny bone.

What of Plautus' style? We have already alluded to his songs. His was the first truly "musical" comedy since the lyrics of Aristophanes had been replaced by the mundane iambics of New Comedy. Plautus was not the only Roman writer to add melody to a simpler text.[19] The operatic impulse seems to have been part of the Italian

---

18. The verb *pergraecari* is used in the *Mostellaria,* lines 22, 64, 960—and in other Plautine comedies. Sometimes Plautus expresses it by *congraecare (Bacchides,* line 743), a similar verb which we may translate as "Greek around." Both these terms influenced the Elizabethan stereotype of a "Merry Greeke"—one who acted frivolously and partied-up.

19. Eduard Fraenkel asserted that, among others, Ennius (239–169 B.C.), in adapting Roman tragedy from Greek models, changed Greek dialogue into Latin lyric, and vice versa (*Plautinisches im Plautus,* now revised by the author and translated into Italian by Franco Munari as *Elementi Plautini in Plauto,* Florence, 1960, pp. 325ff.). The historian Livy, in discussing primitive Roman drama (7.2), mentions a *satura* ("variety show") with assorted rhythmical music.

character from the very beginning.[20] As Plautus developed in the theater, he tended to add more and more songs to his plays. This is, in fact, one method employed by scholars to date his comedies. *The Braggart Soldier*, included in this volume, has no lyrics, and its simple metrical scheme suggests a date of composition early in Plautus' career.[21] *The Brothers Menaechmus* and the *Mostellaria* each have five songs and were doubtless written later on, when Plautus was becoming more Plautine.

Nor, since Aristophanes, had a theater audience heard such vivacious verbal abandon. What a language Plautus' characters speak! Unlike the simple, forthright (good old Roman) style championed by Plautus' conservative contemporary Cato the Elder,[22] his dialogue is purple, but not blue; it is racy, but not dirty. He is repetitive, mock elegant, mock heroic, mock everything. He invents all sorts of delicious new words. As one of his slave characters—surely speaking for his creator—expresses it, *Nil moror vetera et volgata verba* (*Epidicus*, line 350), "To hell with dated, dissipated diction!" Note the alliteration, by the way, a very Roman touch.

Plautus' verbal extravagance ranges from the super-superlative like:

Occisissumus sum omnium qui vivont!
(*Casina*, line 694)
I'm the very dead-dead-deadest man alive!

or Menaechmus' complaint that he is the most "kicked-out" man in the world (line 698, page 167) to the mini-diminutive, such as his famous description of a lovers' embrace:

Papillarum horridularum oppressiunculae.
(*Pseudolus*, line 68)
Touchie-clutchie, itty-bitty-pretty-titty.

---

20. The "melodic urge" inherent in the Roman character has recently been discussed by my colleague Thomas Cole, "Opera in Ancient Rome," *Ventures* (Magazine of the Yale Graduate School) (Spring 1967), pp. 35ff.

21. In the *Braggart*, one brief interlude of anapests ("Aristophanic" or "Gilbertian" meter), lines 1011–1093, interrupts the very simple iambics and trochees. The chief arguments tracing Plautus' development through his increasing use of lyrics are by W. B. Sedgwick. Cf. "The Dating of Plautus' Plays," *Classical Quarterly*, 24 (1930), pp. 102ff.

22. Cato the Censor (234–149 B.C.), stern watch-and-warder over Roman morals, coined this phrase as a formula for Roman speaking style: *Rem tene, verba sequuntur*, "Just stick to the subject, words follow." Plautus, on the other hand, sticks to the words—as many as possible.

Plautus did not "invent" any new comic characters, but he certainly developed certain types with enormous zest and skill. The most vivid are those characters who are in some way the enemies of *la dolce vita:* greedy pimps (Plautus has a whole gallery, the most infamous being Ballio in the *Pseudolus*); bitchy wives (Plautus has a whole henhouse: Mrs. Menaechmus has plenty of company). Then there are the silly old codgers, credulous dupes like Theopropides in the *Mostellaria,* or senile Romeos like Lysidamus in the *Casina.* Clearly, the farcical types are emphasized. Menander sketched; Plautus painted with broad strokes.

But, without a doubt, his most brilliant—and favorite—character is the clever slave. This type did not originate with Plautus (Xanthias in Aristophanes' *Frogs* is a witty bondsman), but never before did the scheming servant take center stage.[23] Pseudolus and Epidicus in the comedies which bear their names, Palaestrio in *The Braggart Soldier,* and Tranio in the *Mostellaria* are all comic catalysts. They are the stars of their shows. If Greek New Comedy is essentially about love,[24] Plautine comedy is essentially about trickery, the *malitia* or "shrewdness" that is celebrated in the brief epilogue to the *Epidicus* (lines 732–733):[25]

> *Hic is homo est qui libertatem* malitia *invenit sua*
> *plaudite et valete. Lumbos porgite atque exsurgite.*

Here's a lad who won his freedom, making good by being bad. Now applaud, arise and stretch. Go home—we've nothing more to add.

The fact that the Roman slave who groveled at the lowest rung of everyday society reigns supreme in Plautus epitomizes the topsy-turvy, Saturnalian quality of his comedy, just the right atmosphere for a Roman holiday.

A thousand handbooks and a million footnotes testify to the

---

23. See the chapter on this subject in Fraenkel's book (cited above in note 19), pp. 223ff.

24. There is Ovid's famous description of Menandrian drama (*Tristia,* 2.369):
Fabula iucundi nulla est sine amore Menandri.

Never did charming Menander write a play without love in it.

25. *Malitia* is not unlike the Greek *poneria,* "resourceful craftiness," which Cedric Whitman considers the distinguishing quality of the Aristophanic protagonist. Cf. his *Aristophanes and the Comic Hero* (Cambridge, Mass., 1964), pp. 30ff.

influence of Plautus throughout the ages.[26] Masters of comedy have increasingly filched from the storehouse of Plautine fun. As recently as 1962, *A Funny Thing Happened on the Way to the Forum* had them rolling in the Broadway aisles the same way Plautus had them in the Roman aisles—and with the very same jokes! Yet, strangely enough, though Plautus' verve and gaiety brightened the stages of countless nations, it could not keep the Roman theater alive after his death. The epigram which marks Plautus' passing well describes the state of Roman Comedy after 184 B.C.:

> *Postquam est mortem aptus Plautus, comoedia luget.*
> *Scaena est deserta, dein risus ludus jocusque*
> *Et numeri innumeri simul omnes conlacrimarunt.*

When the playwright Plautus died,
Comedy broke down and cried.
Then the stage was empty, then all Laughter, Games and Fun
And all his boundless bouncy rhythms—wept as one.

---

26. There is a vast, exhaustive study on Plautine influence by Karl von Reinhardtstoettner, *Plautus: Spätere Bearbeitungen plautinischer Lustspiele* (Leipzig, 1886). All but the super-specialist, however, should be satisfied by the concluding portions of George Duckworth's *The Nature of Roman Comedy* (Princeton, 1952), pp. 396–433 (also Bibliography, pp. 461–464), which cover the later tradition of Plautus in ample detail.

About the Translations and the Text

The renderings are line for line; the Latin text is indicated in the introduction to each play. As far as English allows, I tried to approximate the meter of Plautus. This was a relatively easy task for *The Braggart Soldier:* I merely wrote English lines in iambs and trochees (and in one spot anapests), to correspond to the Latin. I did likewise for the iambic and trochaic lines of the other two comedies, but the meter of their songs only remotely resembles the polymetric lyrics of the Plautine original. In other words, I took a few rhythmic liberties—else the task of translation would have been impossibly complicated.

There is no rhyme in the original Latin (except, perhaps, such rare instances as *Menaechmi,* lines 595ff.), but I have added it where it might be called for in the analogous situation on the English-speaking stage. The prologues are an obvious example. Also, to emphasize Plautus' ternary crescendos like

> *Sine ultro veniat; quaeritet, desideret, expectet*
> (*Miles Gloriosus,* line 1244)

I have rhymed as follows:

Do let her come unbidden, sir: to yearn, to burn, to wait her turn.

On rare occasions, a metaphor has been altered, but always in the service of Plautus' joke. I have zealously tried to avoid anachronisms, and where the dialogue sounds very snappy and modern, I have added footnotes to assure the reader he is getting the real ancient stuff.

I have *not* divided the plays into acts and scenes, for there is no evidence that Plautus himself did so. The divisions we see in modern editions were only made in 1500 by L. B. Pius. Since these translations are also made to be acted, I have suggested where logical intermissions might be placed.[1] There are no stage directions in the ancient manuscripts. Those included here are one translator's intuitive guesses.

With the few exceptions that are signaled below, the translations in this volume were based on the following Latin editions:

For *Miles Gloriosus* the text of Leo-Nixon in the Loeb Classical Library, with assistance from the notes in the school edition by M. Hammond, A. Mack, and W. Moskalew (Cambridge, Mass., 1963).

The *Menaechmi* and *Mostellaria* were based on the texts of W. M. Lindsay (Oxford, 1904). Points in the former were elucidated by the edition of N. Moseley and M. Hammond (Cambridge, Mass., rev. ed., 1968). The edition of the latter comedy by E. Sonnenschein (Oxford, 2nd ed., 1907, rep. 1966) still proved enormously useful. At times the Belles Lettres edition of A. Ernout helped to explain a few puzzling passages.

Miles

Page 49, line 584: Favoring Tyrrell's suggestion of *capitulo* for *populo impio*.

Page 53, line 658: With Lindsay et al., reading *O lepidum semisenem*.

Page 67, line 894: With Ernout, preferring *mala mulier mers*.

Page 75, line 997: *Bitant* for *bitat*.

line 1000: Redistributing the lines as in Ernout.

Page 105, line 1337: With Lindsay et al., reading Palaestrio's line as *Fio miser*.

Page 108, line 1365: With Ernout, Tyrrell, giving line to Pyrgopolynices.

---

1. Interestingly enough, each of the three plays in this volume has a very natural break just about halfway through. Perhaps this requires further scholarly investigation.

Menaechmi

Page 130, line 152–153: *Pulchre habeamus* for *sepulcrum habeamus*.

Page 143: Line 333 redivided.

Page 159, line 613: Line 614 after line 619, following Kiessling, whom Ernout accepts.

Page 180, line 914: Line 914 bracketed by Lindsay.

Mostellaria

Page 224: Lines 286, 290–291 bracketed. See Ernout ad loc.

Page 226: Lines 306–307 omitted. See Sonnenschein ad loc.

Page 244, lines 537–538: Lacuna in lines 537–538 conjectured.

Page 250: Lines 622ff. redistributed as in Leo, Ernout, Sonnenschein.

Page 252, line 645: As in Sonnenschein.

Page 266: Lines 864–866 omitted (fragmentary).

Page 282: Lines 1055–1060 are fragmentary.

The Braggart Soldier

(Miles Gloriosus)

for David Segal

Rogitabant "hicine Achilles est?" inquit mihi.
"Immo eius frater" inquam "est." Ibi illarum altera
"ergo mecastor pulcher est! . . ."

(lines 60–62)

About the Play

The Braggart Soldier does not begin with a prologue. It opens instead with one of the touchstones of comic literature: the hero discussing himself (who else?) with a hired admirer. This is a classic confrontation between *alazon* and *eiron,* the quintessential comic opposites originally described by Aristotle in the *Nicomachean Ethics.*[1] The *alazon* is the overstater, the bluffer, the great balloon of hot air. *Alazoneia,* braggadocio, has been aptly described as the comic counterpart of *hubris,* tragic pride. In contrast, the *eiron* is, as the word suggests, the *ironic* man, the understater, the needle of "I know nothing" which pricks the balloon of the *alazon*'s "I know everything."[2] In all of ancient literature, the greatest *eiron* is Plato's Socrates; the greatest *alazon* is Plautus' Pyrgopolynices.

In a scene of but seventy-nine lines, the Braggart Soldier's outrageous character is exposed to an audience who will wait anxiously through more than half the play to see him reappear. Pyrgopolynices ("terrific tower taker")[3] boasts of such mammoth exploits as having crushed (exactly) seven thousand men in a single day (line 45), also

---

1. Aristotle, *Nicomachean Ethics,* 4.7.
2. In discussing this comic process, we are reminded of Shaw's *Man and Superman,* where Ann punctures the pomposity of Jack Tanner, who, at one point described by Shaw in a stage direction, "collapses like a pricked balloon."
3. There may be a pun on the soldier's (Greek) name in line 1055: "noble king-killer, *sacker of cities.*" As for his boast of killing exactly seven thousand of the foe in a single fray, he is outdone by another of Plautus' boastful warriors, who (in the *Poenulus,* lines 470ff.) claims to have done away with sixty thousand "flying men" (*homines volatici*). He must have had an especially good day.

3

of punching an elephant to smithereens, a behemoth exploit (line 28). He is vain about his attractiveness to women. When his slave suggests that one of his female admirers may be compared in beauty to himself, the soldier can only remark: "Oh, how gorgeous" (line 968).[4] He is also a bit of a parvenu, anxious to drop names of such friends as *King* Seleucus (cf. lines 75, 77, 948–951). In his own way, Pyrgopolynices is the ancestor of Molière's Monsieur Jourdain.

As the soldier struts off to the forum, the tricky slave Palaestrio enters to deliver a long and complicated expository prologue. A fine trick of Plautus' it was to give the audience five minutes of funny dialogue before inflicting upon them the convolutions of plot. Not that Plautus originated the delayed prologue (although he uses it again in his *Cistellaria*); the technique was also practiced by Menander.[5] Palaestrio has lots of complicated story to convey. In "good old Athens," the Braggart Soldier kidnaped his master's girl friend.[6] Loyal slave that he was, Palaestrio set out in pursuit, only to be kidnaped by pirates and given as a gift to none other than the Braggart himself, who had by this time rented a mansion in Ephesus, to set up hausfrau-keeping with the kidnaped girl. By chance, the soldier's mansion is *right next door* to that of an old family friend of Palaestrio's Athenian master. Clearly, the long arm of Fate has a boardinghouse reach. Greek New Comedy dealt constantly with the chance workings of Chance. In this prologue, Plautus mocks the convention.[7]

The *Braggart* is an early play, and Palaestrio is the prototype for such tricky Plautine servants as Pseudolus and Tranio (in the *Mostellaria*). In the prologue he outlines but one of two "mighty machinations" he will set working. This "architect"[8] has cut a passage in the common wall between the two houses, and thus

---

4. This splendid egotism is caught by Stephen Sondheim in one of his lyrics to *A Funny Thing Happened on the Way to the Forum*, when he has a character *named* Miles Gloriosus sing, "I am my Ideal."

5. For example in *The Shearing of Glycera*.

6. "Girl friend" is both anachronistic and inaccurate. "Mistress" is rather Victorian and does not suit a lovely young thing like Philocomasium. *But she is not your sister either.* Since she can be "owned," she is clearly some sort of slave. She is not a pay-as-you-go courtesan like Acroteleutium. We have problems of vocabulary here, not of sociology. I trust the reader will make the necessary adjustments of sensibility.

7. The prologue to the Menander comedy mentioned in note 5 constantly repeats, "It just happened by chance that . . ."

8. Cf. lines 901, 902, 915ff., 1139.

Pleusicles, his Athenian master (newly arrived in Ephesus), can meet in secret with his beloved—kidnaped—sweetheart. This particular hole-in-the-wall is much more satisfying than the one that accommodated Pyramus and Thisbe. As her name suggests, the young girl—Philocomasium, ''lover of revelry''—is the pleasure principle personified. She and Pleusicles are constantly hugging and embracing. In fact, their tireless urge to neck almost undoes them in the finale.

When one of the soldier's slaves happens to spy the young lovers, Palaestrio must convince this thick-witted bondsman that he did not see Philocomasium, but her sister, who *just happened* to arrive in Ephesus the night before. To substantiate this claim, Palaestrio trains the girl to impersonate her own twin sister; by dashing through the hole-in-the-wall, she can appear from either doorway. The twin joke proved successful for Plautus; he presents it again in the *Menaechmi,* where two brothers unwittingly play one (here one girl plays two), and in the *Amphitryon,* where Mercury becomes the slave Sosia's twin and ''steals'' his identity.

All this masquerading scares off the silly slave who had spied on the lovers, but does nothing toward getting Philocomasium away from the soldier. And so Palaestrio needs a second machination.[9] With the help of the old man next door, a zany codger who goes to absurd lengths to prove that he thinks young,[10] he dresses up a courtesan to pretend she is the old man's wife, desperately in love with the soldier, and willing to go to any length—and expense—to get his amatory attentions. Pyrgopolynices will then hurriedly get rid of his present mistress and devote himself to a more profitable amour. The clever slave's scheme has a second purpose as well: to deflate the soldier's gargantuan ego, and show the ''hero'' to be a groveling coward when confronted with the penalty for adultery: castration.

Palaestrio knows his military master. And so he brilliantly couches his proposition in terms which appeal to the soldier's greatest source

---

9. Much scholarly ink has flowed over the fact that Plautus has combined two plots in this play, perhaps derived from two different Greek originals. This process is known as *contaminatio,* a term which has a pejorative connotation. See, for example, the prologues of Terence, for very defensive defenses against this charge. If combining two unrelated plots—from different sources—be an artistic shortcoming, however, all of Elizabethan drama is in terrible jeopardy.

10. Cf. lines 627ff.

of pride: not his valor, not even his beauty, but his wealth (cf. 1063 ff.). The slave feeds the soldier with ambiguous promises of "profit" from this new affair, which he describes as *condicio nova et luculenta* (line 952), a phrase which could be understood either as a new love *or* business affair. He further stokes the fire of the soldier's *alazoneia* by presenting him with a ring which he calls the "first deposit on a love account" (line 957). Moreover, Pyrgopolynices is later offered payment for his sexual services (lines 1059–1062). But ironically *he* pays a great deal. He ends up giving away not only his present mistress, but "all the gold and all the jewels and all the things you dressed her up with" (line 981).

On every field of battle, the clever slave emerges victorious over the allegedly undefeated and unbeatable warrior. The farewell scene, when the girl, her many trunks of baggage and Palaestrio himself are all about to be given away by the soldier, is truly a masterpiece of irony. And there are some very interesting similarities between this ironic leavetaking and the finale of Euripides' *Helen*.[11] This may not prove any direct Euripidean influence, for Plautus himself has a predilection for trickery-by-masquerade. There are, in fact, three masquerades in *The Braggart Soldier* alone: first Philocomasium as her own twin sister, then the courtesan as the amorous wife, then Pleusicles, the young lover, as a ship's captain. Needless to mention, Palaestrio wrote all three scripts.

The *miles gloriosus* is by no means a Plautine invention, although the boastful officer is one of the Roman comedian's favorite characters, and appears in half a dozen of his extant plays. Certainly General Lamachos in Aristophanes' *Acharnians* is a blustering military man of much the same ilk. But the type must have had a very special appeal for the Roman audience, almost all of whom were themselves soldiers.[12] And, as the notes indicate, Plautus has added certain Roman innuendoes: private jokes for general laughter.

The Braggart Soldier has a long heritage on the comic stage. Even

---

11. In Euripides' play, Helen is departing from Egypt in the company of Menelaus, who is disguised as a sailor, as is young Pleusicles here. The Euripidean protagonists have bamboozled King Theoclymenos into giving them not only permission to leave the shore, but rich gifts as well. There are even striking similarities in the dialogue. Compare for example *Helen*, lines 1419–1420, with *Braggart*, lines 1321–1325.

12. In describing the Roman character, the historian Polybius (6.37) observes that they considered boasting of military valor—even if true—to be bad form, a bad show, as it were. This may explain why they considered Plautus' comedy such a good show.

Terence's Thraso—in *The Eunuch*, his most successful play—owes quite a debt to Plautus. We see the same characterization in the various captains of the *commedia dell' arte*, in Corneille's *L'Illusion Comique*, in *Ralph Roister Doister*, in Captain Bobadil of Ben Jonson's *Everyman in His Humor*, and of course, in Falstaff, who is the greatest *alazon* of all time and also bids fair to be the best *eiron* as well![13] If nothing else, the Braggart Soldier has commanded a legion of imitators.

---

13. Cf. Falstaff's famous (and true) self-characterization: "I am not only witty in myself, but the cause that wit is in other men" (*Henry IV, Part II*, I, ii, 10).

Dramatis Personae

PYRGOPOLYNICES, a soldier
ARTOTROGUS, his parasite
PALAESTRIO, slave to the soldier (formerly to Pleusicles)
PERIPLECTOMENUS, an old man of Ephesus
SCELEDRUS, slave to the soldier
PLEUSICLES, a young man from Athens
LURCIO, slave to the soldier
PHILOCOMASIUM, a girl abducted by the soldier
ACROTELEUTIUM, a courtesan
MILPHIDIPPA, her maid
A SLAVE BOY
CARIO, Periplectomenus' cook

*The entire action takes place on a street
in Ephesus, before the adjoining houses of*
PYRGOPOLYNICES *and* PERIPLECTOMENUS.

(Enter PYRGOPOLYNICES,
followed by his parasite ARTOTROGUS†
and several minions who carry his monstrous shield.)

PYRGOPOLYNICES:

(posing pompously, declaiming in heroic fashion)

Look lively—shine a shimmer on that shield of mine
Surpassing sunbeams—when there are no clouds, of course.
Thus, when it's needed, with the battle joined, its gleam
Shall strike opposing eyeballs in the bloodshed—bloodshot!
Ah me, I must give comfort to this blade of mine
Lest he lament and yield himself to dark despair.
Too long ere now has he been sick of his vacation.
Poor lad! He's dying to make mincemeat of the foe.

(dropping the bombastic tone)

Say, where the devil is Artotrogus?

ARTOTROGUS:

                              He's here—
By Destiny's dashing, dauntless, debonair darling,   10

---

†*parasite* . . . From the Greek *parasitos*, which in turn is from *sîtos*, meaning food or
fodder. The parasite is your professional sponger. Treat him to food and he'll treat you
to compliments. Parasites' character names suggest their functions. Here Artotrogus,
"bread muncher"; in the *Menaechmi*, Peniculus, "the sponge"; in the *Stichus*, Gelasimus,
"funny boy."

A man so warlike, Mars himself would hardly dare
To claim his powers were the equal of your own.
PYRGOPOLYNICES:

(preening)

Tell me—who was that chap I saved at Field-of-Roaches,
Where the supreme commander was Crash-Bang-Razzle-Dazzle
Son of Mighty-Mercenary-Messup, you know, Neptune's nephew?

ARTOTROGUS:
Ah yes, the man with golden armor, I recall.
You puffed away his legions with a single breath
Like wind blows autumn leaves, or straw from thatch-roofed
huts.

PYRGOPOLYNICES:
A snap—a nothing, really.
ARTOTROGUS:

Nothing, indeed—that is
Compared to other feats I could recount—*(aside)* as false as
this.   20

(to the audience, as he hides behind the soldier's shield)

If any of you knows a man more full of bull
Or empty boastings, you can have me—free of tax.
But I'll say this: I'm crazy for his olive salad!
PYRGOPOLYNICES:
Hey, where are you?
ARTOTROGUS:
   (popping up)   Here! And then that elephant in India—
The way your fist just broke his arm to smithereens.
PYRGOPOLYNICES:
What's that—his *arm*?
ARTOTROGUS:

I meant his leg, of course.
PYRGOPOLYNICES:
I gave him just an easy jab.
ARTOTROGUS:

A jab, of course!
If you had really tried, you would have smashed his arm
Right through his elephantine skin and guts and bone!   30

PYRGOPOLYNICES:
  No more of this.
ARTOTROGUS:
                  Of course. Why bother to narrate
  Your many daring deeds to me—who knows them all.

  (aside, to the audience)

  It's only for my stomach that I stomach him.
  While ears are suffering, at least my teeth are suppering.
  And so I yes and yes again to all his lies.
PYRGOPOLYNICES:
  What was I saying?
ARTOTROGUS:
                  Oh, I know precisely what.
  It's done, by Hercules.
PYRGOPOLYNICES:
                  What's done?

ARTOTROGUS:
                              Well, something is.

PYRGOPOLYNICES:
  Have you—
ARTOTROGUS:
                  Your tablets? Yes, of course, a stylus too.
PYRGOPOLYNICES:
  How expertly you suit your mind to know my own.
ARTOTROGUS:
  I ought to know your habits well-rehearsedly   40
  And see to it I sniff your wishes in advance.
PYRGOPOLYNICES:
  How good's your memory?
ARTOTROGUS:
                              It's perfect, sir. In Cilicia,
  A hundred fifty. In Saudi I-robya, hundreds more.
  Add thirty Sardians, those Macedonians, and there's
  The total men you've slaughtered in a single day.
PYRGOPOLYNICES:
  "The total men," your final sum is—
ARTOTROGUS:
                              Seven thousand.

PYRGOPOLYNICES:

I believe you're right. You're good at your accounts.†

ARTOTROGUS:

I didn't even write it down; it's all by heart.

PYRGOPOLYNICES:

My god, you've got a memory!

ARTOTROGUS:

Food feeds it.

PYRGOPOLYNICES:

Well, if you keep behaving as you have, you'll eat   50
Eternally. I'll always have a place for you at dinner.

ARTOTROGUS:

(inspired by this)

And then in Cappadocia, you would have slain
Five hundred with one blow—except your blade was dull.

PYRGOPOLYNICES:

Just shabby little soldiers, so I let them live.

ARTOTROGUS:

Why bother to repeat what every mortal knows—
There's no one more invincible in all the earth
In duties or in beauties than—Pyrgopolynices!
Why, all the women love you—who can blame them, either—
Since you're so . . . so attractive? Why, just yesterday
Some women grabbed me by the tunic—

PYRGOPOLYNICES:

Yes, what said
they?

ARTOTROGUS:

They badgered me with asking—"Isn't that Achilles?"   60
"No," said I, "it's just his brother." "Ah," said one,
"That's why he looks so beautiful and so genteel!
Just look at him—that handsome head of hair he has!
Oh, blessed are the women that can sleep with him!"

PYRGOPOLYNICES:

They really said all that?

---

†*your accounts* . . . The Latin *recte rationem tenes* suggests "accurate bookkeeping."
The mercenary soldier ironically reveals his preoccupation with money. As we will see,
Palaestrio will play upon this avarice to trick him later on (cf. line 952).

ARTOTROGUS:

> And then both begged me
> To parade you by today so they could see you.

PYRGOPOLYNICES:

> How wretched to be such a handsome man.

ARTOTROGUS:

> How true.
> They are a bother, screeching and beseeching me
> For just one little look at you. And sending for me! 70
> That's why I can't give all my time to serving you.

(Suddenly, duty calls.)

PYRGOPOLYNICES:

> Now is the hour, fall in! On to the forum
> To seek the mercenaries I conscripted yesterday.
> I must distribute salaries to all enlisted.
> King Seleucus† has urgently appealed to me
> To gather fighting men for him and sign them up.
> I have decreed this day devoted to the king's demands.

ARTOTROGUS:

> Then off we go!

PYRGOPOLYNICES:

> Faithful fellows—follow!‡

*(PYRGOPOLYNICES leads his minions off.
Enter PALAESTRIO.)*

PALAESTRIO:

(to the audience)

> Now, folks, if you'll be kind enough to hear me out, 80
> Then I'll be kind and tell you what our play's about.
> Whoever doesn't want to listen, let him beat it
> And give a seat to one of those in back who need it.
> I'll tell you why we've gathered in this festive spot,

---

†*King Seleucus* . . . It is not known which of the Syrian kings of this name is intended. The comic point here is that the soldier is boasting of his regal connections by mentioning a *king* (which he does once again in line 77).

‡*follow!* . . . The soldier himself acts regally by referring to his followers as *satellites*, the term used for members of a royal retinue.

What comedy we will enact, its name and plot.
This play is called the *Alazon* in Greek,
A name translated "braggart" in the tongue we speak.
This town is Ephesus; that soldier is my master
Who's just gone to the forum. What a shameless crass
                                        bombaster!
He's so full of crap† and lechery, no lies are vaster.   90
He brags that all the women seek him out en masse.
The truth is, everywhere he goes they think he's just an ass.
The local wenches claim they've tired out their lips,
But not from kissing him—from making nasty quips.
   Not very long have I been slaving as his slave,
I want you all to know how I became his knave,
And whom I slaved for prior to this slavish lot.
So listen very closely, folks, here comes the plot!
   My master back in Athens was a fine young man.
In good old Athens,‡ he was crazy for a courtesan.   100
She loved him too. Yes, that's the kind of love that's best.
Then he was sent to Naupactus—a governmental quest
Of great importance. While my master served the state,
The soldier came to Athens—by some trick of Fate.
He made advances to my master's little friend.
He played up to her mother and began to send
Cosmetics, costly catered cookery and wine—
The soldier and the bawd were getting on just fine.
Right when the soldier saw his chance for something shady
He bamboozled the old bawd—the mother of the lady   110
(That's the girl my master loved). He took her daughter
In secret on a ship, and made for open water.
To Ephesus—against her will—is where he brought her.
   Now when *I* learn he's kidnaped Master's concubine,
As fast as possible, I get a ship of mine.
I head for Naupactus to tell him of the fact,
But just when we get out to sea we are attacked—
And pirates take the ship. Fate's will be done,   120

---

†*full of crap* . . . The Latin is *stercoreus*, meaning "full of crap." Such explicit
scatology is extremely rare in Plautus, who is quite unlike Aristophanes in this respect.
‡*good old Athens* . . . It was typical of Roman comedy to stress its "good old Athens"
origins. Cf. Introduction, p. xiv.

And I was finished, though I scarcely had begun.
    The pirate made the soldier here a gift of me
And when the soldier took me home—what do I see?
The girl from Athens—my old master's concubine—
Who, when she saw me, winked and gave a sign
Not to address her. Later, when the coast was clear,
She wept and told me how unhappy she was here.
She longed to flee to Athens—in a phrase:
She loved my master from the good old days
And hated no one as she did this military guy. 130
On learning of the woman's inner feelings, I
Compose a letter, sign and seal it secretly
And get a merchant to deliver it for me
To my old master—he who still adored
This girl here. And my note to come was not ignored!
He came! He's staying with a neighbor right next door—
A wonderful old man his family knew before,
Who's been a blessing to my amorous young man,
Promoting our affair in every way he can.
    Now here within I've started mighty machinations 140
To make it easy for the lovers' . . . visitations.
The soldier gave the girl a bedroom of her own.
No one but she can enter it, it's hers alone.
So in this bedroom I have tunneled through the wall.
Right to the other house in secret she can crawl.
Our neighbor knows of this—in fact, he planned it all!
    So good for nothing is this fellow slave of mine—
The one the soldier picked to guard the concubine—
That with our artful artifice and wily ways
We'll coat this fellow's eyeballs with so thick a glaze,
We'll make him sure he doesn't see what's really there!
Don't *you* be fooled: one girl today will play a *pair*. 150
And so the girl that comes from either house will share
A single face, the same one claiming to be twins.
We'll fool that guard of hers until his head just spins!
But wait—I hear the creaking of our neighbor's door.
Here comes that nice old fellow I described before.

(Old PERIPLECTOMENUS *comes out of his house,*
still shouting back angrily at the slaves within.)

PERIPLECTOMENUS:

After this, by Hercules, if you don't beat the daylights out of
Anyone who's on our roof, I'll make your raw sides into
rawhides!

(in exasperation, to the audience)

Now my neighbors see the show of all that happens in my
house—
Looking right down through my skylight!† *(back to his slaves)*
Listen, I command you all:
Anyone you see on our roof, coming from the soldier's
house—
That's excepting for Palaestrio—throw 'em down into the
street!   160
Should they claim to be pursuing monkeys, pigeons or the
like,
You'll be finished if you don't just pound and pummel 'em to
pulp!
Make it so they won't be able to infringe upon our gambling
laws.
See to it they won't have even bones enough for rolling dice!‡

PALAESTRIO:

Someone from our house has done a naughty thing, from
what I hear—
The old man's commanded that my fellow slaves be beaten
up.
Well, he said except for me—who gives a hoot about the
rest?
I'll go see him.

(PALAESTRIO steps into view.)

---

†*skylight* . . . The *impluvium* was an opening in the roof of Roman houses through
which the sun could shine and the rain fall (the latter would be gathered for household
use).

‡*bones. . . dice* . . . The metaphor sounds extremely modern, but it is not only in
Plautus' Latin (*talus* can mean an ankle bone *or* a die), but may even have been in his
Greek original (*astragalos* has the very same double meaning).

PERIPLECTOMENUS:

        Isn't this Palaestrio now coming toward me?

PALAESTRIO:

  How are you, Periplectomenus?

PERIPLECTOMENUS:

           There aren't many men I'd
Rather meet right now than you, Palaestrio.

PALAESTRIO:

          What's going
                on?   170
Why are you in such an uproar with our household?

PERIPLECTOMENUS:

          We're all finished!

PALAESTRIO:

  What's the matter?

PERIPLECTOMENUS:

    It's discovered!

PALAESTRIO:

        What's discovered?

PERIPLECTOMENUS:

           On my
           roof—
Someone from your household has been spying on us, through
            the skylight,
Where he saw Philocomasium in my house, with my guest—
Kissing.

PALAESTRIO:

  Who saw this?

PERIPLECTOMENUS:

      A fellow slave of yours.

PALAESTRIO:

          But which, I
          wonder.

PERIPLECTOMENUS:

I don't know, the fellow got away too fast.

PALAESTRIO:

         Oh, I suspect
           —that
I'm a dead man.

PERIPLECTOMENUS:

As he fled, I cried, "Why are you on my
roof?"
He replied, still on the run, "I had to chase our little monkey."

PALAESTRIO:

Pity me—I'll have to die—all for a worthless animal!   180
But the girl—is she still in your house?

PERIPLECTOMENUS:

She was when I
came out here.

PALAESTRIO:

Quick—have her cross back to our house, so the slaves can
see her there.
Make her hurry—that's unless she'd rather see her faithful
slaves
Just for her affair become fraternal brothers—on the cross!†

PERIPLECTOMENUS:

She'll be told. *(going off)* If that is all . . .

PALAESTRIO:

It isn't. Also tell
the girl to
See to it she doesn't lose her woman's ingenuity.
Have her practice up her tricks and female shrewdness.

PERIPLECTOMENUS:

What's
this for?

PALAESTRIO:

She must force the fellow who found her into full forget-
fulness.
Even if he saw her here a hundred times, have her deny it.
She has cheek, a lot of lip, loquacity, audacity,
Also perspicacity, tenacity, mendacity.
If someone accuses her, she'll just outswear the man with
oaths.   190
She knows every phony phrase, the phony ways, the phony
plays.

---

†*on the cross* . . . Plautus' comedy abounds in grim threats of torture and crucifixion for
misbehaving slaves. Note Sceledrus' fear in line 310, and Palaestrio's increasing of this
fear in 359–360.

Wiles she has, guiles she has, very soothing smiles she has.
"Seasoned" women† never have to get their spices at the
                                                       grocer's—
Their own garden grows the pepper for their sharp and
                                                       saucy schemes.

PERIPLECTOMENUS:

I'll convey this all to her, if she's still there. *(stops, amazed)*
                                                 What's going on?
What are you debating there inside yourself?

PALAESTRIO:

                                                 Some silence,
                                                       please,
While I call my wits to order to consider what to do
In retaliation: to outfox my foxy fellow slave, who
Saw her kissing in your house. We've got to make the seen
                                                       . . . *un*seen.

PERIPLECTOMENUS:

              (starts to head for his house)

Cogitate—while I withdraw and go in here. *(turns)* Well,
                                          look at him!   200
Standing pensive, pondering profundities with wrinkled brow.
Now he knocks upon his head—he wants his brains to answer
                                                       him.
Look—he turns. Now he supports himself with left hand on
                                          his left thigh.
Now he's adding something with the fingers of his right hand.
                                                 Now he
Slaps his right thigh—what a slap! What to-do for what
                                          to do!
Now he snaps his fingers, struggles, changes posture every
                                                       second.
Look—he shakes his head. No, no, what he's invented doesn't
                                          please him.

---

†*"Seasoned" women* . . . Both the metaphor and the tone are typically Plautine. All his
comedies express a cynical distrust, even dislike at times, of female behavior. Cf.
Palaestrio's remark in line 786, and Periplectomenus' ''what mangy merchandise a
woman is'' in line 894. This attitude may in part be derived from Euripides, who often
expresses his cynical mistrust of women's wiles.

He'll cook up a plan that's well done—not half baked—I'm
sure of that.
Look—he's going in for building—with his chin he crowns
a column.
Cut it out! That type of building doesn't please me—not at
all.   210
For I hear a foreign poet† also has his face so columned—
But he has two guards to keep him columned like that all the
time.
Bravo! *Molto bello,* standing slavewise and theatrically.‡
He won't rest at all today until he finds the plan he's seeking.
Now I think he has it. Hey—get busy, man, don't slip to
sleep.
That's unless you'd rather be on guard right here and *(points
to his back)* scarred right here.
Hey, have you been drinking? Hey, Palaestrio, I'm talking to
you.
Rouse yourself! Wake up, I say; it's dawn, I say.

PALAESTRIO:
(still rapt in thought)   I   hear
you, sir.

PERIPLECTOMENUS:
Don't you see the enemy is threatening that back of yours?
Think!
Get us aid and reinforcements. No more napping; let's get
scrapping!   220
Ready an offensive for the foe; prepare defenses too!
Cut the enemy's supply line, then we'll fortify our own.
So our rations and equipment get to you and to our legions
Safely: do it quickly. What we need is instant action!
Tell me that you'll take command yourself and then I'll rest
secure,

---

†*foreign poet . . .* The "foreign poet" may be Plautus' colleague Naevius, who, as the
legend goes, was chained up in prison for slandering an influential Roman family. Since
this comedy supposedly takes place in Greece, the Roman poet—whoever he may
be—is ironically referred to as "foreign," *barbarus.*
‡*slavewise and theatrically . . .* Plautus frequently alludes to theatrical matters, as part
of his tongue-in-cheek irony. Thus one of his characters assures the audience near the
conclusion of the *Pseudolus* that he will not ambush his tricky slave as is the typical
practice "in other comedies" (line 1240). Tranio in the *Mostellaria* is extremely well
versed in the comic tradition (cf. lines 1149ff.).

Knowing we can crush the foe.

PALAESTRIO:

    (magnanimously)   I do accept the office and do   230
Take command!

PERIPLECTOMENUS:

              I think you'll win the prize you seek.

PALAESTRIO:

                     (paternally and gratefully)   May
                                     Jupiter
Shower blessings on you.

PERIPLECTOMENUS:

                Won't you share your plans?

PALAESTRIO:

                        Be silent, sir,
While I show you through the landscape of my "plot," so
                           you'll be sharing
Equally in all the plans.

PERIPLECTOMENUS:

              I'll guard them as I would my own.

PALAESTRIO:

Master hasn't normal skin—it's thicker than an elephant's.
He's about as clever as a stone.†

PERIPLECTOMENUS:

              That much I know myself.

PALAESTRIO:

Here's the whole idea, here's the notion that I'll set in motion:
I will say Philocomasium has got a real twin sister
Who has just arrived from Athens with a young man she's
                           in love with.
These two "sisters" are alike as drops of milk. We'll say the
                           lovers   240
Stay at your house, as your guests.

PERIPLECTOMENUS:

                  Bravo—it's a brilliant
                        plan!

PALAESTRIO:

Should this fellow slave of mine make accusations to the
                          soldier,

---

†*clever as a stone* . . . The soldier's intellect is again likened to stone in line 1024.

Claiming that he saw the girl there kissing someone else,
                                                    why then
I'll accuse my fellow slave of having spied on you and seen
                                                            the
Sister with her lover, kissing and embracing.

PERIPLECTOMENUS:

                                        Oh, that's fine!
If the soldier questions me, I'll back you up.

PALAESTRIO:

                                        Remember
                                            that the
Sisters are identically alike. Remind the girl as well, so
When the soldier asks her, she won't foul it up.

PERIPLECTOMENUS:

                                            A perfect
                                                ploy!

                    (suddenly)
Wait—what happens if the soldier wants to see 'em both
                                            together?
What do we do then?

PALAESTRIO:

                        It's easy; there are thousands of
                                        excuses: 250
"She's not home, she took a walk, she's sleeping, dressing,
                                                    washing,
Dining, drinking, busy, indisposed, it's just impossible."
If we start this on the right foot, we can put him off forever.
Soon he'll get to thinking all the lies we tell him are the truth.

PERIPLECTOMENUS:
This is just terrific.

PALAESTRIO:

                    Go in—if the girl is there, then have her
Hurry home. And train her, make things plainer and explain
                                                    her all.
She must fully comprehend our plan, the web we're weaving
                                                    with her
New twin sister.

PERIPLECTOMENUS:
                    You shall quickly have a girl who's very quick.

What else?

PALAESTRIO:

Be off.

PERIPLECTOMENUS:

I'm off.

*(The old man rushes off into his house,
leaving* PALAESTRIO *to ponder his next move.)*

PALAESTRIO:

Now I myself must go back home
And by secret subterfugitive investigation find out   260
Who of my fellow servants chased that monkey on the
roof today.
Surely he'll have shared the secret with the other household
slaves,
Whispering of Master's mistress, telling people how he saw
her
Here—within our neighbor's house—embracing some un-
known young man.
"I can't keep it secret, I'm the only one who knows," he'll say.
When I find the man who saw her, my equipment will be
ready.†
All is ready; I'm resolved to storm and take the enemy.
If I can't discover him, I'll sniff just like a hunting dog
Till I can pursue the little fox by following his footprints.
Wait—our door is creaking—I had better quiet down for now.   270
Look—here comes my fellow slave, the one they picked to
guard the girl.

(Enter SCELEDRUS, *one of the soldier's household slaves.
Normally a nervous nail-biter,
he is now completely bewildered.)*

SCELEDRUS:

If I wasn't walking in my sleep today up on that roof, I
Know for sure, by Pollux, that I saw Philocomasium,
Master's mistress, right here in our neighbor's house—in
search of trouble.

---

†*my equipment* . . . The Latin refers specifically to Roman siege machines.

PALAESTRIO:

(aside)

There's the man who saw her kissing. I can tell from what he
                                                            said.

SCELEDRUS:
Who is that?

PALAESTRIO:
                Your fellow slave. How goes it, Sceledrus?

SCELEDRUS:
                                                Palaestrio!
I'm so glad to see you.

PALAESTRIO:
                Why? What's up? What's wrong?
                                Please let me know.

SCELEDRUS:
I'm afraid—

PALAESTRIO:
        Of what?

SCELEDRUS:
                    Today I fear we slaves are really
                                            leaping into
Trouble and titanic tortures!

PALAESTRIO:
                        So leap solo, you yourself—
I don't care the slightest bit for any leaping—up or down.   280

SCELEDRUS:
Maybe you don't know the crime committed in our house
                                                    today.

PALAESTRIO:
Crime? What sort of crime?

SCELEDRUS:
                    A dirty one!

PALAESTRIO:
                        Then keep it to
                                yourself.
I don't want to know it.

SCELEDRUS:
                    Well, I won't allow you *not* to
                                    know it!

Listen: as I chased our monkey over neighbor's roof today—
PALAESTRIO:
Sceledrus, I'd say one worthless animal pursued another.
SCELEDRUS:
Go to hell!
PALAESTRIO:
       You ought to go—on with your little tale, I mean.

      (SCELEDRUS *glares at* PALAESTRIO,
      then goes on with his story.)

SCELEDRUS:
On the roof, I chanced by chance to peek down through our
                  neighbor's skylight—
And what do I see? Philocomasium! She's smooching with
                         some
Utterly unknown young man!
PALAESTRIO:
      (*horrified*)   What scandal, Sceledrus, is
                        this?
SCELEDRUS:
There's no doubt of it, I saw her.
PALAESTRIO:
                Really?
SCELEDRUS:
                    With my own two
                    eyes.   290
PALAESTRIO:
Come on, this is all illusion, you saw nothing.
SCELEDRUS:
                Look at me!
Do my eyes look bad to you?
PALAESTRIO:
            Ask a doctor; don't ask me!

(*He now becomes the friendly adviser.*)

By the gods, don't propagate this tale of yours so indiscreetly.
Now you're seeking trouble head-on, soon it may seek you—
                head off!
And unless you can suppress this absolutely brainless banter,

Double death awaits you!

SCELEDRUS:

What's this "double" death?

PALAESTRIO:

Well, I'll explain it:
First, if you've accused our master's mistress falsely, you must
die.
Next, if what you say *is* true, you've failed as guard—you
die again.

SCELEDRUS:

I don't know my future, but I know I'm sure of what I saw.

PALAESTRIO:

Still persisting, wretch?

SCELEDRUS:

Look, I can only tell you what I saw.
Why—   300
She's inside our neighbor's house right now.

PALAESTRIO:

(with mock surprise)   What's that,
she's not at home?

SCELEDRUS:

You don't have to take my word. Go right inside and look
yourself.

PALAESTRIO:

Yes, indeed I will!

(He strides with severity into the soldier's house.)

SCELEDRUS:

And I'll wait here and ambush her, the
Minute our young filly trots from pasture to her storehouse
stall.†

(He reflects a moment, then groans.)

What am I to do? The soldier chose me as her guardian.
If I let this out—I die. Yet, if I'm silent, still I die,
Should this be discovered. Oh, what could be wickeder than
women?
While I was on the roof there, she just left her room and went
outside!

---

†*storehouse stall* . . . The Latin *stabulum* can mean either stable or whorehouse.

Bold and brazen badness, by the gods! If master learns of this,
Our whole household will be on the cross, by Hercules. Me
too!   310

(resolves himself)

Come what may, I'll shut my mouth. Better stilled than
killed, I say.

(exasperated, to the audience)

I can't guard a girl like this who's always out to sell herself!

*(PALAESTRIO marches out of the soldier's house,
a very stern look on his face.)*

PALAESTRIO:

Sceledrus! Is there a man more insolent in all the earth, or
Born beneath more angry or unfriendly stars—

SCELEDRUS:

What's
wrong? What's wrong?

PALAESTRIO:

You should have your eyes dug out for seeing what was
never there.

SCELEDRUS:

Never where?

PALAESTRIO:

I wouldn't give a rotten nut for your whole
life!

SCELEDRUS:

Tell me why—

PALAESTRIO:

You even dare to ask me?

SCELEDRUS:

Well, why can't I
ask?

PALAESTRIO:

You should really have that tattletaling tongue of yours cut
off.

SCELEDRUS:
  Should I—why?

PALAESTRIO:

                    My friend, the girl's *at home*—the one you
                                             said you saw
  In our neighbor's house with some young man, hugging and
                                        kissing him.   320

SCELEDRUS:
  It's amazing you don't eat your carrots.† Why, they're cheap
                                                        enough.

PALAESTRIO:
  Carrots, why?

SCELEDRUS:

              To aid your eyesight.

PALAESTRIO:

                              Gallows bird! It's you
                                    who needs 'em.
  You're the blind man, my sight's perfect—and I'm sure the
                                         girl's at home.

SCELEDRUS:
  She's at home?

PALAESTRIO:

              At home she is.

SCELEDRUS:

                            Oh, cut it out; you're fool-
                                          ing with me.

PALAESTRIO:
  Then my hands are very dirty.

SCELEDRUS:

                          Why?

PALAESTRIO:

                              Because I fool with
                                          filth.

SCELEDRUS:
  Damn your hide!

---

†*carrots* . . . The Latin states, in a roundabout way, that Sceledrus has been eating
food (*lolium*, darnel) which is bad for his eyes.

PALAESTRIO:

> No, Sceledrus, it's *your* hide that is now at
> stake.
That's unless you make some changes in your visions and
> derisions.
Wait—our door is creaking.

SCELEDRUS:

> *(at the old man's door)*

> I shall stay right here and block
> *this* door,
For it's sure she can't cross over if she doesn't use the door!

PALAESTRIO:

What's caused all this scurvy scoundrelism, Sceledrus? She's
> home.   330

> *(SCELEDRUS keeps blocking the old man's door,
> looking straight ahead, trying to reassure himself.)*

SCELEDRUS:

I can see . . . I know myself . . . I trust myself implicitly.
No one bullies me to make me think she isn't in this house.

> *(He spreads his arms across the doorway.)*

Here—I'll block the door. She won't sneak back and catch
> me unawares.

PALAESTRIO:

> *(to the audience)*

There, he's where I want him. Now I'll push him off the
> ramparts.

> *(to SCELEDRUS)*

Do you want me to convince you of your stupi-vision?†

SCELEDRUS:

> Try it!

PALAESTRIO:

And to prove that you don't know what eyes or brains are
> for?

---

†*stupi-vision* . . . Plautus has coined the adjective *stultividus*.

SCELEDRUS:

                                    Well, prove it!

PALAESTRIO:

Now . . . you claim the concubine's in there.

SCELEDRUS:

                                  Why, I *insist*
                                       she is,

And I saw her kissing some young man as well—a perfect
                                       stranger.

PALAESTRIO:

There's no passage from this house to our house, you know
                                       that—

SCELEDRUS:

                         (impatiently)   I know it.

PALAESTRIO:

There's no balcony or garden, just the skylight—

SCELEDRUS:

                                       I know
                                    that too!   340

PALAESTRIO:

Well . . . if she's in *our* house and I bring her out so you can
                                     see her,

Would you say you're worthy of a whipping?

SCELEDRUS:

                            (nods)   Worthy.

PALAESTRIO:

                                  Guard the door—
See she doesn't sneak out on the sly and slip across to our
                                       house.

SCELEDRUS:

That's my plan.

PALAESTRIO:

                    I'll have her standing in the street here right
                                      away.

    (PALAESTRIO dashes into the soldier's house.)

SCELEDRUS:

(muttering to himself)

Go ahead and do it! I'll soon know if I saw what I saw.
Or if—as he says he will—he'll prove the girl is still at home.

(tries to reassure himself)

After all, I have my eyes. I never borrow someone else's. . . .

(having second thoughts)

Yet he's always playing up to her—and he's her favorite:
First man called to dinner, always first to fill his face with
food.
And he's only been with us about three years—not even that.†   350
Still, I tell you, no one's slavery could be more savory.
Never mind, I'd better do what must be done, that's guard
this door.
Here I'll stand, by Pollux. Never will they make a fool of me!

*(SCELEDRUS stands with his arms spread across the doorway
to the old man's house.
PALAESTRIO enters from the soldier's house,
leading the girl PHILOCOMASIUM.)*

PALAESTRIO:
Remember your instructions.

PHILOCOMASIUM:

I'm astonished I'm admonished
so.

PALAESTRIO:
I'm worried you're not slippery enough.

PHILOCOMASIUM:

What? I could make
A dozen decent damsels devils with my surplus shrewdness!

PALAESTRIO:
Now concentrate on trickery. I'll slip away from you.

---

†*not even that* . . . Sceledrus claims that Palaestrio has been with their household for
three years, yet Palaestrio himself stated that he had only been there a very short while
(line 95, *nam ego hau diu apud hunc servitutem servio*). Plautus has been criticized for
this kind of inconsistency, but it is doubtful whether his audience noticed it.

(PALAESTRIO strides jauntily up to SCELEDRUS,
who is still blocking the old man's door
with all possible concentration.)

How are you, Sceledrus?
SCELEDRUS:

(staring straight ahead)

I'm on the job. Speak—I have ears.

(PALAESTRIO looks at SCELEDRUS' pose, amused.)

PALAESTRIO:
You know, I think you'll travel soon in that same pose—
beyond the gates
With arms outstretched—to bear your cross.
SCELEDRUS:

Oh yes? What
for?   360

PALAESTRIO:
Look to your left. Who is that woman?
SCELEDRUS:

Oh—by all the
gods—

That girl—she's the master's concubine!
PALAESTRIO:

You know, I think
so too.

Well, hurry, now's your time—
SCELEDRUS:

What should I do?

PALAESTRIO:

Don't dally
—die!

PHILOCOMASIUM:
Where is this "loyal" slave who falsely brands an honest
woman
With unchastity?
PALAESTRIO:

(points to SCELEDRUS)

Right here! He told me all the things I told
you.

PHILOCOMASIUM:

You say you saw me—rascal—kissing in our neighbor's
house?

PALAESTRIO:

And with an unknown man, he said.

SCELEDRUS:

By Hercules, I did.

PHILOCOMASIUM:

You saw me?

SCELEDRUS:

With these eyes, by Hercules.

PHILOCOMASIUM:

You'll lose them
soon—

They see more than they see.

SCELEDRUS:

By Hercules, I won't be
frightened

Out of seeing what I really saw!

PHILOCOMASIUM:

I waste my breath   370

Conversing with a lunatic. I'll have his head, by Pollux!

SCELEDRUS:

Oh, stop your threats! I know the cross will be my tomb.
My ancestors *all* ended there—exactly like my forefathers—
and five-fathers.†

And so these threats of yours can't tear my eyes from me!

(meekly motioning PALAESTRIO *to one side)*

But—could I have a word with you, Palaestrio? . . . Please
tell me:

Where *did* she come from?

PALAESTRIO:

Home, where else?

---

†*forefathers—and five-fathers* . . . A special Roman joke, for legally speaking, slaves
were *nullo patre*, that is, considered as having no father at all. Hence when Plautus lets
Sceledrus speak of multiancestors, he compounds the impossibility and increases the fun.

SCELEDRUS:

From home?

PALAESTRIO:

(checking SCELEDRUS' *eyes)* You see me?

SCELEDRUS:

Sure.

But it's amazing how she crossed from one house to the other!
For certainly we haven't got a balcony, no garden,
Every window's grated. *(to* PHILOCOMASIUM*)* Yet I'm sure
I saw you here inside.

PALAESTRIO:

What—criminal—you're still accusing her?

PHILOCOMASIUM:

By Castor, now   380
I think it must have been the truth—that dream I dreamed
last night.

PALAESTRIO:

What did you dream?

PHILOCOMASIUM:

I'll tell you both, but please pay close
attention:
Last night it seemed as if my dear *twin sister* had arrived
In Ephesus from Athens—with a certain man she loved.
It seemed as if they both were staying here next door as
guests.

PALAESTRIO:

(aside)

Palaestrio dreamed all this up. *(to* PHILOCOMASIUM*)* Go
on—continue, please.

PHILOCOMASIUM:

It seemed—though I was glad my sister came—because of
her,
There seemed to be a terrible suspicion cast upon me.
Because it seemed that, in my dream, one of our slaves accused me,

(to SCELEDRUS*)*

Just as you're doing now, of having kissed a strange young
man,   390

When really it was my *twin sister* kissing her beloved.
And so I dreamt that I was falsely and unjustly blamed.

PALAESTRIO:

What seemed like dreams now happen to you wide awake!
By Hercules—a real live dream! *(to* PHILOCOMASIUM*)* Go
                              right inside and pray!

                    (casually)

I think you should relate this to the soldier. . . .

PHILOCOMASIUM:

                              Why, of
                              course!
I won't be falsely called unchaste—without revenge!

              (She storms into the soldier's house.
              PALAESTRIO *turns to* SCELEDRUS.*)*

SCELEDRUS:

I'm scared. What have I done? I feel my whole back itching.

PALAESTRIO:

You know you're finished, eh?

SCELEDRUS:

                    Well, now at least I'm sure
                    she's home.
And now I'll guard our door—wherever she may be!

    *(*SCELEDRUS *plants himself astride the soldier's door
in the same position he used to block the old man's doorway.)*

PALAESTRIO:

                    (sweetly)   Sceledrus—
That dream she dreamt was pretty similar to what went on—   400
Even the part where you suspected that you saw her kissing!

SCELEDRUS:

I don't know what I should believe myself. I thought I saw
A thing . . . I think . . . perhaps . . . I didn't see.

PALAESTRIO:

                              You're waking
                              up—
Too late. When Master hears of this, you'll die a dandy death.

SCELEDRUS:

I see the truth at last. My eyes were clouded by some fog.

PALAESTRIO:

I knew it all along. She's always been inside the house.

SCELEDRUS:

I can't say anything for sure. I saw her, yet I didn't . . .

PALAESTRIO:

By Jupiter, your folly almost finished us for good!
In trying to be true to Master, *you* just missed disaster!
But wait—our neighbor's door is creaking. I'll be quiet now.   410

> *(Enter* PHILOCOMASIUM *again,
> this time from the old man's house.)*

PHILOCOMASIUM:

> *(in a disguised voice)*

Put fire on the altar; let me joyfully give thanks
To Diana of Ephesus.† I'll burn Arabian incense.
She saved me in the turbulent Neptunian territory,
When I was buffeted about, beset by savage seas.

SCELEDRUS:

Palaestrio, Palaestrio!

PALAESTRIO:

> *(mimicking him)*

> O Sceledrus! What now?

SCELEDRUS:

That girl that just came out—is that our master's concubine,
Philocomasium? Well—yes or no?

PALAESTRIO:

                              It seems like her,
Yet it's amazing how she crossed from one house to the other.
If it is she . . .

---

†*Diana of Ephesus* . . . The temple of Diana at Ephesus was one of the seven wonders
of the world. When Shakespeare translates *The Brothers Menaechmus* into *The Comedy
of Errors*, he transfers the locale of the play from Epidamnus to Ephesus, where Emilia,
long-lost mother of the twins, is the abbess at the priory which is descended from
Diana's temple.

SCELEDRUS:
　　　　　　　You mean you have your doubts?

PALAESTRIO:
　　　　　　　　　　　　　　　It seems
　　　　　　　　　　　　　　　like her.

SCELEDRUS:
　Well, let's accost her. Hey, what's going on, Philocomasium?　420
　What were you doing in that house? Just what's been going
　　　　　　　　　　　　　　　　　　　on?

　Well, answer when I talk to you!

PALAESTRIO:
　　　　　　　　　　　You're talking to your-
　　　　　　　　　　　self—

　She doesn't answer.

SCELEDRUS:
　　　　　　　You! I'm speaking to you, wicked
　　　　　　　　　　　　　　　woman!

　So naughty with the neighbors—

PHILOCOMASIUM:
　　　　　　　(coldly)　　　Sir, with whom are you
　　　　　　　　　　　　　　conversing?

SCELEDRUS:
　Who else but you?

PHILOCOMASIUM:
　　　　　　　　Who are you, sir? What do you want
　　　　　　　　　　　　　　with me?

SCELEDRUS:
　Asking me who am I?†

PHILOCOMASIUM:
　　　　　　　　Why not?—I don't know you, so I
　　　　　　　　　　　　　　ask.

PALAESTRIO:
　I suppose you also don't know who *I* am.

PHILOCOMASIUM:
　　　　　　　　　　　Well, you *and*
　　　　　　　　　　　he—

　Are both a nuisance.

---

†*who am I?* . . . There is an abrupt change from iambic to trochaic verse here.

SCELEDRUS:

You don't know us?

PHILOCOMASIUM:

Neither one.

SCELEDRUS:

I'm
scared, I'm scared.

PALAESTRIO:

Scared of what?

SCELEDRUS:

I think we've lost our own identities somewhere—
Since she says she doesn't know us!

PALAESTRIO:

(very seriously)   Let's investigate this
further.   430
Sceledrus—are we ourselves—or are we other people now?
Maybe, unbeknownst to us, one of our neighbors has *transformed* us!

(SCELEDRUS *ponders this for a split second.*)

SCELEDRUS:

I'm myself for sure.

PALAESTRIO:

Me too. Hey, girl—you're going after
trouble.

(PHILOCOMASIUM *ignores him completely.*)

PALAESTRIO:

Hey, Philocomasium!

PHILOCOMASIUM:

(coolly)   What madness motivates you, sir, to
Carelessly concoct this incoherent name to call me?

PALAESTRIO:

(sarcastically)   Well now,
Tell me—what's your real name, then?

PHILOCOMASIUM:

My name is Dicea.

SCELEDRUS:

                      No, you're wrong, the
Name you're forging for yourself is phony, Philocomasium.
You're not *de*cent, you're *in*decent†—and you're cheating on
                             my master!

PHILOCOMASIUM:
  I?

SCELEDRUS:
  Yes, you.

PHILOCOMASIUM:
         But I only arrived from Athens yesterday,
With my faithful lover, an Athenian young man.

SCELEDRUS:

                        Then tell
                          me—   440
What's your business here in Ephesus?

PHILOCOMASIUM:

                      Looking for my dear
                            twin sister.
Someone said she might be here.

SCELEDRUS:
              (sarcastically)   Oh, you're a clever girl!

PHILOCOMASIUM:
No, I'm foolish, by the gods, to stand here chattering with
                             you two.
  I'll be going. . . .

SCELEDRUS:
         No, you won't be—*(He grabs her.)*

PHILOCOMASIUM:
                      Let me go!

SCELEDRUS:

                        You're
                  caught red-handed!
  I won't let you—

PHILOCOMASIUM:
         Then beware the noise—when my hand
                      meets your cheek.

---

†*decent . . . indecent . . .* Plautus puns on the Greek words *dikaia* and *adikos*, "right" and "wrong." To have the pun sound right in English, pronounce Dicea to rhyme with "Lisa."

Let me go!
SCELEDRUS:

> *(to* PALAESTRIO*)*

>>   You idiot, don't stand there; grab her other arm!
PALAESTRIO:
I don't want to get my back involved in this.† Who knows—
Maybe she's our girl . . . or maybe someone else who *looks*
>>>   like her.

PHILOCOMASIUM:
Will you let me go or not?
SCELEDRUS:

>>   You're coming home, no matter
>>>   what!
If you don't, I'll drag you home.
PHILOCOMASIUM:

>>   My home and master are
>>>   in Athens—   450
Athens back in Attica. I'm only staying as a guest here.

> *(pointing to the soldier's house)*

I don't know and I don't care about that house—or who you
>>>   are!

SCELEDRUS:
Go and sue me!‡ I won't ever let you go unless you swear
>>>   that
If I do you'll come inside.
PHILOCOMASIUM:

>>   Whoever you are, you're forcing
>>>   me.
All right, if you let me go, I give my word to go inside.
SCELEDRUS:
Go then. *(releases her)*
PHILOCOMASIUM:

>>   Go I shall . . . goodbye!

---

†*back involved in this* . . . i.e., for a whipping.
‡*Go and sue me* . . . Though it sounds like Nathan Detroit's song in *Guys and Dolls*,
the phrase literally translates Plautus' *lege agito*.

(She dashes into the old man's house.)

SCELEDRUS:

That's typical: a woman's word.

PALAESTRIO:

Sceledrus, you let the prize slip through your fingers. No mistaking—
She's our master's mistress. *Now*—you want to be a man of action?

SCELEDRUS:

(timidly)

Tell me how.

PALAESTRIO:

(boldly) Bring forth a sword for me!

SCELEDRUS:

(frightened) What will you do with it?

PALAESTRIO:

(imitating his master's bombastic manner)

I'll burst boldly through these portals and the man I see inside   460
Kissing Master's mistress, I shall slash to slivers on the spot!

SCELEDRUS:

(meekly)

So you think it's she?

PALAESTRIO:

There's no two ways about it.

SCELEDRUS:

What an actress—
So convincing . . .

PALAESTRIO:

(shouts) Bring me forth my sword!

SCELEDRUS:

I'll do it right away.

(SCELEDRUS *dashes headlong into the soldier's house.*
PALAESTRIO, *convulsed with laughter, addresses the audience.*)

PALAESTRIO:

All the king's horses and all the king's men could never act
with such great daring,
Never be so calm, so cool, *in anything,* as one small *woman!*
Deftly she delivered up a different accent for each part!
How the faithful guard, my foxy fellow slave, was fully flim-
flammed!
What a source of joy for all—this passage passing through
the wall!

(PALAESTRIO *laughs gleefully*
as SCELEDRUS *peeks out of the soldier's house,*
then sheepishly approaches.)

SCELEDRUS:

Say, Palaestrio . . . forget about the sword.

PALAESTRIO:

What's that?
Why so?

SCELEDRUS:

She's at home . . . our master's mistress.

PALAESTRIO:

Home?

SCELEDRUS:

She's lying
on her couch.   470

PALAESTRIO:

(*building up to a frightening crescendo*)

Now it seems you've found the trouble you've been looking
for, by Pollux!

SCELEDRUS:

Why?

PALAESTRIO:

Because you dared disturb a lady who's our neighbor's
guest.

SCELEDRUS:

Hercules! How horrible!

PALAESTRIO:

Why, there's no question, she must
be the
Real twin sister of our girl—and *she's* the one that you saw
kissing!

SCELEDRUS:

Yes, you're right. It's clearly she, just as you say. Did I come
close to
Getting killed! If I'd said a word to Master—

PALAESTRIO:

Now, be
smart:
Keep this all a secret. Slaves should always know more than
they tell.
I'll be going. I don't want to get mixed up in all your mischief.
I'll be at our neighbor's here. I don't quite care for your
confusions.
If when Master comes he needs me, he can send for me in
here.   480

(PALAESTRIO strides into the old man's house.)

SCELEDRUS:

At last he's gone. He cares no more for Master's matters
Than if he weren't slaving here in slavery!
Well, *now* our girl's inside the house, I'm sure of that;
I personally saw her lying on her couch.
So now's the time to pay attention to my guarding.

(SCELEDRUS paces before the soldier's door,
concentrating on his guarding.
PERIPLECTOMENUS *rushes out angrily from his own house.)*

PERIPLECTOMENUS:

By Hercules, those men must take me for a sissy—
My military neighbor's slaves insult me so!
Did they not lay their hands upon my lady guest—
Who yesterday arrived from Athens with my friend?

(indignantly to the audience)

A free and freeborn girl—manhandled and insulted!   490

SCELEDRUS:

Oh, Hercules, I'm through. He's heading to behead me.
I'm scared this thing has got me into awful trouble—
At least that's what I gather from the old man's words.

PERIPLECTOMENUS:

(aside)

Now I'll confront him. *(to* SCELEDRUS*)* Scurvy soundrel
                                          Sceledrus!
Did you insult my guest right by my house just now?

SCELEDRUS:

(near panic)

Dear neighbor, listen please—

PERIPLECTOMENUS:

                    I listen? *You're* the slave!

SCELEDRUS:

I want to clear myself—

PERIPLECTOMENUS:

                    How can you clear yourself,
When you've just done such monstrous and disgraceful
                                          things?
Perhaps because you're used to plundering the foe
You think you're free to act here as you please, scoundrel?   500

SCELEDRUS:

Oh, please, sir—

PERIPLECTOMENUS:

                    May the gods and goddesses not love me
If I don't arrange a whipping for you—yes,
A good long-lasting lengthy one, from dawn to dusk.
For one, because you broke my roof tiles and my gutters,
While you chased another monkey—like yourself.
And then for spying on my guest in my own house,
While he was kissing and embracing his own sweetheart.
And *then* you had the gall to slander that dear girl
Your master keeps—and to accuse me of atrocious things!
And *now* you maul my lady guest—right on my doorstep!   510
Why, if I don't have knotted lashes put to you,
I'll see to it your master's hit by more disgrace
Than oceans are by waves during a mighty storm!

(SCELEDRUS *trembles with fright.*)

SCELEDRUS:

I'm so upset, Periplectomenus, I just don't know
Whether I'd better argue this thing out with you,
Or else—if one is not the other—she's not *she*—
Well then, I guess I should apologize to you.
I mean—well, now I don't know *what* I saw at all!
Your girl looks so much like the one we have—that is,
If they are not the same—

PERIPLECTOMENUS:

      (*sweetly*)   Look in my house; you'll see.   520

SCELEDRUS:

Oh, could I?

PERIPLECTOMENUS:

       I insist. Inspect—and take your time.

SCELEDRUS:

Yes, that's the thing to do.

    (*He dashes into the old man's house.*)

PERIPLECTOMENUS:

      (*calling at the soldier's house*)

Philocomasium, be quick!
Run over to my house—go at a sprint—it's vital.
As soon as Sceledrus goes out, then double quick—
Run right back to your own house at a sprint!

      (*getting a bit excited himself*)

Oh, my goodness, now I'm scared she'll bungle it.
What if he doesn't see her? Wait—I hear the door.

   (SCELEDRUS *re-enters, wide-eyed and confused.*)

SCELEDRUS:

O ye immortal gods, there never were two girls more similar,
More similar—and yet I know they're not the same.   530
I didn't think the gods could do it!

PERIPLECTOMENUS:

          Well?

SCELEDRUS:

I'm whipped.

PERIPLECTOMENUS:
  Is she your girl?
SCELEDRUS:

It is and yet it isn't her.

PERIPLECTOMENUS:
  You saw . . . ?
SCELEDRUS:

I saw a girl together with your guest,
  Embracing him and kissing.
PERIPLECTOMENUS:

Was it yours?

SCELEDRUS:

Who knows?

PERIPLECTOMENUS:
  You want to know for sure?
SCELEDRUS:

Yes!

PERIPLECTOMENUS:

Hurry to your house
  And see if your girl's there within. Be quick—
SCELEDRUS:

I will.
  That's good advice. Wait—I'll be back here right away.

(SCELEDRUS *rushes into the soldier's house.*)

PERIPLECTOMENUS:
  By Pollux, never was a man bamboozled better,
  More wittily, in wilder or more wondrous ways.
  But here he comes. . . .

(SCELEDRUS *re-enters, on the brink of tears,
  and throws himself at* PERIPLECTOMENUS' *feet.*)

SCELEDRUS:

Periplectomenus, I beg of you,   540
  By all the gods and men—by my stupidity—
  And by your knees.

PERIPLECTOMENUS:

What do you beg of me?

SCELEDRUS:

Forgive
My foolishness and my stupidity. At last
I know that I've been thoughtless—idiotic—blind!

(sheepishly)

Philocomasium . . . is right inside.

PERIPLECTOMENUS:

Well, gallows bird—
You've seen them both?

SCELEDRUS:

I've seen.

PERIPLECTOMENUS:

Would you please call your
master?

SCELEDRUS:

(beseeching)

I do confess I'm worthy of a whopping whipping,
And I do admit that I abused your lady guest.
But I mistook her for my master's concubine—
The soldier has appointed me her guardian.   550
Two drops of water from a single well could not be drawn
Much more alike than our girl's like your lady guest.

(quietly)

I also peeked down into your house through the skylight,
I do confess.

PERIPLECTOMENUS:

Why not confess? I saw you do it!
And there you saw my guests—a man and lady—kissing—
Correct?

SCELEDRUS:

Yes, yes. Should I deny the things I saw?
But, sir, I thought I saw Philocomasium.

PERIPLECTOMENUS:

Did you consider me a man so vile and base

To be a party to such things in my own house,
And let my neighbor suffer such outrageous harm?   560

SCELEDRUS:

At last I see how idiotically I've acted.
I know the facts now. But it wasn't done on purpose.
I'm blameless—

PERIPLECTOMENUS:

             But not shameless. Why, a slave should have
His eyes downcast, his hands and tongue in strict control—
His speech as well.

SCELEDRUS:

          If I so much as mumble, sir,
From this day on—and even mumble what I'm sure of—
Have me tortured. I'll just give myself to you.
But now I beg forgiveness.

PERIPLECTOMENUS:

    (*magnanimously*)   I'll suppress my wrath
And think you really didn't do it all on purpose.
So—you're forgiven.

SCELEDRUS:

          May the gods all bless you, sir!   570

PERIPLECTOMENUS:

Now, after this, by Hercules, you guard your tongue
And even if you know a thing, *don't* know a thing—
And *don't* see even what you see.

SCELEDRUS:

           That's good advice.
I'll do it. Have I begged enough?

PERIPLECTOMENUS:

         Just go away!

SCELEDRUS:

Do you want something else?†

PERIPLECTOMENUS:

        Yes—*not* to know you!

(PERIPLECTOMENUS *turns away from* SCELEDRUS *in disgust
        and walks aside.*)

---

†*Do you want something else?* . . . A literal rendering of the Latin, which was a Roman way
of saying ''Goodbye.'' It is not meant to be taken literally as Periplectomenus does here.

SCELEDRUS:

(suspiciously)

He's fooling me. How easily he just excused me.
He wasn't even angry. But I know what's up:
The minute that the soldier comes home from the forum,
They'll grab me in the house. He and Palaestrio,
They have me up for sale—I've sensed it for a while now. 580
By Hercules, I won't snap at their bait today.
I'll run off somewhere, hide myself a day or two,
Till this commotion quiets and the shouting stops.
I've earned myself much more than one man's share of
                                     troubles.

(SCELEDRUS runs off.)

PERIPLECTOMENUS:

Well, he's retreated. Now, by Pollux, I'm quite sure
A headless pig has far more brains than Sceledrus.
He's been so gulled he doesn't see the things he saw.
His eyes, his ears, his every sense has now deserted him
To join our cause. Well, up to now, so far so good. 590
That girl of ours came up with quite a fine performance.
Now to our little senate,† for Palaestrio
Is there inside my house and Sceledrus is gone.
We now can have a meeting with the whole committee.
I'd better go inside before they vote without me!

(He goes into his own house.
The stage is empty for a moment,
then PALAESTRIO tiptoes out of the old man's house.)

PALAESTRIO:

(motioning to the others who are still inside)

Pleusicles, have everybody wait inside a little longer.
Let me reconnoiter first to see if there are spies around to

---

†*our little senate* . . . It is characteristić of Plautus' slave heroes that they see themselves as leading Roman senators. Cf. Tranio in *Mostellaria*, line 688. Note that they
might vote without an elder statesman, for Palaestrio is the leader!

Stop the meeting we're about to have. We need a place that's
                                                      safe,

Some place where no enemy can plunder any plans we've
                                                      made.

What you plan out will not pan out, if your enemy can use it.   600

Useful things for enemies become abuseful things for you.

Clearly, if the enemy should somehow learn about your plans,
                                                      they'll

Turn the tables on you, shut your mouth and tie your hands.
                                                      And so

Whatever you had planned to do to them, they'll do to you
                                                      instead!

Now I'll peek around, look right and left, to see there's no
                                                      one here, no

Hunter using ears for nets so he can "catch" our secret plans.

(looks to either side)

Good—the coast is clear all up and down the street. I'll call
                                                      them out.

Hey, Periplectomenus and Pleusicles, produce yourselves!†   610

(They come out eagerly.)

PERIPLECTOMENUS:
Here—at your command.

PALAESTRIO:
                    Commanding's easy when your
                              troops are good.

How about it now—that plan we figured out inside—shall we
                                                      now

Carry on with it?

PERIPLECTOMENUS:
                    We couldn't do it better.

PALAESTRIO:
                                        What do you
                                              think,

Pleusicles?

---

†*produce yourselves!* . . . Palaestrio was extremely long-winded here, even by Plautine
standards. Moreover, his verbosity is of dubious comic value. Perhaps *The Braggart
Soldier*, the longest of Plautus' comedies, has come down to us in its rough-draft version.

PLEUSICLES:

          (mindlessly devoted)

      What could be fine with you and not be fine with
                                    me?
No one's more my friend than you are.

PALAESTRIO:

                        Nicely and precise-
                        ly put.

PERIPLECTOMENUS:

  That's the way he should be talking.

PLEUSICLES:

                      Yet it makes me mis-
                      erable; it
Troubles and torments me too—

PERIPLECTOMENUS:

                  What troubles you? Speak
                  up, my boy!

PLEUSICLES:

  That I burden someone who's as old as you with childish
                              trifles.
These concerns are so unworthy of your noble qualities—
Asking you for so much help in what is really my concern: 620
Bringing reinforcements to a lover, doing different duties,
Duties which most men of your age would prefer to dodge—
                            not do!
I'm ashamed to bring annoyance to you in your twilight
                            years.

PALAESTRIO:

  You're a novel lover if you blush at doing anything!
  You're no lover—just the palest shadow of what lovers
                      should be.

PLEUSICLES:

  Troubling a man of his age with a youthful love affair?

PERIPLECTOMENUS:

  What's that? Do I seem so six-feet-under to you—is that so?
  Do I seem to be so senile, such a coffin candidate?
  After all, I'm barely fifty-four years old—not even that.
  I've got perfect vision still, my hands are quick, my legs are
                      nimble.   630

PALAESTRIO:

    Maybe he's white-haired on top, but not inside his head—
                                that's sure.

    All the qualities that he was born with haven't aged a bit.

PLEUSICLES:

    I know that, by Pollux, what you say is true, Palaestrio.
    He's been absolutely youthful in his hospitality.

PERIPLECTOMENUS:

    Try me in a crisis, boy. The more I'm pressed the more you'll
                                  note how

    I'll support your love affair—

PLEUSICLES:

                      No need to note—I know it
                            well.

PERIPLECTOMENUS:

                (casually boasting)

    Experience, experience . . . the only way of finding out.
    Only he who's loved himself can see inside a lover's soul.
    Even I still have a little lively loving left in me.   640
    All my taste for joy and pleasure hasn't dried up in me yet.
    I'm the perfect party guest—I'm quick with very clever quips.
    And I never interrupt another person when he's talking.
    I refrain from rudeness, I'm restrained with guests and never
                                  rowdy.
    I remember to contribute just my share of conversation.
    And I also know to shut my mouth when someone else is
                                  talking.
    I'm no spitter, I'm no cougher and I'm not forever sneezing.
    I was born in Ephesus, I'm not an Animulian.†

PALAESTRIO:

    Mezzo-middle-aged at most, with all the talents he describes!
    Certainly a Muse has shown this man how to be so amusing.   650

PERIPLECTOMENUS:

    I can show you that I'm even more amusing than you say:

---

†*Animulian* . . . Most critics suggest that the inhabitants of Animulia, a small town in
Apulia, southeastern Italy, had a bad reputation for one reason or another. Or perhaps
Plautus is punning on the word *animal*, the old man arguing that he is not a beast, but
very civilized. Cf. the enigmatic joke on the town of Sarsina, *Mostellaria*, line 770.

Never at a party do I screw around with someone's girl,
Never do I filch the food or take the goblet out of turn.
Never do I let the wine bring out an argument in me.
Someone gets too nasty? I go home and cut the conversation.
Give me love and loveliness and lots of laughter at a party.

PALAESTRIO:

All your talents seem to tend toward charm and graciousness,
                                                    by Pollux.
Show me three men with such talents and I'll pay their weight
                                                    in gold!

PLEUSICLES:

Never—you won't find another man as old as he who is so
Thoroughly delightful and so good a friend to anyone.   660

> (PERIPLECTOMENUS *is enjoying the compliments,
> but he doesn't like being called an old man.*)

PERIPLECTOMENUS:

I'll make you admit I'm really just a youngster in my way.
Wait until you see the countless splendid services I'll render:
Do you need a lawyer—one that's fierce and angry? Here I
                                                    am.
Do you need a mild one? I'll be smoother than the silent sea.
I'll be oh so softer than the southern breeze in early spring.
I can also be the most lighthearted of your dinner guests,
Or the perfect parasite, or else supply a super supper.
As for dancing—even fruity fairies† haven't got *my* grace.

(Acting very impressed, PALAESTRIO *turns to* PLEUSICLES.*)*

PALAESTRIO:

> *(to* PLEUSICLES*)*

What else could you wish for if you'd even wish for some-
                                                    thing else?

PLEUSICLES:

Just the talent to express my gratitude for everything.   670

---

†*fruity fairies* . . . The Latin words are *cinaedus*, which refers to boy ballet dancers of
dubious sexuality, and *malacus*, meaning "delicate." Interestingly enough, as Hammond,
Mark and Moskalew note in their edition (p. 133), both these Latin words are taken directly
from the Greek. This was a typical practice of the Romans when they wished to describe
"people or practices which they regarded as characteristic of degenerate Greeks, but
not of themselves."

Thanks to you *(to* PERIPLECTOMENUS*)* and thanks to you,
                for taking such good care of me.
I must be a burdensome expense to you—

PERIPLECTOMENUS:

                          You silly boy!
What you spend for enemies or for a nasty wife's expense,
What you lay out for a guest, a real true friend of yours, is
                              profit!†
Thank the gods I can afford to entertain you as I'd like to.
Eat! Drink up! Indulge yourself, let laughter overflow the
                              brim!
Mine's the house of freedom—I am free—I live my life for
                              me.
Thank the gods, I'm rich enough. I could've married very well,
Could've led a wealthy wife of high position to the altar.   680
But I wouldn't want to lead a barking dog into my house!‡

PALAESTRIO:

Yet remember—children can be pleasant—and it's fun to
                              breed 'em.

PERIPLECTOMENUS:

You can breed 'em, give me freedom! *That,* by Hercules, is
                              fun!

PALAESTRIO:

You're a good adviser—for yourself as well as other people.

PERIPLECTOMENUS:

Sure it's sweet to wed a *good* wife—if there's such a thing on
                              earth.
I'd be glad to marry someone who would turn to me and ask
                              me,
"Dearest husband, buy some wool, so I can make some cloth-
                              ing for you,
First a tunic, soft and warm, and then a cloak for winter
                              weather,
So you won't be cold." You'd never hear a wife say things
                              like that!
Why, before the cock would crow, she'd shake me from my
                              sleep and say,   690

---

†Line 675 omitted.
‡Cf. *Brothers Menaechmus,* lines 713–718, on wifely "bitchiness."

"Husband! Give me money for a New Year's gift to give my
mother!
It's Minerva's festival, so give to give the fortuneteller,
Dream interpreter, diviner, sorceress and soothsayer!
She tells fortunes from your eyebrows—it's a crime to leave
her out!
How about the laundry girl? She couldn't do without a gift.
Look how long it's been since we have tipped the grocer's
wife—she's angry with us.
And the midwife has complained—we didn't send her quite
enough!
What! Will we send nothing to the one who's nursed our
household slaves?"
These and other ruinations that a woman brings have kept me
Single, so I'm not subjected to this sort of sordid speeches. 700

PALAESTRIO:

All the gods have blessed you, for, by Hercules, if you let go
of
Freedom just one second, it's no easy thing to get it back.

PLEUSICLES:

Don't you think it's noble for a man of wealth and high
estate to
Bring up children as a sort of monument to his good name?†

PERIPLECTOMENUS:

I have relatives aplenty, so what need have I of children?
I live happily and well, I suit myself, do what I please.
When I die, my relatives can split the money that I leave 'em.
Now they're up at dawn to come and ask me if I've slept all
right. 709
When they sacrifice, they give me bigger portions than their
own.
And they take me out to banquets, have me home for lunch,
for dinner.
They're so sad if they can send me only something small and
simple.

---

†*to his good name* . . . This discussion of children has a faintly Roman touch. But
Periplectomenus' rejoinder that he doesn't want offspring of his own (line 705) is a most
un-Roman sentiment. Think of what Aeneas suffers, all for the sake of his son's future!

They compete in giving, as I secretly repeat inside:
"Let them chase my money; they're all eagerly supporting
me!"

PALAESTRIO:

Ah, you really know the way to live; you know what life is
for.

If you're having fun, it's just as good as having twins or
triplets.

(PERIPLECTOMENUS *seems anxious to talk on any topic,*
so he now pursues this one.)

PERIPLECTOMENUS:

If I really had 'em, I'd be miserable because of them—
Worrying about their health. Why, if my son had fever, I
would   720

Think he's dying. If he drank too much or tumbled off his
horse,

I would always be afraid he broke his neck or broke a leg.

PALAESTRIO:

Here's a man who rightfully has riches. He should live forever.
He keeps wealthy, ever healthy—and he's out to help his
friends.

PLEUSICLES:

What a charming chap! By all the gods and goddesses above,
Gods should all decide how long we live by a consistent
system.

Just as the inspector fixes selling prices in the market,
Merchandise of quality is priced according to its merits,
Merchandise that's rotten gets a price that makes its owner
poorer,

That's the way a person's life should be determined by the
gods.   730

Men with charm and lots of talent should have long and
lengthy lives;

Rotten men and rogues should be deprived of life without
delay.

We'd be minus many scoundrels if the gods would use this
system,

And the dirty deeds committed would be fewer. Furthermore,

Men would be of quality—and life would be a better bargain.

(PERIPLECTOMENUS is flattered,
but he playfully chides the young man.)

PERIPLECTOMENUS:

Only silly fools find fault with what the gods above decree.
Only fools would scold the gods. Let's stop this stupid stuff
                                         for now.

(He starts to go off.)

Now I'll buy the groceries to entertain my guest with some-
                                                thing
Worthy of us both, a welcome of good wishes *and* good
                                                dishes!

PLEUSICLES:

Please—I've been a terrible expense to you already. Surely
No guest can accept such friendly treatment as you've offered
                                         me and   740
Not become an inconvenience after three days in a row.
After *ten* days, he becomes an *Iliad* of inconvenience!
Even if his host is willing, still the servants start to mutter.

PERIPLECTOMENUS:

I've instructed servants in this house to stick to serving me,
Not to give me orders or to have myself depend on them.
                                                Why, if
What I want displeases them—too bad! I'm captain of the
                                                ship.
Willy-nilly, they'll do what they're ordered—or be beaten up.
Now I'd better get on with the groceries. . . .

(He starts to amble off.)

PLEUSICLES:

                                    Well, if you
                                    must—
Please don't buy extravagantly—anything is fine for me.   750

(PERIPLECTOMENUS now stops to discuss this topic.)

PERIPLECTOMENUS:

Stop that kind of talk, that stale cliché is older than the hills.

Really, now you're talking like the hoi-polloi—you know the
                                                kind, who
When they're at the table and the dinner's set before 'em say,
"Did you go to all this trouble just for *me*—you shouldn't
                                                have.
Hercules, it's madness. Why, there's food enough for ten at
                                                least!"
Much too much for them! But while they're frowning, they
                                        are drowning it!

PALAESTRIO:

That's the way it is exactly. *(to* PLEUSICLES*)* He speaks
                                soundly and profoundly.

PERIPLECTOMENUS:

Never will you hear these people, when a feast is set before
                                                'em,
Say, "Remove this . . . take this plate away . . . take off the
                                ham . . . I simply couldn't.
Take this bit of pork away . . . this eel would be much better
                                                cold."   760
"Take" . . . "remove" . . . "be off" are words you'll never
                                hear from one of them.
No, they leap to reach the food, with half their bodies on the
                                                table.

PALAESTRIO:

Bad behavior well described.

PERIPLECTOMENUS:

                                I haven't told the hundredth
                                                part of
What I could expound upon if only we had time to talk—

            *(PALAESTRIO seizes this opportunity
            to cut* PERIPLECTOMENUS' *monologue short.)*

PALAESTRIO:

Right! But we had better turn our thoughts to what we're
                                                doing now.
Listen closely, both of you. *(to* PERIPLECTOMENUS*)* I'll
                                need your services in this,
Periplectomenus. I've figured out a lovely scheme to help us

Take our curly-headed soldier to the barber's for a trimming.†
And we'll give our lover here the chance to get his sweetheart
                                                           back, and
Take her off from here for good!

PERIPLECTOMENUS:

                              Now there's a plan I'd
                                   like to hear!   770

PALAESTRIO:
First, I'd like to ask you for that ring of yours.

PERIPLECTOMENUS:

                    (suspiciously)   How will you
                                              use it?

PALAESTRIO:
When I have the ring you'll have the reason—and my whole
                                                   invention.

PERIPLECTOMENUS:
Here's the ring.

PALAESTRIO:

                    And here's your reason in turn, the little
                                              scheme that
I've been setting up.

PLEUSICLES:

                    We're listening to you with well-washed
                                                   ears.

PALAESTRIO:
Master is the wildest wenching wanton man who ever was—
Or who ever will be for that matter.

PERIPLECTOMENUS:

                              I believe it too.

PALAESTRIO:
He supposes he surpasses Paris in his handsomeness.
He thinks all the women here just cannot help pursuing him.

PERIPLECTOMENUS:
I know several husbands here who wish that statement were
                                              the truth!‡

---

†*for a trimming* . . . "Trimming" sounds modern, but Plautus' *admutiletur* has precisely that tonsorial tone. Much of Plautus' vocabulary for trickery sounds very up-to-date.
‡*were the truth* . . . The old man means that lots of unhappily married husbands would be glad to have the soldier relieve them of their onerous connubial responsibilities. Plautus is full of anti-wife jokes, roundabout and direct.

But proceed, I know too well he's what you say, Palaestrio.   780
Get on to the point, be brief, don't beat around the bush, my
boy.

PALAESTRIO:
Could you find a woman for me—someone beautiful and
charming,
Someone full of cleverness and trickery from tip to toe?

PERIPLECTOMENUS:
Freed or freeborn girl?

PALAESTRIO:
It doesn't matter, just be sure and get
me
One who's money-loving, and who earns her keep by being
kept.
One who's got a mind—she doesn't need a heart—no woman
has one.

PERIPLECTOMENUS:
Do you want a . . . green one . . . or a ripe one?

PALAESTRIO:
Just be
sure she's juicy.
Get the freshest, most appealing girl you possibly can find.

PERIPLECTOMENUS:
Say—I have a client—luscious, youngish little courtesan!
But—why do you need her?

PALAESTRIO:
Bring her home to your house,
right away.   790
Have her in disguise, so she'll look like a married woman—
Hair combed high, with ribbons and the rest.† She must
pretend that
She's your wedded wife. Now train the girl!

PERIPLECTOMENUS:
I'm lost. What's
all this for?

PALAESTRIO:
You'll soon see. Now, does she have a maid?

---

†*ribbons and the rest* . . . You could tell by her hairdo if a Roman woman was married
or single.

PERIPLECTOMENUS:

                                    A very clever
                                         one.

PALAESTRIO:

    We'll have need of her as well. Now tell the woman and her
                                         maid the
    Mistress must pretend that she's your wife—who's dying for
                                         the soldier boy.
    We'll pretend she gave her little maid this ring—to give to
                                         me.
    I'll give it to him, pretending I'm the go-between.

PERIPLECTOMENUS:

                                    I hear you—
    Don't assume I'm deaf. I know my ears are both in fine
                                         condition.†

PALAESTRIO:

    I'll pretend it's been presented as a present from your wife so   800
    She could . . . get together with him. I know him—he'll be in
                                         flames!
    Nothing gets that lecher more excited than adultery!

PERIPLECTOMENUS:

    If you asked the Sun himself to find the girls you've asked
                                         me for,
    He could never find a pair more perfect for the job. Relax!

                        (He exits.)

PALAESTRIO:

    Fine, hop to it then. We need 'em right away. Now,
                                    Pleusicles—

PLEUSICLES:

    At your service.

PALAESTRIO:

                    When the soldier gets back home, remember
                                         not to
    Call your girl Philocomasium.

PLEUSICLES:

                        What should I call her then?

---

†*in fine condition* . . . The text is uncertain here. The translator has given the general
sense of it.

PALAESTRIO:
  Dicea.

PLEUSICLES:
      Yes, of course, the name we just agreed upon.

PALAESTRIO:
                                              Now go.

*(PLEUSICLES remains stationary for a moment,
        "memorizing" the name.)*

PLEUSICLES:
  I'll remember. *(to PALAESTRIO)* But I'd like to ask you *why*
                                    I should remember.

PALAESTRIO:
  When you have to know, I'll tell you. For the moment, just
                                  keep still,   810
  While the old man does his part—and very soon you'll play
                                  your role.

PLEUSICLES:
  Then I guess I'll go inside.

              (He starts to walk off.)

PALAESTRIO:

              (calling after him)
                      And follow orders carefully!

      *(PLEUSICLES walks slowly into the house,
              rehearsing to himself.)*

PALAESTRIO:

      (to the audience, with a broad smile)

  What storms I'm stirring up—what mighty machinations!
  Today I'll snatch that concubine back from the soldier—
  That is, if all my troops† remain well disciplined.   815
  Now I'll call him. Hey, Sceledrus! If you've got time
  Come out in front. Palaestrio is calling you.

---

†*all my troops* . . . Palaestrio speaks of *manuplares*, specifically Roman troop divisions.
Cf. note on *Mostellaria*, line 312. In performance, this is an ideal spot for the
intermission.

(A pause.
Not SCELEDRUS, *but another slave,* LURCIO *by name,*
appears at the door, extremely drunk.)

LURCIO:

He's busy now.†

PALAESTRIO:

        At what?

LURCIO:

                He's pouring . . . as he sleeps.

PALAESTRIO:

Did you say "pouring"?

LURCIO:

                "Snoring" 's what I meant to say.

But snoring, pouring—isn't it about the same?   820

(LURCIO starts to reel offstage. PALAESTRIO stops him.)

PALAESTRIO:

Hey—Sceledrus inside asleep?

LURCIO:

                Except his nose.

That's making quite a noise. *(confidentially)* He took some
                        secret snorts

'Cause he's the steward and was spicing up the wine.

(LURCIO again turns to go; PALAESTRIO *again stops him.)*

PALAESTRIO:

But wait, you scoundrel, you're the guy's substeward—wait!

LURCIO:

Your point?

---

†*He's busy now* . . . The translator is hard pressed to explain the purpose of the Lurcio-Palaestrio repartee (lines 816–869). The plot is not advanced, and Lurcio never appears again. At least Artotrogus in the opening scene serves as a foil to the soldier, and aids exposition somewhat.

Perhaps one of Plautus' actors needed some extra time to change costume. This explanation has been offered for several moments in his comedies which seem otherwise to be needless padding. It is also possible that a member of the troupe which performed this play was popular for his drunk bit, and Plautus simply had to accommodate a comedian, as Shakespeare did many a time. If we accept this explanation, we then may imagine that the same actor who plays Lurcio here was so successful that Plautus wrote him another drunken part—Callidamates in the *Mostellaria*. See pp. 226ff.

PALAESTRIO:

(indignantly)

How could he let himself just go to sleep?

LURCIO:

He closed his eyes, I think.

PALAESTRIO:

I didn't ask you that!

Come here! You're dead if I don't know the truth at once!

Did you serve him the wine?

LURCIO:

I didn't.

PALAESTRIO:

You deny it?

LURCIO:

I do, by Hercules. He told me to deny it.   830

I also didn't pour four pints into a pitcher.

He also didn't drink 'em all warmed up at dinner.

PALAESTRIO:

You also didn't drink?

LURCIO:

Gods blast me if I did.

I wish I'd drunk.

PALAESTRIO:

How come?

LURCIO:

Because I *guzzled* it instead.

The wine was overheated and it burned my throat.

PALAESTRIO:

Some slaves get drunk, while others get weak vinegar!

Our pantry has some loyal steward and substeward!

LURCIO:

You'd do the same, by Hercules, if you had charge.

You're acting jealous now 'cause you can't copy us.   840

(He turns to go once again.)

PALAESTRIO:

Wait, wait, you scoundrel! Has he drunk like this before?

And just to help your thinking let me tell you this:

If, Lurcio, you lie, you'll suffer horribly.

LURCIO:

Oh, really now? Then you can tattle what I've told
To get me kicked out from my storeroom stuffing job,
And pick a new substeward when *you're* put in charge.

PALAESTRIO:

By Pollux, no, I won't. Come on, be brave and speak.

LURCIO:

He never poured a drop, by Pollux. That's the truth.
He'd order me to do it—and I'd pour for him.

PALAESTRIO:

That's why the jars were always standing on their heads!   850

LURCIO:

By Hercules, that isn't why the jars were jarred.
Inside the storeroom was this very slippery spot.
A two-point pot was leaning on the casks nearby;
It often would get all filled up—ten times or so.
I saw it filled and emptied. Mostly it got filled.
And then the pot danced wildly† and the jars were jarred.

PALAESTRIO:

Get in! You held that storeroom bacchanal yourselves.
By Hercules, I'll go bring master from the forum.

(PALAESTRIO *takes a few steps toward the forum,
then stops to listen to* LURCIO'*s lament.*)

LURCIO:

I'm dead. Master will crucify me when he comes
And finds out what's been done because I didn't tell him.   860
I'll run off somewhere so I can postpone the pains.

(*to the audience*)

---

†*danced wildly* . . . Here and in line 857 below we find a topical allusion to bacchana-
lian behavior, that is, the orgiastic dancing involved in the worship of the wine god
Bacchus. This wild worship was newly introduced to Italy in Plautus' day, and was
outlawed by a decree of the senate in 186 B.C. *Bacchor*, the verb for "dance wildly,"
appears here, I believe, for the very first time in Latin literature. Virgil uses this verb at
significant moments in the *Aeneid*, with very great dramatic effect. For example:

Saevit inops animi, totamque incensa per urbem bacchatur (4.301)

[Dido] rages, out of her mind, reeling in flames, in a dance through the city.

Cf. also *Aeneid*, 6.78 and 7.385.

Folks, please don't tell Palaestrio, I beg of you.

(He starts to tiptoe off. PALAESTRIO *scares him with a shout.)*

PALAESTRIO:
Hey—where're you going?

LURCIO:
   (nervously) I'll be back. I'm on an errand.

PALAESTRIO:
For whom?

LURCIO:
   Philocomasium.

PALAESTRIO:
     Go—rush right back!

LURCIO:
Do me a favor, will you? If while I'm away
There's punishment distributed . . . please take my share.

  (LURCIO scampers off.)

PALAESTRIO:
(to the audience) Ah, now I understand our young girl's
           strategy.
With Sceledrus asleep, she sends his underling
Off on some business while she sneaks across.

  (looks offstage to his left)

But here's our neighbor with the girl I requisitioned— 870
And, oh, is she good-looking! All the gods are with us.
She's dressed so finely—most unprostitutishly.
This whole affair now seems most charmingly in hand!

 (PERIPLECTOMENUS enters with a girl on either arm.
  One is the courtesan ACROTELEUTIUM,
   a reasonably young old pro,
  and the other is her maid MILPHIDIPPA.*)*

PERIPLECTOMENUS:

   (to the girls)

Now I've explained this whole thing to you both from start
           to finish,

Acroteleutium and Milphidippa. If you haven't grasped
This artful artifice as yet, I'll drill you once again.
But if you understand it all, then we can change the subject.

ACROTELEUTIUM:

Now don't you think I'd be a stupid idiot to undertake
An unfamiliar project or to promise you results,
If I were unacquainted with the whole technique—the art of
being wicked? 880

PERIPLECTOMENUS:

Forewarned's forearmed, I say.

ACROTELEUTIUM:

Not to a real professional—
A layman's words are little use. Why, didn't I myself,
The minute that I drank the smallest drop of your proposal,
Didn't *I* tell *you* the way the soldier could be swindled?

PERIPLECTOMENUS:

But no one ever knows enough. How many have I seen
Avoid the region of good sense—before they even found it.

ACROTELEUTIUM:

But when it's wickedness or wiles that's wanted of the
woman,
Why, then she's got a monumentally immortal memory.
It's only when it comes to something fine or faithful
That suddenly she's scatterbrained—and can't remember. 890

PERIPLECTOMENUS:

Well, that's what I'm afraid of. Here your job is double edged:
For when you do the soldier harm, you're doing *me* a favor.

ACROTELEUTIUM:

Relax, you're safe as long as we don't know we're doing good.

PERIPLECTOMENUS:

What mangy merchandise a woman is.

ACROTELEUTIUM:

Just like her cus-
tomers.

PERIPLECTOMENUS:

That's typical. Come on.

PALAESTRIO:

I ought to go ahead and meet them.
It's good to see you, sir, so charmingly accompanied.

PERIPLECTOMENUS:

Well met, Palaestrio. Look—here they are—the girls
You ordered me to bring—and in their costumes.

PALAESTRIO:

        (pats him on the back)   You're my
           man!

Palaestrio salutes Acroteleutium.

ACROTELEUTIUM:

        Who's this   900
Who speaks to me as if he knew me?

PERIPLECTOMENUS:

        He's our . . . archi-
          tect.

ACROTELEUTIUM:

My greetings to the architect.

PALAESTRIO:

        The same to you. Has he
Indoctrinated you?

PERIPLECTOMENUS:

        The girls I bring are well rehearsed.

PALAESTRIO:

I want to hear how well. The fear of failure frightens me.

PERIPLECTOMENUS:

I didn't add a thing to those instructions that you gave me.

*(*ACROTELEUTIUM *approaches* PALAESTRIO *and speaks to him
in a very blasé manner.)*

ACROTELEUTIUM:

Now look, you want the soldier to be swindled, right?

PALAESTRIO:

        That's right!

ACROTELEUTIUM:

Neatly, sweetly and completely—everything's arranged.

PALAESTRIO:

I want you to pretend to be his wife—

ACROTELEUTIUM:

        I *am* his wife.

PALAESTRIO:

Pretend that you're enamored of the soldier—

ACROTELEUTIUM:

So I will be.

PALAESTRIO:

Pretend that I'm the go-between for this—with Milphidippa.

ACROTELEUTIUM:

You should have been a prophet—all you say will soon come
true.   910

PALAESTRIO:

Pretend this ring was given by your little maid to me
To offer to the soldier with your compliments.

ACROTELEUTIUM:

That's true!

PERIPLECTOMENUS:

Why bother to remind the girls of things they know?

ACROTELEUTIUM:

It's good.

Remember if you're dealing with a first-rate architect,
And if this man designs a ship with well-drawn plans,
You'll build the ship with ease if everything's laid out and
set.
Now we've a keel that's accurately laid and nicely set,
Our architect has helpers who are not exactly . . . amateurs,
So if our raw material is not delayed en route,   920
I know our capabilities—we'll have that ship in no time.

PALAESTRIO:

(to ACROTELEUTIUM)

I guess you know my military master—

ACROTELEUTIUM:

What a question!!

How could I *not* know such a public menace, such a big-
mouth,
Fancy-hairdoed, perfumed lecher?!

PALAESTRIO:

Hmm— does he know
you?

ACROTELEUTIUM:

He never saw me, so how could he?

PALAESTRIO:

Ah, that's lovely talk.
I'm sure the action will be lovelier.

ACROTELEUTIUM:

Now just relax—
Leave him to me. If I don't make a fancy fool of him,
Then put the blame on me completely.

PALAESTRIO:

Fine, now go inside
And concentrate completely on this project.

ACROTELEUTIUM:

(going)   Just relax.

PALAESTRIO:

Periplectomenus, take them inside. I'm for the forum.   930
I'll find my man, I'll offer him this ring and I'll insist
That it was given to me by "your wife," who's dying for him.

>   *(pointing to* MILPHIDIPPA)

As soon as we get back here from the forum, send her out,
Pretending she was sent to him in secret.

PERIPLECTOMENUS:

Fine—relax.

PALAESTRIO:

Just keep on the alert. I'll bring him here already stuffed.

>   (PALAESTRIO *rushes out toward the forum.*)

PERIPLECTOMENUS:

Now walk and talk successfully! Oh, if we work this out,
And if my guest gets back the soldier's concubine today,
I'll send you such a gift—

ACROTELEUTIUM:

(casually)   Say—is the girl cooperating?   940

PERIPLECTOMENUS:

Absolutissimo, bellissimo.

ACROTELEUTIUM:

(facetiously)   Swellissimo.
When all our roguery is pooled together, I'm convinced,
We'll never meet defeat by any trickier deceit.

PERIPLECTOMENUS:

Let's go inside and then rehearse our parts with care.

We all must follow our instructions nicely and precisely,
So when the soldier comes, there'll be no blunders.

ACROTELEUTIUM:

You're the slow one.

(PERIPLECTOMENUS *leads the two women into his house.*
The stage is empty for a brief moment
[musical interlude?],
then enter PYRGOPOLYNICES,
smiling with pleasure at his accomplishments this morning.
PALAESTRIO *follows at his heels,*
trying to get his master's attention.)

PYRGOPOLYNICES:

(smiling smugly)

What a pleasure when affairs go well—exactly as you planned
them.
I've already sent a parasite of mine to King Seleucus,
Leading mercenaries I conscripted for His Majesty.
While they guard his kingdom, I shall have a little relaxation.   950

PALAESTRIO:

Come now, think of your affairs, not King Seleucus'. Why,
look, a
Promising new venture's† been proposed to me as go-between.

PYRGOPOLYNICES:

(condescendingly)

Well, I'll put the other things aside and give you my attention.
Speak—I now surrender both my ears to you and to this
venture.

PALAESTRIO:

(suspiciously)

Reconnoiter first—is there a snare to catch our conversation?
I'm commanded to pursue this business with all secrecy.

---

†*Promising new venture's* . . . The Latin is *condicio nova et luculenta,* which might also
be rendered as "a new and profitable business." Note how Palaestrio employs commercial
terms to get the greedy soldier interested in love affairs. Cf. line 957, "the first deposit
on a love account," in which a very technical term, *arrabo* (down payment), is used.

*(PYRGOPOLYNICES "scouts" the area,
then whispers to PALAESTRIO.)*

PYRGOPOLYNICES:
  No one.
PALAESTRIO:

(gives the ring)

  Take this—it's the first deposit on a love account.
PYRGOPOLYNICES:
  What's this? Where'd you get it?
PALAESTRIO:

  From a lovely and lively
  lady
  Who adores you and who longs to have your handsome
  handsomeness.
  She has had her maid give me this ring to forward on to you.   960
PYRGOPOLYNICES:
  But who is she—is she freeborn or some manumitted slave?
PALAESTRIO:
  Feh! How could I dare negotiate for you with freedwomen—
  You're already swamped with offers from the well-born girls
  who want you!

(PYRGOPOLYNICES smiles and continues his questions.)

PYRGOPOLYNICES:
  Wife or widow?
PALAESTRIO:
  Wife *and* widow.
PYRGOPOLYNICES:
  Tell me how a woman can be
  Both a wife and widow?
PALAESTRIO:
  Easy: she is young, her husband's
  old!

PYRGOPOLYNICES:
  Goody!
PALAESTRIO:
  She's delectable and dignified.

PYRGOPOLYNICES:

Tell me no lies—

PALAESTRIO:

She alone could be compared to *you* in beauty.

PYRGOPOLYNICES:

Oh, how
gorgeous!

Who is she?

PALAESTRIO:

The wife of old Periplectomenus, next door.
How she's dying for you, longing to escape—she hates the
old boy.   970
I've been asked to beg you—to beseech you—let her have a
chance to
Give herself completely.

PYRGOPOLYNICES:

Hercules, why not? If she is willing—

PALAESTRIO:

Willing? *Thrilling!*

PYRGOPOLYNICES:

(suddenly remembering)

Say—what shall we do about the girl at
home?

PALAESTRIO:

Let her go—wherever she would like to. *And it just so
happens*
Her twin sister and her mother have arrived to fetch the girl.

PYRGOPOLYNICES:

What—her mother's come to Ephesus?

PALAESTRIO:

Those who saw so
say so.

PYRGOPOLYNICES:

Hercules—the perfect chance for me to kick the woman out!

PALAESTRIO:

Yes, but you should do it in the "perfect" way.

PYRGOPOLYNICES:

All right,
what's your advice?

PALAESTRIO:

Don't you want to have her hurry from your house with no
hard feelings?

PYRGOPOLYNICES:

Yes yes yes.

PALAESTRIO:

Here's what to do: you're rich enough, so let
the girl have   980
All the gold and all the jewels and all the things you dressed
her up with.
Better not upset her; let her take the stuff where she would
like.

PYRGOPOLYNICES:

That sounds good. But watch out when I let her go this
other woman
Doesn't change her mind!

PALAESTRIO:

Oh, feh! Don't be absurd—the
girl adores you!

PYRGOPOLYNICES:

(preening)
Venus loves me!

PALAESTRIO:

Quiet now—the door is open—hide yourself.

(MILPHIDIPPA enters from the old man's house.)

That one coming out is madam's clipper ship, the go-between
who
Brought the ring that I just gave to you.

PYRGOPOLYNICES:

By Pollux, she's not
bad, not
Bad at all!

PALAESTRIO:

A chimpanzee—a harpy set beside her mistress!

Look at her there—hunting with her eyes and using ears as
                                                    traps.   990

MILPHIDIPPA:

(to the audience)

There's the circus where I must perform my little act right
                                                    now.

I'll pretend that I don't see them—I won't even know they're
                                                    there.

PYRGOPOLYNICES:

(whispering to PALAESTRIO)

Shh . . . let's listen in to see if there's a mention made of *me*.

MILPHIDIPPA:

Are there men about who care for others' business, not their
                                                    own,

Idlers who don't earn their supper, who might spy on what
                                                    I'm doing?

I'm afraid of men like these, lest they obstruct me or delay
                                                    me—

If they come while mistress crosses over—burning for *his*
                                                    body.

How she loves that man—too beautiful, too too magnificent,
                                                    the

Soldier Pyrgopolynices.

PYRGOPOLYNICES:

(aside)

This one's mad about me too!
She just praised my looks.

PALAESTRIO:

By Pollux, her speech needs no
                                                    further rubbing.   1000

PYRGOPOLYNICES:

How is that?

PALAESTRIO:

Because her words are bright enough—already
                                                    polished.

And why not? She speaks of you—she has a shining subject,
                                                    too!

PYRGOPOLYNICES:

Say, her mistress surely is a gorgeously attractive woman.
Hercules, I'm getting sort of warm for her already, boy.

PALAESTRIO:

Even when you haven't seen her yet?

PYRGOPOLYNICES:

(ogling MILPHIDIPPA*)*

I take your word for
it.

Meanwhile, "clipper ship" here whets my appetite for love.

PALAESTRIO:

No, you don't, by Hercules!
Don't you fall in love with her—that girl's engaged to *me*.
If you should
Wed the mistress, *she* becomes my bride at once.†

PYRGOPOLYNICES:

(impatiently)   Then speak to her.

PALAESTRIO:

All right, follow me.

PYRGOPOLYNICES:

I'll be your follower.

(They approach MILPHIDIPPA,
who still pretends not to see them.
She gets even more melodramatic.)

MILPHIDIPPA:

Would I could find
him—
Find the man I've left the house to meet. Oh, heaven grant
me this!‡   1010

PALAESTRIO:

All you dreamed will appear, you can be of good cheer—
there is certainly no cause for fearing,

---

†she *becomes my bride.* . . Strange words from Palaestrio's mouth! Neither before this
nor at any time later does he speak of his own love affairs. It may just be a tossed-off
line, simply to get the soldier to concentrate on Milphidippa's mistress. Yet in Renais-
sance comedies master and man wooing mistress and maid became a staple plot item,
influenced by the "zany" of the *commedia dell' arte,* the servant who apes his master.
‡*heaven grant me this* . . . We must imagine some brief musical introduction to this
one and only "sing scene" in the play.

For the person that's speaking knows just who you're seek-
                                                   ing—

MILPHIDIPPA:

My goodness—who is this I'm hearing?

PALAESTRIO:

Of your council a sharer—and also a bearer of counsel,
                           should you be confiding it.

MILPHIDIPPA:

Oh no, heaven forbid, what I'm hiding's not hid!

PALAESTRIO:

Well, you
may or may not still be hiding it.

MILPHIDIPPA:

Tell me how that can be?

PALAESTRIO:

It's not hidden from me—but I'm
trusty, a tacit and mum one.

MILPHIDIPPA:

Can you give me a sign that you know our design?

PALAESTRIO:

Let us say that a woman loves someone.

MILPHIDIPPA:

There are hundreds who do—

PALAESTRIO:

Ah, but ever so few send a
gift given straight from their finger.

MILPHIDIPPA:

Ah, now I understand, I've the lay of the land now—and no
                          more uncertainties linger.

Are there spies hereabouts?

PALAESTRIO:

(pointing to the soldier)

We're both with and without.

(MILPHIDIPPA motions PALAESTRIO to one side.)

MILPHIDIPPA:

I must see you alone, so I beckoned.

PALAESTRIO:

  Well, for many or few words?

MILPHIDIPPA:

                   I only want two words.

PALAESTRIO:

                (to the soldier)   I'll be
            back with you in a second.   1020

PYRGOPOLYNICES:

  What of me—hey, explain—must I stand here in vain, looking
           fiery, fierce . . . fascinating?

PALAESTRIO:

  Yes, sir, stand there in view—I'm just working for you.

PYRGOPOLYNICES:

  (in great heat)   But I'm wasting away with this waiting!

PALAESTRIO:

  But it's best to go slow, for I'm sure you well know of the
           kind of low mind that her stock has.

PYRGOPOLYNICES:

  Yes yes yes—on with your quest—do what you think is best.

PALAESTRIO:

  (aside to MILPHIDIPPA*)* This man has no more brains
            than a rock has!

  Now I'm back here with you—ask me.

MILPHIDIPPA:

                  What shall I do?
    What's your method for storming our Troy here?†
  Can you give me a plan?

PALAESTRIO:

             Just pretend if you can, that you're
               dying with love—

MILPHIDIPPA:

             (nodding) For our boy here!

PALAESTRIO:

  Don't forget when you speak, praise his face and physique—
           and his courage in every endeavor.

---

†*storming our Troy here?* . . . The metaphor of storming a city, meaning to outwit
someone, appears frequently in Plautus. Cf. *Epidicus*, line 163; *Bacchides*, line 829;
Pseudolus, lines 585ff.; 761ff. It is most significant that it is always a *slave* who plans
the assault on the citadel.

MILPHIDIPPA:

Now you don't have to harp, I've got everything sharp. As I
                    showed you before, I'm quite clever.

PALAESTRIO:

In respect to the rest, you resolve what is best—hunt a hint
                    in whatever I'm saying.

PYRGOPOLYNICES:

(chafing at the bit)

Well, I wish we would start and you'd tell me my part in all
                    this—come back here—you're delaying!   1030

(PALAESTRIO scampers back to the soldier's side.)

PALAESTRIO:

Here I am, don't be nervous, I'm back at your service—

PYRGOPOLYNICES:

                    Tell me what she has said—

PALAESTRIO:

                              It's her mistress—
Why, the poor dear's been sighing and crying—near dying—
                    in short, she's in terrible distress.
For she's crazy about you and can't live without you, so she
                    sent out her maid on this mission.

PYRGOPOLYNICES:

Let her come—

PALAESTRIO:

                    Why so pliant? Do act more defiant, disdain-
                              ful of this proposition.
Shout—why did I annoy you, debase, hoi-polloi you?—pre-
                    tend that this whole affair piques you.

PYRGOPOLYNICES:

Say, there is something to that, I'll certainly do that.

PALAESTRIO:

(aloud)   Shall I call this woman who seeks you?

PYRGOPOLYNICES:

Let her come if she wants something.

PALAESTRIO:

                              Come if you want
                              something, woman.

MILPHIDIPPA:

> *(hurling herself at the soldier's feet)*
>
>> O beauty so beaming!

PYRGOPOLYNICES:
  What a clever young dame—she remembers my name.

> *(to* MILPHIDIPPA*)*
>
> May the gods grant whatever you're dreaming—

MILPHIDIPPA:
  Why, to live out this life as your own wedded wife.

PYRGOPOLYNICES:

>> That's too
>> much!

MILPHIDIPPA:

>> Oh, it's not *my* desire—
> It's for mistress I woo—she's just dying for you.

PYRGOPOLYNICES:

>> My dear girl,
>> there are thousands on fire.   1040

  And there just isn't time—

MILPHIDIPPA:

>> Oh, by Castor, sir, I'm quite aware
>> that you've so high a rating.
> You're a man so attractive, in action so active—and "fiery,
>> fierce . . . fascinating."

> *(aloud to* PALAESTRIO*)*

  And there never could be one more godlike than he—

PALAESTRIO:

>> He's *not* human
>> —you're right, no debating.

> *(aside)*

  Why, it couldn't be plainer—a vulture's humaner than he is.

PYRGOPOLYNICES:
  > *(not hearing this)*   I'll act more imposing.
  I must put on a show since she's praising me so—

PALAESTRIO:

>> *(aside to* MILPHIDIPPA*)*   What an ass
>> —will you look at him posing!

> *(aloud, to the soldier)*

Will you deign a reply to her mistress's cry? You remember,
>> I spoke a while back of it.

PYRGOPOLYNICES:

I don't quite understand—from *which one*? The demand is so
>> great that I cannot keep track of it.

MILPHIDIPPA:

Well, she took from her hand something grand, something
>> handsome, to hand you in elegant fashion.
Look—you're wearing the ring I was bidden to bring—from
>> a woman who's burning with passion.

PYRGOPOLYNICES:

All right, what's her request—speak out, woman, I'm pressed.

MILPHIDIPPA:

>> How she wants you—oh, please don't reject her!   1050
She lives only for you—who knows what she may do—she's
>> near death—but *you* could resurrect her!

PYRGOPOLYNICES:

What's her wish now?

MILPHIDIPPA:

>> To touch you, to clasp you, to clutch
>> you—she cries for complete consummation.
And unless you relieve her, I truly believe her to be very near
>> desperation.
O Achilles so fair, won't you answer my prayer—save this
>> pretty one all the world pities.
Oh, produce something kind from your merciful mind—
>> noble king-killer, sacker of cities!

PYRGOPOLYNICES:

Ah, these girls who adore me do nothing but bore me.
(to PALAESTRIO*)* You shouldn't be letting me near all this.
Do you think it's your job—giving me to the mob?

PALAESTRIO:

>> *(to* MILPHIDIPPA*)*   Hey there,
>> woman, I hope that you hear all this!

Look, I've told you before—must I tell you once more? This
                          great stud always must be rewarded.
He can't give out his seed to just any old breed—it's too
                          valuable not to be hoarded!   1060

MILPHIDIPPA:

Let him make his demand; we have cash here on hand.

PALAESTRIO:

                                        Well . . .
                          one talent—not silver, but golden.
And he never takes less—

MILPHIDIPPA:

                          By the gods, I confess that he's
                          cheap at that price; we're beholden!

PYRGOPOLYNICES:

Oh, I'm not one for greed, I've got all that I need. To be
                          frank, I've got wealth beyond measure:
Golden coins by the score—by the thousands and more—

PALAESTRIO:

                          Not to mention a storehouse of treasure!
Silver too, not in pounds, no, not even in mounds, but in
                          mountains, like Aetna—or higher.

MILPHIDIPPA:

(aside)   Oh, ye gods, how he's lying!

PALAESTRIO:

                    (aside to her)   And how I'm supply-
                                        ing him fuel—

MILPHIDIPPA:

                                        And I'm stoking the fire!
But do hurry, I pray, send me back right away.

PALAESTRIO:

                              (aloud)   Will you deign,
                                        sir, to give her an answer?
Say you do or you don't, say you will or you won't—

MILPHIDIPPA:

                          Save a suffering wretch while you can, sir!
Why torment her so long? She has done you no wrong.

PYRGOPOLYNICES:

(magnanimously)   Have her come here to me for a view-
                                        ing.

You may say that I'm willing; I'll soon be fulfilling her
                                                    dreams—

MILPHIDIPPA:

          (excitedly)   Just as you should be doing!   1070
Being very astute you will do what is mutual—

PALAESTRIO:

          (waving her off)   Experts need no
                     further cuing.

MILPHIDIPPA:

You're so kind to be heeding my passionate pleading and
          letting me speak to your soul myself!

          (aside to PALAESTRIO*)*
Well, speak up—how's my act?

PALAESTRIO:

          (aside to MILPHIDIPPA*)*   As a matter of fact, I have
                all I can do to control myself!

MILPHIDIPPA:

That's why I turned aside. I was trying to hide— *(She breaks
                into giggles.)*

PYRGOPOLYNICES:

          (completely involved in self-praise)

          Do you know this occasion is stellar?
Do you know the great honor I lavish upon her?

MILPHIDIPPA:

                I know, and
                I'll certainly tell her.

PALAESTRIO:

The demand is so great I could ask for his weight in pure
                gold—

MILPHIDIPPA:

              By the gods, you'd receive it!

PALAESTRIO:

And the women he lies with he fecundifies with real heroes
             —and would you believe it—
The children he rears live for eight hundred years—

MILPHIDIPPA:

(aside)   Oh, please stop it, you joker—I'm crying!

PYRGOPOLYNICES:

My dear boy, there are many who live a millennium—from
age to age without dying!

PALAESTRIO:

Oh, I knew it but hid it—and I underdid it so she wouldn't
think I was lying.

MILPHIDIPPA:

Oh, I'm simply aghast—why, how long will *he* last—if his
sons are of such great duration?   1080

PYRGOPOLYNICES:

Jove was born of the Earth† just preceding my birth—I was
born one day after Creation.

PALAESTRIO:

And what is more—had he been born before, *he* would be in
the heavens now, reigning!

MILPHIDIPPA:

(aside to PALAESTRIO*)*

Please—one more and I'll crack! By the gods, send me back
—let me go with some breath still remaining.

PALAESTRIO:

(aloud)

Don't stand lazily by—go—you've got your reply.

MILPHIDIPPA:

Yes—I'll go
and I'll bring back madam now.
How her spirits will soar!

(to PYRGOPOLYNICES*)*

Do you want something more?

PYRGOPOLYNICES:

To be no handsomer than I am now.
It is so aggravating to be devastatingly handsome. . . .

PALAESTRIO:

Go on,
girl!

---

†*born of the Earth* . . . In the Latin *Ops*, the mother figure analogous to the Greek Rhea.

MILPHIDIPPA:

                                        I'm going.

PALAESTRIO:

Now remember, be smart—use your head and your heart.
        Have *her* heart fairly dance, have her glowing!

            (aside to MILPHIDIPPA*)*

And if our girl's in there, have her cross and prepare—say
                the soldier's returned to his station.

MILPHIDIPPA:

She's with mistress inside; they found someplace to hide
        where they took in our whole conversation.   1090

PALAESTRIO:

That was smart—what they're hearing will help them in
        steering their own course with good navigation.

MILPHIDIPPA:

Come—you're holding me back—

PALAESTRIO:

                        I'm not holding you ac-
                            tually, nor am I—

            (gives a knowing glance)

                        no further mention now.

            *(*MILPHIDIPPA *exits)*

PYRGOPOLYNICES:

Have your mistress make haste, I have no time to waste. I
        shall give this my foremost attention now.

*(*PYRGOPOLYNICES *paces back and forth, deep in thought,
        then turns to* PALAESTRIO.*)*

Palaestrio, you're my adviser, what about
My concubine? For clearly it's impossible.
To ask the new one in before the other's out!

PALAESTRIO:

Why ask me for advice on what to do? I've told you
How to do it gently—with the most compassion:
Let her keep the jewels and fancy clothes you gave her.
Tell her to prepare 'em, wear 'em, bear 'em off.   1100

Say the time is ripe for her to go back home—
Her mother's here with her twin sister—say that too.
It's fitting she go home accompanied by them.

PYRGOPOLYNICES:

(worried)

How do you *know* they're here?

PALAESTRIO:

Why, with these very eyes
I saw our lady's twin.

PYRGOPOLYNICES:

And have the sisters met?

PALAESTRIO:

Yes.

PYRGOPOLYNICES:

(lecherously)
How's the twin—good-looking?

PALAESTRIO:

Sir! You want
To grab at everything!

PYRGOPOLYNICES:
    (more lechery)   Where did she say the mother is?

PALAESTRIO:

Aboard the ship, in bed with swollen and infected eyes.
The skipper told me—that's the man who brought 'em here.
He happens to be staying as our neighbor's guest.   1110

PYRGOPOLYNICES:

How's *he*—is he good-looking?

PALAESTRIO:

Cut it out! Indeed—
You really have been quite the model stud—
Pursuing both the sexes—male and female!†
Enough of this!

PYRGOPOLYNICES:

(a bit cowed, changing the subject)

_____

†*male and female . . .* Homosexual jokes or allusions are very rare in Plautus. We do
find another one in *Mostellaria*, line 890.

           Now this advice you've given me—
I would prefer your speaking to her of the matter.
You seem to get on well with her in conversation.

PALAESTRIO:

    What better than to go yourself; it's your affair.
    Just say that it's imperative you take a wife.
    Say your relations tell you and your friends compel you.

PYRGOPOLYNICES:

    You think so?

PALAESTRIO:

            Would I tell you what I didn't think?   1120

PYRGOPOLYNICES:

    I'll go inside. Meanwhile, you stay before the house
    And guard. As soon as *she* appears, you call me out.

PALAESTRIO:

(confidently)

    Just do your own part well.

PYRGOPOLYNICES:

            Consider it as done!
    If she's unwilling, then I'll kick her out by force!

PALAESTRIO:

    Oh, do be careful. It's much better that she leave
    With no hard feelings. So just give her what I told you—
    The gold, the jewels and all the stuff you dressed her up with.

PYRGOPOLYNICES:

    Ye gods, I hope she'll go!

PALAESTRIO:

            I think that you'll succeed.
    But go inside—don't wait.

PYRGOPOLYNICES:

            I'll follow your advice.

(PYRGOPOLYNICES dashes into his house.
PALAESTRIO smiles broadly as he watches his master,
then turns to the audience.)

PALAESTRIO:

    Well, folks, did I exaggerate a while ago   1130

In what I said about this concupiscent captain?
Now I need Acroteleutium, or else
That little maid of hers, or Pleusicles. By Jupiter!
My luck is coming through for me at every turn!
For just the ones I wanted most of all to see,
I see—coming together from the house next door!

(Enter ACROTELEUTIUM *from the old man's house,*
leading MILPHIDIPPA *and* PLEUSICLES.)

ACROTELEUTIUM:

(to the others)

Follow me and look around to see there's no one spying on us.
MILPHIDIPPA:
I see no one here—except the man we want to see.
PALAESTRIO:

Well met!

MILPHIDIPPA:
How're you doing, architect?
PALAESTRIO:

Feh, I'm no architect.

MILPHIDIPPA:

What's that?

PALAESTRIO:
Why, compared to you, my talent couldn't bang two boards
together.   1140
MILPHIDIPPA:
Come now, don't exaggerate—
PALAESTRIO:

(smiling)   Why, you're a filly full of
felony!
And you polished off the soldier charmingly.
MILPHIDIPPA:

We haven't fin-
ished.

PALAESTRIO:
Smile a little; this affair is well in hand—at least for now.
Simply keep on giving helpful help as you have done so far.
Soldier boy is there inside, beseeching her to go away:

"Please go back to Athens with your mother and your sister!"

PLEUSICLES:

Great!

PALAESTRIO:

And he gave her all the gold, the jewels, the stuff he dressed
her up with
As a gift—to go away. He's following the plan I gave him!

PLEUSICLES:

It looks easy: he is all insistence—she gives no resistance.

PALAESTRIO:

Don't you know that when you're climbing upward in a well
that's deep,
You're in greatest danger of a fall when nearest to the top.   1150
We have almost drawn this from the well, but if he gets
suspicious,
We'll get nothing out of him—so now's the time to be our
sharpest.
We have raw materials aplenty for the job, that's clear.
Three girls, *(to* PLEUSICLES*)* you're a fourth, and I'm a fifth
—the old man is a sixth.
We six have a large reserve of rogueries to draw upon.
Name a city—we could storm and conquer it with all our
tricks.†

Pay attention now—

ACROTELEUTIUM:

That's why we've come——to find out
what you want.

PALAESTRIO:

Nice of you to say. Now I'll command you in your line of
duty.

ACROTELEUTIUM:

You'll command commendably. I'll do my best for your
request.   1160

PALAESTRIO:

Lightly . . . brightly . . . and in spritely fashion—fool the
soldier boy.

I command it.

---

†*with all our tricks* . . . See note on line 1025.

ACROTELEUTIUM:

       Your command's a pleasure.

PALAESTRIO:

                    You've got the
                          way?

ACROTELEUTIUM:

I pretend I'm torn apart for love of . . . him, that I've divorced
                   my present husband,
Since I'm burning so to marry . . . him.

PALAESTRIO:

              (smiling)   It's all in order
                          now.
One more thing—this house is *yours*—since it was in your
                   dowry.† Say the
Old man has gone off already, since the separation's final.
We don't want our man afraid to enter someone else's house.

ACROTELEUTIUM:

Well advised.

PALAESTRIO:

           When he comes out, be hesitant—don't come
                      too close.
Act as if you're too ashamed to place your beauty near his
                      own.   1170
Be in awe of all his riches; lavish praise upon his looks, his
Splendid face and figure, charm, his personality, et cetera.
Have you been rehearsed enough?

ACROTELEUTIUM:

                    Of course. Won't it be
                      quite enough to
Render you a polished piece of work? I know you'll find it
                      flawless.

PALAESTRIO:

Fine. *(to* PLEUSICLES*)* It's your turn now to be commanded
                   in your line of duty.
When what we've discussed is done, and she goes in—you
                   come at once.

---

†*in your dowry* . . . The Roman legal process of *divortium* (referred to in line 1167)
provided for the return of the wife's dowry upon separation.

Get yourself disguised the way the skipper of a ship would
                                                        dress:
Have a wide-brimmed hat—rust-brown—and on your eye a
                                                woolen patch.
Also have a rust-brown cloak—since that's the color sailors
                                                         wear.
Fasten it to your left shoulder, tie it round with one arm
                                                bare.   1180
One way or another, you must seem the master of a ship.
All these clothes are there inside—the old man owns some
                                                fishing boats.

             (PLEUSICLES *nods,*
     having taken great pains to memorize all this.)

PLEUSICLES:
   Well, when I am here . . . all dressed up like you just described
                                            . . . what then?
PALAESTRIO:
   Come here—and pretend you're fetching Philocomasium for
                                                her mother.
   Say that if she's going to Athens she must hurry to the
                                                    harbor.
   Also have them carry all the things she wants to take on
                                                      board.

          (*affecting an old-salt accent*)

   If she doesn't come, you'll cast off anyway—the wind is fair.
PLEUSICLES:
   Pretty picture—please proceed.
PALAESTRIO:

                          Then right away he'll urge
                                    the girl to
   Hasten, hurry—don't keep Mother waiting.
PLEUSICLES:
          (*admiringly to the others*)   He's poly-percep-
                                                  tive!   1190
PALAESTRIO:
   I'll have her request my aid in taking luggage to the harbor.

He'll command me to escort her. When I'm there, be sure of
                                                      this—
Straightaway I'll be away, straight . . . back to Athens.

PLEUSICLES:

                                    When you're there,
You won't be a slave for three days longer. I'll release you.

PALAESTRIO:

Quickly now, and dress yourself.

PLEUSICLES:

                              There's nothing else?

PALAESTRIO:

                                                    Just
                                    don't forget.

PLEUSICLES:

I'll be going. . . . *(He goes.)*

PALAESTRIO:

                    (to the women)

                You two hurry in as well, since any minute
He'll be coming out again, I know.

ACROTELEUTIUM:

                    (taking leave)   Your wish is our com-
                                                    mand.

PALAESTRIO:

Everybody go—retreat! *(turns)* And just in time—our door
                                                is open!

                    (to the audience)

Here he comes—so chipper—he's "succeeded"! Fool—he
                                        gapes at nothing!

(PYRGOPOLYNICES bursts out, overjoyed with himself.)

PYRGOPOLYNICES:

I've succeeded! I got what I wanted as I wanted it—   1200
Sweetly and completely she agreed.

PALAESTRIO:

                              What took so long in
                                        there?

PYRGOPOLYNICES:

Never was I loved as madly as that little woman loves me.

PALAESTRIO:

Oh?

PYRGOPOLYNICES:

I needed countless words; she was the toughest nut to
crack.
Finally, I triumphed. Did I give her gifts! I gave her
Everything that she demanded. *(sheepishly)* I even had to
give her . . . you.

PALAESTRIO:

(mock shock)

Even me! How could I live away from you?

PYRGOPOLYNICES:

Stiff upper lip.
I would like to have you back, and yet there was no other
way. I
Couldn't get the girl to go without you—I tried everything,
she
Overwhelmed me.

PALAESTRIO:

(dramatically)

Well, I trust the gods—and you, of course.
I know that
After this, though 'twill be bitter, parted from the best of
masters,   1210
This at least will comfort me: that your surpassing beauty
will have—
Through my humble efforts—won that lady. I will now ar-
range it.

PYRGOPOLYNICES:

Ah, what need of words. If you succeed, you'll be a free
man—
And a rich man.

PALAESTRIO:

I'll succeed.

PYRGOPOLYNICES:

    (impatiently)   I'm bursting—hurry!

PALAESTRIO:

                    Self-control!
Take it easy, don't be so . . . hot-blooded. Wait—she's coming
                          out.

        (PALAESTRIO pulls the soldier aside,
        as MILPHIDIPPA *leads* ACROTELEUTIUM
           from the old man's house.)

MILPHIDIPPA:

        (aside to ACROTELEUTIUM*)*

Oh, mistress, there's the soldier.

ACROTELEUTIUM:

              Where?

MILPHIDIPPA:

              Right to your left.

ACROTELEUTIUM:

                I see.

MILPHIDIPPA:

Take just a hasty glance so he won't know we're looking at
                        him.

ACROTELEUTIUM:

All right, by Pollux, now's the time for bad girls to be worse
                       girls.†

MILPHIDIPPA:

You take the lead.

ACROTELEUTIUM:

        (melodramatically)

      Please tell me—did you see the man in
                  person?

        (aside)

Don't speak too softly—let 'im hear.

---

†Cf. Mae West: "When I'm good I'm very good, but when I'm bad I'm better."

MILPHIDIPPA:

        (proudly)   I spoke to him myself, 1220
Quite calmly, easily—and just as long as I desired.

PYRGOPOLYNICES:

  You hear?

PALAESTRIO:

       I hear. She's overjoyed just to have talked to you.

ACROTELEUTIUM:

  Oh, what a lucky woman!

PYRGOPOLYNICES:

             How they love me.

PALAESTRIO:

                   You deserve it.

ACROTELEUTIUM:

  What a miracle—you got to him and begged him to sub-
                       mission.
  I heard òne needed letters, or a page—like for a king.

MILPHIDIPPA:

  Indeed, it took a bit of effort getting through to him.

PALAESTRIO:

  You're a legend with the women.

PYRGOPOLYNICES:

               I accept the will of Venus.

ACROTELEUTIUM:

           (picking up a cue)

I give my thanks to Venus and I beg her and beseech
That I may be successful with the one I love and long for.
May he be kind to me and not deny me my desire.   1230

MILPHIDIPPA:

  I hope so too. And yet so many women long for him.
  He spurns them all, despises them—except for you alone.

ACROTELEUTIUM:

  I'm terribly tormented, since he's so discriminating,
  That, seeing me, his eyes will make him change his mind.
  Why, his own splendidness will spurn with speed my plain
                     appearance.

MILPHIDIPPA:

  He won't. Be of good cheer.

PYRGOPOLYNICES:

    (taken—and taken in)   How she disparages herself.

ACROTELEUTIUM:

  I'm frightened you exaggerated my good looks to him.

MILPHIDIPPA:

  Oh, I was careful—you'll be prettier than I described.

ACROTELEUTIUM:

  If he won't take me for his wife, then I'll embrace his knees
  And I'll implore him. Otherwise, if I can't win him over,   1240
  I am resolved to die. I know I cannot live without him.

  (PYRGOPOLYNICES *starts toward her with open arms.*)

PYRGOPOLYNICES:

  I must prevent that woman's death. I'll go—

PALAESTRIO:

(restraining him)

                          Oh, not at all!
  You're cheapening yourself to give yourself so liberally.
  Do let her come unbidden, sir: to yearn, to burn, to wait her
                                    turn.
  Now, do you want to lose your reputation? Don't do that!
  No man was *ever* loved by woman thus—except for two:
  Yourself and Phaon, Sappho's lover on the Isle of Lesbos.†

ACROTELEUTIUM:

  Dear Milphidippa, call him out—or I'll go in myself!

MILPHIDIPPA:

  Let's wait at least till someone else comes out.

ACROTELEUTIUM:

                            But I can't wait—

  I'm going in!

MILPHIDIPPA:

        The doors are locked.

---

†*Isle of Lesbos* . . . Sappho, the famous poet who dwelt on the Isle of Lesbos in the late
seventh and early sixth century B.C., was not the ''lesbian'' simplistic tradition has made
her out to be (she was married, had a child, etc.). She was, however, quite a passionate
person. The legend here alluded to concerns Sappho's wild infatuation for a ferryman
named Phaon. When Phaon rejected her advances, she committed suicide. Let us not
speculate as to why he rejected her. Not all ferrymen are attracted by aging schoolteachers.

ACROTELEUTIUM:

I'll break 'em.

MILPHIDIPPA:

(She rushes to the soldier's door.)

You're insane! 1250

ACROTELEUTIUM:

But if he's ever loved, or if his wisdom match his beauty,
Then he'll forgive whatever I may do because of love.

PALAESTRIO:

(to the soldier)

The poor girl's burning up for love of you.

PYRGOPOLYNICES:

(trembling) It's mutual!

PALAESTRIO:

(hushing him)

Don't let her hear!

MILPHIDIPPA:

You're standing stupefied—why don't
you knock?

ACROTELEUTIUM:

The man I love is not inside.

MILPHIDIPPA:

How do you know?

ACROTELEUTIUM:

I smell.

My nose would sense it if he were inside.

PALAESTRIO:

A prophetess!

PYRGOPOLYNICES:

She loves me, therefore Venus gave her powers of prophecy.

ACROTELEUTIUM:

He's near—somewhere—the man I long to see. I smell him!

PYRGOPOLYNICES:

She sees more with her nose than with her eyes.

PALAESTRIO:

She's blind
with love.

(ACROTELEUTIUM *begins an elaborate fainting act.*)

ACROTELEUTIUM:
Oh, hold me!

MILPHIDIPPA:
Why?

ACROTELEUTIUM:
I'm falling!

MILPHIDIPPA:
Why?

ACROTELEUTIUM:
Because I can't stand up! 1260
My soul's retreating through my eyes—

MILPHIDIPPA:
By Pollux, then you've
seen

The soldier!

ACROTELEUTIUM:
Yes!

MILPHIDIPPA:
I don't see—where?

ACROTELEUTIUM:
You'd see him if you
loved him!

MILPHIDIPPA:
What's that? Why, if you'd let me, I would love him more
than you do!

PALAESTRIO:
It's obvious that every woman loves you at first sight.

PYRGOPOLYNICES:

(in a confidential tone)

I don't know if I told you, but my grandmother was . . .
Venus.†

ACROTELEUTIUM:
Dear Milphidippa, please go up to him.

---

†*my grandmother was . . . Venus.* . . . Is Plautus mocking the Aeneas legend, then
newly introduced in Rome? Aeneas was, of course, the son of Venus. Lucretius warmly
hails this very Roman goddess in the very first words of his *De Rerum Natura* as
Aeneadum genetrix, the originator of the race of Aeneas.

PYRGOPOLYNICES:

                    (preening)   How she reveres me!

PALAESTRIO:

Well, here she comes.

MILPHIDIPPA:

                    I want you—

PYRGOPOLYNICES:

                    (aside)   I want *you*!

MILPHIDIPPA:

                                        As you com-
                                        manded,

I've brought my mistress out.

PYRGOPOLYNICES:

                    I see.

MILPHIDIPPA:

                    Well, tell her to approach.

PYRGOPOLYNICES:

Your pleas have forced me not to hate her as I do the others.

(PYRGOPOLYNICES *starts toward* ACROTELEUTIUM,
    but MILPHIDIPPA *suddenly blocks his way.*)

MILPHIDIPPA:

If she approaches nearer you—she couldn't speak a word.   1270
For when she simply looks at you, her eyes cut off her tongue.

PYRGOPOLYNICES:

I'll cure milady's malady.

MILPHIDIPPA:

                    Oh, how she shaked and quaked

When she beheld you.

PYRGOPOLYNICES:

                    Mighty men in armor do the same—
I do not wonder that a woman does. What does she want?

MILPHIDIPPA:

She wants to live a lifetime with you, so—come to her house.

PYRGOPOLYNICES:

                    (hesitantly)

I—to her house? She's married—why—her husband—he
                                        might catch me!

MILPHIDIPPA:

But, sir, for love of you, she's thrown her husband out.

PYRGOPOLYNICES:

How could she?

MILPHIDIPPA:

(smiling)

This house was in her dowry.

PYRGOPOLYNICES:

Yes?

MILPHIDIPPA:

Yes, sir.

PYRGOPOLYNICES:

Then take her
home—

I'll be there in a second.

MILPHIDIPPA:

Please don't keep her waiting long—

Don't break her heart.

PYRGOPOLYNICES:

I won't—of course. Be off!

MILPHIDIPPA:

We're off. 1280

*(MILPHIDIPPA helps her ''fainting'' mistress
back into the old man's house.)*

PYRGOPOLYNICES:

(looking offstage)

What do I see?

PALAESTRIO:

What do you see?

PYRGOPOLYNICES:

Someone's approaching,
dressed

In sailor's clothes.

PALAESTRIO:

He's heading for our house—it's clear he
wants you.

Why, that's the skipper—

PYRGOPOLYNICES:

Come to fetch the girl, no doubt.

PALAESTRIO:

No doubt.

*(Enter PLEUSICLES,
looking very uncomfortable in his elaborate sailor's costume.
Among other items of apparel,
he has a huge patch over his left eye.)*

PLEUSICLES:

If I were not aware how many others have
Done awful things because of love, I'd be afraid
To march around dressed up like this to win my love.
Yet, since I know of many others who committed things
Both shady and dishonest for the sake of love . . .
Why mention how Achilles† let his Greeks be killed? . . .
But there's Palaestrio—he's standing with the soldier.   1290
I'd better change my language to a different style.

(affecting the accent PALAESTRIO demonstrated earlier)

Why, woman's born the daughter of Delay herself.
For any other plain delay of equal length
Seems less of a delay than waiting for a woman.
I really do believe it's in their constitution.
But now to fetch this girl Philocomasium.
I'll knock. Hey—anybody home?

PALAESTRIO:

(rushing up to him)   Young man—what's up?
What are you knocking for?

PLEUSICLES:

I want Philocomasium.
Her mother sent me. If she's coming, let her come.
The girl's delaying everyone—we're anxious to set sail.   1300

---

†*Achilles* . . . Here the misogynistic playwright reduces the cause for the wrath of
Achilles to *propter amorem*, "all for love." Needless to say, this is not Homer's view.
We are reminded of Shakespeare's cynical reduction of the Trojan War as expressed by
Thersites in *Troilus and Cressida* (II, iii, 67ff.): "All the argument is a whore and a
cuckold—a good quarrel to draw emulous factions and bleed to death on."

(PYRGOPOLYNICES *dashes over nervously.*)

PYRGOPOLYNICES:

   Oh, everything's all ready. Go, Palaestrio—
   Get helpers to transport her stuff onto the ship—
   The gold, the jewels, the clothes and all the fancy things.
   The gifts I gave her are all packed. Now let her take them!

PALAESTRIO:

   I'm off.

PLEUSICLES:

     For heaven's sake be quick!

PYRGOPOLYNICES:

     (trying to placate him)   He won't be long.
   But tell me, sir, what happened to that eye of yours?

PLEUSICLES:

        (pointing to his unbandaged eye)

   Why, this one's fine.

PYRGOPOLYNICES:

         I mean your left one.

PLEUSICLES:

                 It's like this:
   The *ocean* caused me to use this eye less. And yet
   Were it not for *dev*-otion,† I could use it now.
   But they're delaying me too long—

PYRGOPOLYNICES:

                Ah—here they come! 1310

(PALAESTRIO *leads a tearful* PHILOCOMASIUM
out of the soldier's house.)

PALAESTRIO:

   Will there ever be an end to all this weeping?

PHILOCOMASIUM:

        (woefully)   Can I help it?
   I must leave this beautiful existence. . . .

---

†dev-*otion* . . . "Ocean-devotion." Not a very good pun in the Latin either. Plautus is punning on *maris*, "sea" (line 1308), and *amare*, "to love" (line 1309). Most editors, in fact, believe the word play too feeble to be Plautine, and read *amoris*, "love," in line 1308.

PALAESTRIO:

This man's come
for you

From your mother and your sister.

PHILOCOMASIUM:

Yes, I see.

PYRGOPOLYNICES:

(impatiently) Palaestrio!

PALAESTRIO:

Yes?

PYRGOPOLYNICES:

Command that all the stuff I gave the girl be carried off!

PLEUSICLES:

Greetings, Philocomasium.

PHILOCOMASIUM:

The same to you.

PLEUSICLES:

Mother and sister

Also bade me tell you . . . greetings.

PHILOCOMASIUM:

Greetings to them
both as well.

PLEUSICLES:

(delivering his carefully memorized speech)

They beseech you . . . come ahead . . . the wind is fair . . .
the sails are full.
If your mother's eyes were better, she'd have come along
with me.

PHILOCOMASIUM:

Though I long to stay, one must obey one's mother.

PLEUSICLES:

Very wise.

PYRGOPOLYNICES:

(confidentially to PLEUSICLES)

If she hadn't lived with me, she'd be a half-wit to this day! 1320

PHILOCOMASIUM:

That's what pains me so—the separation from so great a man.

Why, with your abilities, you could . . . enrich . . . most
anyone.

(At this moment,
PALAESTRIO *appears from inside the soldier's house,*
carrying a treasure chest.)

And because I used to be with you, I held my head up high.
Now . . . I have to lose that one distinction.

PYRGOPOLYNICES:

Do not cry.

PHILOCOMASIUM:

I must—

When I look at you. . . .

PYRGOPOLYNICES:

Stiff upper lip.

PHILOCOMASIUM:

Oh, if you knew
my feelings!

PALAESTRIO:

I don't wonder, girl, that you lived happily with him, and that
his
Beauty's blaze, his noble gaze, his manly ways have held you
rapt, for
Even I—slave that I am—am brought to tears at leaving him.

PHILOCOMASIUM:

(to the soldier)

May I hug you one more time before I go for good?

PYRGOPOLYNICES:

You may.

*(*PYRGOPOLYNICES *readies himself for her embrace.*
She starts toward him with open arms, then staggers, wailing.)

PHILOCOMASIUM:
Oh, my darling . . . oh, my soul . . . oh. . . .

(She begins an elaborate faint.
PALAESTRIO *catches her "just in time,"*
and hands her to PLEUSICLES.)*

PALAESTRIO:

Hold this woman
please; she may do   1330
Damage to herself!

PYRGOPOLYNICES:

What's going on?

PALAESTRIO:

Because she has to
leave you, the
Poor girl's fainted dead away!

PYRGOPOLYNICES:

Well, run inside and get some
water!

PALAESTRIO:

Never mind the water—she needs rest.

(The soldier starts toward her.)

No—don't come any
closer!
Please—let her recover.

*(PYRGOPOLYNICES eyes PLEUSICLES and PHILOCOMASIUM
with suspicion.)*

PYRGOPOLYNICES:

Say—their heads are awfully close
together!
I don't like the looks of this. Hey, sailor—take your lips
from hers!

PLEUSICLES:

I just tried to see if she was breathing.

PYRGOPOLYNICES:

Use your ear for
that!

PLEUSICLES:

If you'd like, I'll let her go—

PYRGOPOLYNICES:

No no—hold on!

PALAESTRIO:

(weeping) Oh, woe is me!

PYRGOPOLYNICES:

> *(calling inside his house)*

Men! Come out—bring forth her stuff—bring everything I
> gave the girl!

(Various LACKEYS *enter with* PHILOCOMASIUM's *luggage
and assorted gifts,*
as PALAESTRIO *readies himself for an impassioned valedictory.)*

PALAESTRIO:

Ere I go . . . let me salute you once again . . . ye Household
> Gods.

And to you, my male and female fellow slaves . . . hail and
> farewell.   1340

Please don't speak too badly of me 'mongst yourselves when
> I am gone.

PYRGOPOLYNICES:

Come, Palaestrio, buck up!

PALAESTRIO:

> Alas, I cannot help but cry—

I must leave you.

PYRGOPOLYNICES:

> Take it like a man.

PALAESTRIO:

> Oh, if you knew my
> feelings!

*(*PHILOCOMASIUM *suddenly "regains consciousness.")*

PHILOCOMASIUM:

What? Where am I? What's been going on. Who are you?
> *(aside)*   Hello, darling!

PLEUSICLES:

Ah, you have revived, *(aside)* my darling.

PHILOCOMASIUM:

> Goodness! Who
> am I embracing?

Who's this man? I'm lost—I must have fainted.

PLEUSICLES:

> *(aside)*   Never fear,
> my dearest.

(She puts her head on PLEUSICLES' *chest.)*

PYRGOPOLYNICES:
What's all this?
PALAESTRIO:

(trying to cover up)

It's nothing . . . nothing . . . just another
fainting spell.
Oh, I shiver and I quiver. *(to the lovers)* This is getting *far
too public!*

PYRGOPOLYNICES:
What'd you say?
PALAESTRIO:

Uh—carrying this stuff in public—through
the city—

It might hurt your reputation.
PYRGOPOLYNICES:

Well, it's mine to give and no
one else's.   1350

I don't care what others think. Now depart—the gods be with
you.

PALAESTRIO:
I was looking out for you.
PYRGOPOLYNICES:

I know.

PALAESTRIO:

Farewell.

PYRGOPOLYNICES:

Farewell to you.

PALAESTRIO:

(aside to PLEUSICLES*)*

Hurry, I'll be with you in a second. *(aloud)* Just two words
with Master.

(He goes to the soldier.)

Though you have thought other servants far more faithful
than myself,
Still and all, I'm very grateful to you, sir . . . for everything.

And, if you'd seen fit to, I would rather have been slave to you
Than a freedman, working for another.

PYRGOPOLYNICES:

              Come—stiff upper lip.

PALAESTRIO:

   (sudden burst of passion)

Fond farewell to following a fiery, ferocious fighter!
Now I'm flunky to a frilly female . . . fortitude forgot.

   (He breaks into sobs.
   PYRGOPOLYNICES *pats him on the shoulder,*
   barely able to restrain his own tears.)

PYRGOPOLYNICES:
Good old fellow.

PALAESTRIO:

       Oh, I can't go on—I've lost my will to live! 1360

PYRGOPOLYNICES:
Go, go—follow them—no more delay.

PALAESTRIO:

            Farewell.

PYRGOPOLYNICES:

               Farewell to
               you.

(PALAESTRIO turns to go, then whirls back toward the soldier.)

PALAESTRIO:
Don't forget me, sir, for if perchance I should be freed
               someday,
I will send you word. You won't forsake me?

PYRGOPOLYNICES:

            Ah, that's not
            my style.

PALAESTRIO:
Always and forever think how faithful I have been to you.
Then at last you'll know who's been a loyal slave and who
               has not.

PYRGOPOLYNICES:
I'm aware. I've noticed often—never quite so much till now.

PALAESTRIO:

    Yes, today at last you'll know the kind of slave I really am.

    (PALAESTRIO *turns and starts to walk slowly off.*)

PYRGOPOLYNICES:

    I can hardly stop myself from keeping you—

PALAESTRIO:

                (frantically)   Oh, don't do that!

    There'd be talk—they'd say you didn't keep your word—
                                untrustworthy.

    They would say you had no faithful slaves at all—except for
                                  me.   1370

    If I thought it could be done the proper way—why, I'd
                                  insist—

    But you simply can't—

PYRGOPOLYNICES:

                Be off then.

PALAESTRIO:

                      I shall bear whatever comes.

PYRGOPOLYNICES:

    So, farewell.

PALAESTRIO:

                I'd better hurry off.

PYRGOPOLYNICES:

                (impatiently)   All right—farewell already!

    (PALAESTRIO *races offstage—with a broad smile.*)

PYRGOPOLYNICES:

       (Reflecting, to the audience)

    Till today I always thought he was the very worst of slaves.
    Now I see he was devoted to me. When I think it over,
    I was foolish giving him away. But now I'll head inside,
    Now's the time for love! Wait—I perceive a sound—made by
                                the door.

    (A SLAVE BOY *enters from the old man's house.*)

BOY:

       (to those inside the house)

    Stop coaching me, please. I remember what to do.

(getting melodramatic)

Wheresoever in the world he be, I'll find him.
Yes, I'll track him down; I won't spare any effort.   1380

PYRGOPOLYNICES:

This one seeks me. I'll go up and meet the boy.

BOY:

Aha, I'm looking for you. Hail, you gorgeous creature!
O man of every hour, beyond all other men
Beloved of two gods—

PYRGOPOLYNICES:

                    Which two?

BOY:

                              Venus and Mars.†

PYRGOPOLYNICES:

A clever boy.

BOY:

              She begs of you to go inside.
She yearns, she burns, expectantly expecting you.
Bring solace to the lovelorn, don't wait—go!

PYRGOPOLYNICES:

                    (hungrily)   I will!

(He dashes full speed ahead into the old man's house.)

BOY:

                    (to the audience)

Well, now he's trapped himself, caught in his own devices.
The ambush is prepared: the old man's standing staunchly
To attack this lecher who's so loud about his loveliness,   1390
Who thinks that every woman loves him at first sight,
When really they detest him, men as well as women.
Now I'll rejoin the uproar—there's a shout inside!

                    (He runs back into the house.
                    Sounds of a scuffle from within,
                    then enter PERIPLECTOMENUS,

---

†*Venus and Mars . . . The* Roman gods. Cf. lines 11–12, where the soldier is said to
surpass the fighting talents of the god of war. Surely Pyrgopolynices is some sort of
Roman caricature.

followed by his servants, who are carrying PYRGOPOLYNICES.
Among them is CARIO, *the cook, who has a long, sharp knife.)*

PERIPLECTOMENUS:

   Bring 'im out! If he won't come, then pick him up and throw
                                    him out!
   Make a little seat for him—right in mid-air. Tear him apart!
PYRGOPOLYNICES:

   Please—I beg—by Hercules!
PERIPLECTOMENUS:

                        By Hercules, you beg in vain.
   Cario, see to it that that knife of yours is sharp enough.
CARIO:

   Why, it's long been eager to remove this lecher's vital parts,†
   And to hang 'em like a baby's string of beads—around his
                                              neck.

PYRGOPOLYNICES:

   Oh, I'm dead!
PERIPLECTOMENUS:

             Not yet—you speak too soon.
CARIO:

             (brandishing that knife)   Can I go at
                                    him now?   1400
PERIPLECTOMENUS:

   First let him be pummeled by your clubs a little more.
CARIO:

                                    Much more!

   (The SLAVES *pound* PYRGOPOLYNICES *much more.)*

PERIPLECTOMENUS:

   So! You dared to make advances to another's wife—you pig!
PYRGOPOLYNICES:

   By the gods, she asked me first—she came to me!
PERIPLECTOMENUS:

                                    He lies—
                                    hit on.

PYRGOPOLYNICES:

   Wait a second—let me talk.

---

†*this lecher's vital parts* . . . In the Latin, Cario threatens to slice the soldier's
abdomen. But since the punishment for adultery was castration, both the Braggart—and
the audience—knew very well what was in jeopardy.

PERIPLECTOMENUS:
   (to the slaves) Why do you stop?
PYRGOPOLYNICES:
            Please—may I
             speak?

PERIPLECTOMENUS:
 Speak.
PYRGOPOLYNICES:
  The woman begged me—
PERIPLECTOMENUS:
        But you dared to go—hit
           him again!

PYRGOPOLYNICES:
 Stop—stop—stop—I'm pounded plenty. Please, I beg—
CARIO:
           When do I cut?

PERIPLECTOMENUS:
 At your own convenience. Spread 'im out and stretch 'im all
          the way.

PYRGOPOLYNICES:
 Please, by Hercules, I beg you, hear my words before he cuts!
PERIPLECTOMENUS:
 Well?
PYRGOPOLYNICES:
   I didn't want to—Hercules—I thought she was di-
          vorced!
 I was told as much—her maid—that little bawd—she lied to
           me! 1410

PERIPLECTOMENUS:
 Swear that you won't harm a single person for this whole
          affair, or
 For the pounding you've received today—and will receive—if
          we now
 Let you go intact—sweet little grandson of the goddess
          Venus.

PYRGOPOLYNICES:
 Yes! I swear by Jupiter and Mars, I'll never harm a soul.
 And my beating up today—I grant it was my just reward.
 As a favor, let me leave with testimony to my manhood!

PERIPLECTOMENUS:

  If you break your promise after this?

PYRGOPOLYNICES:

                            Then may I live . . .
                                    detested.

CARIO:

  I suggest we wallop him a final time and let him go.

PYRGOPOLYNICES:

  Thank you—may the gods all bless you, sir, for speaking up
                                    for me.

CARIO:

  Also give us gold—a hundred drachmae.†

PYRGOPOLYNICES:

                            Why?

CARIO:

                            To let you go— 1420
  Without giving testimony—grandson of the goddess Venus.
  Otherwise, you'll never leave.

PYRGOPOLYNICES:

                      You'll get it.

CARIO:

                            Now you're being
                                  smart.
  And you can forget about your cloak, your tunic and your
                                    sword.

                  (to PERIPLECTOMENUS)

  Should I pound or let him loose?

PYRGOPOLYNICES:

                      Your pounding's made me
                            loose already!
  Please—I beg of you—no more.

PERIPLECTOMENUS:

                      Release the man.

PYRGOPOLYNICES:

                                  Oh, thank
                            you, thank you.

PERIPLECTOMENUS:

  If I catch you after this, you'll never testify again!

PYRGOPOLYNICES:

  How can I object?

---

†*a hundred drachmae* . . . This is an enormous sum of money. Greek workmen
were paid a single drachma a day.

PERIPLECTOMENUS:

Come, Cario, let's go inside.

(The OLD MAN *takes his* SLAVES *inside,
just as* SCELEDRUS *appears, with the soldier's* LACKEYS,
returning from the harbor.)

PYRGOPOLYNICES:

Look now—I
See my slaves. Quick, tell me, has the girl set sail—well, has
she, has she?

SCELEDRUS:

Long ago—

PYRGOPOLYNICES:

Damn!!

SCELEDRUS:

If you knew what I know, that's not all
you'd say. That
Fellow with the woolen patch on his left eye . . . was no real
sailor!   1430

PYRGOPOLYNICES:

What? Who was he?

SCELEDRUS:

Your own sweetheart's lover.

PYRGOPOLYNICES:

How'd you
know?

SCELEDRUS:

I know.
Why, the minute they were past the city gates, right then
and there, they
Started kissing and embracing—constantly.

PYRGOPOLYNICES:

Oh, pity me!
Now I see I've been bamboozled. Oh, that rogue Palaestrio!
He enticed me into this. And yet . . . I find the verdict's just.

(philosophically)

There would be less lechery if lechers were to learn from this;
Lots would be more leery and less lustful. *(to his slaves)*
Let's go in! *(to the audience)* Applaud!

(All exit into the soldier's house.)

The Brothers Menaechmus

(Menaechmi)

for Richard Rodgers

Iube igitur tribus nobis apud te prandium accurarier.
(line 208)

"Songbirds always eat."
—*The Boys from Syracuse*

About the Play

This is Plautus' only comedy of errors. His Hellenistic predecessors wrote so many that "Miss Ignorance," a personification who speaks one of Menander's prologues,[1] has been called the presiding deity of New Comedy. Plautus usually preferred wit to ignorance, shrewd deceptions to naïve blunders. People in a comedy of errors are mere puppets; Plautus admired puppeteers, creative plotters like Palaestrio and Tranio. Since no one in the *Menaechmi* is clever, the laughter it arouses provides strong argument for that popular theory of the comic which sees the cue for guffaws as a feeling of audience superiority.[2] Indeed, who would not feel superior to these fools who wander the streets of Epidamnus, where the presiding deity must surely be Miss Ignorance's dull-witted twin, "Misunderstanding"?

Yet this is a fine, if untypical, Plautine comedy. It has enjoyed unceasing popularity over the ages, and not only in famous adaptations like Shakespeare's *Comedy of Errors* and Rodgers and Hart's *Boys from Syracuse*. It has always been the most-performed play *of Plautus*. Clearly, it has a very special appeal—in its Plautine assets of song and snappy patter, and in its atmosphere of holiday abandon, of carnival release from everyday rules. Moreover, it presents more simply than any comedy before or since the greatest of all wish fulfillments: the surrogate self, the alter ego with no superego, the

---

1. The goddess Agnoia in Menander's *Shearing of Glycera*.
2. "Superiority" theories run the gamut from Aristotle's view of comic characters as being inferior to ourselves (*Poetics* V) to Hobbes' famous description of laughter as a "sudden glory" (*Leviathan*, chapter VI).

man who can get his pleasure free in every sense, because he is "Jack in town and Earnest in the country." Indeed, Plautus' twin-brother comedy might be aptly subtitled "The Importance of Being Menaechmus."

The two houses onstage represent the conflicting forces in the comedy. They are not unlike the statues of Artemis and Aphrodite which frame the setting of Euripides' *Hippolytus*. In both dramas the action takes place in a magnetic field between poles of restraint and release. It is no coincidence that the house of Menaechmus I stands at the exit nearer the forum. For the local twin is bound by the business of everyday life, restrained by legal, financial and social ties, especially by a wife who is constantly "on the job."[3] Across the stage, and nearer the harbor whence visitors come, dwells a lady of pleasure aptly named Erotium, "Passionella," if you will.[4] It should be noted that Menaechmus' lawfully wedded spouse has no name at all; she is merely called "wife." Shakespeare, in his adaptation, reverses this, making the courtesan the lady with no name, and calling the twin's wife Adriana.[5]

Plautus, of course, intends no allegory; he never intends anything but entertainment. And yet, without any conscious attempt on the part of the playwright, we see in the two onstage houses in the *Menaechmi* a contrast between the atmosphere of everyday and that of holiday, or, as Freud would express it, the Reality Principle versus the Pleasure Principle. Needless to say, Pleasure emerges triumphant, for that is the essential theme of all comedy. But it is especially interesting to see why Menaechmus I needs a twin in order "to win."[6]

The local, married brother is the hero of the play. Plautus gives him the larger and more lyrical role.[7] We first meet Menaechmus I

---

3. All throughout the play, Plautus associates the word *industria*, "work," with Menaechmus' wife (line 123 and elsewhere). To emphasize the contrast, he constantly refers to Erotium as *voluptas*, "pleasure." I discuss this antinomy further in "The *Menaechmi*: Roman Comedy of Errors," *Yale Classical Studies* XXI, pp. 77ff.

4. *Eros*, of course, means passion, and *-ium* is an affectionate diminutive suffix. Ergo Erotium means "Passion-ella." Plautus loves to give his heroines such sensual names, viz., Philocomasium in *The Braggart Soldier*, and Philematium in the *Mostellaria*.

5. In contrast to Plautus' callous attitude toward the wife—and to marriage in general—Shakespeare usually celebrates the joys of wedded bliss, especially in his *Comedy of Errors*.

6. As we will see below, Menaechmus I only "wins" vicariously. A Pyrrhic—not empiric—victory.

7. Per contra, Shakespeare emphasizes the visiting twin.

in the midst of a domestic battle, describing himself as a hardened
soldier in the war called marriage (lines 127, 129). He craves Rest
and Recreation from this campaign; this is, in fact, what the play is
about.[8] Menaechmus takes several steps in this direction, i.e.,
toward the other side of the stage, where passion lives incarnate. He
orders a banquet, the bill of fare of which emphasizes various
delicacies which were *forbidden to the Romans* (lines 209ff.).[9]
Plautus even concocts comic names for these illegal dishes, to
emphasize how much Menaechmus is savoring the prospect of his
breaking-of-the-rules banquet. And, of course, dessert will be Erotium,
also rather unlawful. The plans are elaborate, explicit and titillating.
Why, then, does Menaechmus leave the stage and head for—of all
places—*the forum*, not to return till the party is over?

The very moment that the local brother exits toward the business
district, his long-lost twin enters from the harbor. This boy from
Syracuse belongs to a great comic tradition: the lowly stranger who
arrives in town, is mistaken for someone else of greater importance,
and receives the cardinal comic joys: food, sex and money. Xanthias
in Aristophanes' *Frogs* is an earlier such type, a later one is Gogol's
Klestakhov, the lowly government clerk who is mistaken for the
Inspector General. Like the Russian hero, Menaechmus II has come
to town virtually penniless. As Messenio, his loyal slave, expresses
it, "We're traveling for summer—very, very light" (line 255). The
sudden bounty seems too good to be true. Menaechmus II expresses
his happy amazement as he emerges drunk and garlanded from the
house of Erotium:

By all the gods, what man in just a single day
Received more pleasures, though expecting none at all:
I've wined, I've dined, I've concubined, and robbed her blind![10]
No one but me will own this dress after today.

> (lines 473–477)

He also receives some of Erotium's jewelry, which, like the dress,

---

8. Cf. Menaechmus' plan of action:

   Clam uxoremst ubi pulchre habeamus atque hunc comburamus diem.

   > (line 152)

   Hidden from my wife we'll live it up and burn this day to ashes.

9. Cf. Pliny, *Natural History*, 8.78 *passim*.

10. The significance of the visiting brother's "wining, dining and concubining" is
emphasized by its repetition on lines 1131–1142.

has been stolen by Menaechmus I from his wife. Two comic fantasies are here fulfilled. Not only does someone else pick up the tab for the banquet, but the whore ends up paying the customer for sex![11]

But what has kept our protagonist offstage? He arrives, in fact, just in time to be too late, and though he sings elaborately of what has detained him, the cause may be summarized in a single word: *business*. While he was in the forum, a client stopped him and forced him to act as advocate in a complicated lawsuit.[12] Moreover, Menaechmus' punishment—for going to work on a day set for play—is not yet complete. He is about to have an unpleasant encounter with his nameless wife, who will lock him out of his house, after which Erotium too will lock her door. He is then *exclusissimus* (line 698), the most "kicked-out" man in the world. To add diagnosis to other injuries, he is then pronounced insane by a psychiatrist gloriosus, a hilarious quack whose professional questions are not unlike those posed by "Socrates" in Aristophanes' *Clouds*. When one Menaechmus is at the acme of delight, the other is at the nadir of despair. The counterbalance is deliberate, and helps to explain the "meaning" of the entire comedy.

The hero of this play is a married man, a solid citizen of this town, who longs to go on a wild revel. In point of fact somebody named Menaechmus does enjoy all the forbidden delights the hero dreams of. But it is *another Menaechmus*, who, although a mirror image (line 1062), is still different in three vital aspects: he is unmarried, unattached and a noncitizen. In these three noncapacities, unmarried Menaechmus II can enjoy sex without "sin," play without neglecting duty (he has no clients), and can even eat whatever he wants—foreigners are not subject to local dietary restrictions. In brief, Menaechmus II is *free*.

He is also nonexistent. He is the creature of someone's imagination—specifically Menaechmus I's. He is the workaday Roman, caught up in the forum, dreaming of getting away—from everything

---

11. We recall the Braggart Soldier, at the height of his *alazoneia*, drunk with joy at the prospect of being paid for his sexual attentions (cf. lines 1059ff.).

12. Molière based his comedy *Les Fâcheux, The Annoying People*, on this same comic premise: a man on his way to an amorous rendezvous, delayed by all sorts of blocking characters. Molière may have been inspired not only by Menaechmus I's plight, but by Horace's *Satire*, I.9, where an annoying fan dogs the poet.

and with everything. *The Brothers Menaechmus* is Roman comedy par excellence, and demonstrates once again that even when he departs slightly from his usual comic domain, Plautus never loses sight of his public's desires. Here he has given them exactly what they and Menaechmus I longed for: a Roman holiday.

Dramatis Personae

PENICULUS, a parasite
MENAECHMUS I
MENAECHMUS II, his twin brother (born Sosicles)
MESSENIO, slave to Menaechmus II
EROTIUM, a lady of pleasure
CYLINDRUS, a cook in Erotium's employ
MAID, also in Erotium's employ
WIFE of Menaechmus
OLD MAN, father-in-law of Menaechmus
DOCTOR

The scene is a street in Epidamnus.
There are two houses.
On the right (from the audience's view)
is MENAECHMUS' house;
on the left, EROTIUM'S house.
The forum is offstage to the audience's right.
The harbor is offstage to the audience's left.

(Enter the CHIEF ACTOR *to speak the prologue.)*

Now first and foremost, folks, I've this apostrophe:
May fortune favor all of you—and all of me.
I bring you Plautus. *(pause)* Not in person, just his play.
So listen please, be friendly with your ears today.
Now here's the plot. Please listen with your whole attention
                                span;   5
I'll tell it in the very fewest words I can.

(a digression)

Now comic poets do this thing in every play:†
"It all takes place in Athens, folks," is what they say.
So that way everything will seem *more Greek* to you.
But I reveal the real locations when I speak to you.   10
This story's Greekish, but to be exact,
It's not Athenish, it's Sicilyish, in fact.

(smiles)

That was a prelude to the prologue of the plot.
I now intend to pour a lot of plot for you.
Not just a cupful, fuller up, more like a pot.   15
Such is our storehouse, brimming full of plot!

---

†*in every play* . . . Plautus criticizes other Roman playwrights for boasting of their "authenticity," their fidelity to the Greek models, a practice which evidently had some snob appeal (to judge from Terence's prologues, in a later age). Plautus, as he here ironically proves, preferred mob appeal. See Introduction, pp. xiii–xiv.

(finally, to business)

There was at Syracuse a merchant old and worn
To whom a pair of baby boys—two twins—were born.
The babies' looks were so alike their nurse confessed
She couldn't tell to which of them she gave which breast.   20
Nor even could their own real mother tell between them.
I've learned about all this from someone who has seen them.
I haven't seen the boys, in case you want to know.
Their father, 'round the time the boys were seven or so,
Packed on a mighty ship much merchandise to sell—   25
The father also packed one of the twins as well.
They went to Tarentum to market, with each other,
And left the other brother back at home with mother.
A festival chanced to be on there when they docked there,
And piles of people for the festival had flocked there.   30
The little boy, lost in the crowd, wandered away.
An Epidamnian merchant, also there that day,
Made off with him to Epidamnus—there to stay.
The father, learning that he'd lost the lad,
Became depressed, in fact he grew so very sad   35
A few days later he was dead. It was that bad.
    When back to Syracuse this news was all dispatched,
The grandpa of the boys learned one was snatched,
And word of father's death at Tarentum then came.
The grandpa took the other twin and changed his name.   40
He so adored the other twin, who had been snatched,
He gave the brother still at home a name that matched:
Menaechmus. That had been the other brother's name.
It was the grandpa's name as well, the very same.†
In fact, it's not a name you quickly can forget,   45
Especially if you're one to whom he owes a debt.‡
I warn you now, so later you won't be confused:

(emphatically)

For both of the twin brothers one same name is used.

(starts to cross the stage)

---

†*the very same* . . . This "explanation" is also calculated to add a bit to the comic
confusion about which Menaechmus is which.
‡*he owes a debt* . . . The text is uncertain. This is the translator's guess.

Meter by meter† to Epidamnus now I must wend,
So I can chart this map unto its perfect end.   50
If any of you wants some business handled there,
Speak up, be brave, and tell me of the whole affair.
But let him give me cash, so I can take good care.
If you don't offer cash, then you're a fool, forget it.
You do— *(smiles)* then you're a bigger fool, and you'll regret

                 it.   55
I'll go back whence I came—still standing on this floor—
And finish up the story I began before:
   That Epidamnian who snatched the little lad,
He had no children; lots of cash was all he had.‡
So he adopted him he snatched, became his dad.   60
And gave his son a dowried female for his bride.
And then—so he could make the boy his heir—he died.*
By chance, out in the country in a rain severe,
He tried to cross a rapid stream—not far from here.
The rapid river rapt the kidnaper, who fell,   65
Caught in the current, heading hurriedly to hell.
The most fantastic riches thus came rolling in
To him who lives right in the house—the kidnaped twin.
   But *now,* from Syracuse where he had always been,
Today in Epidamnus will arrive the other twin,   70
With trusty slave, in search of long-lost brother-twin.
   This town is Epidamnus, while the play is on.
But when we play another play, its name will change
Just like the actors living here, whose roles can range
From pimp to papa, or to lover pale and wan,   75
To pauper, parasite, to king or prophet, on and on.
[And on and on and on . . .]**

     (Enter the parasite PENICULUS.
     He speaks directly to the audience.)

---

†*Meter by meter* . . . The Latin *pedibus* could mean human feet or feet of verse. A pun.
‡*was all he had* . . . There was a pun in the Greek original which Plautus has not succeeded in rendering in Latin. The same Greek word, *tokos,* means both children and money.
*he died . . . This blithe attitude toward death, and lack of sympathy for the adoptive father, is echoed verbatim by Plautus in line 77 of the *Poenulus.*
**and on and on . . . Plautus' prologue is incomplete, lacking at least one verse. The translator has added this line, which at least has the virtue of giving the prologue-actor something to say as he strolls offstage.

PENICULUS:

By local boys I'm called Peniculus the sponge,
For at the table, I can wipe all platters clean.

(a philosophical discourse)

The kind of men who bind their prisoners with chains,
Or clap the shackles on a slave that's run away,   80
Are acting very foolishly—in my own view.
If you compound the wretchedness of some poor wretch,
Why, all the more he'll long to flee and do some wrong.
For one way or another, he'll get off those chains.
The shackled men will wear the ring down with a file,   85
Or smash the lock. This kind of measure is a joke.
But if you wish to guard him so he won't run off,
You ought to chain the man with lots of food and drink.
Just bind the fellow's beak right to a well-stocked table,
Provide the guy with eatables and drinkables,   90
Whatever he would like to stuff himself with every day.
He'll never flee, though wanted for a murder charge.
You'll guard with ease by using chains that he can chew.
The nicest thing about these chains of nourishment—
The more you loosen them, the more they bind more tightly. 95

(end of discourse)

I'm heading for Menaechmus; he's the man to whom
I've had myself condemned. I'm hoping that he'll chain me.
He doesn't merely feed men, he can breed men and
Indeed men are reborn through him. No doctor's better.
This is the sort of guy he is: the greatest eater,   100
His feasts are festivals.† He piles the table so,
And plants so many platters in the neatest piles
To reach the top, you have to stand up on your couch.
And yet we've had an intermission for some days
And tabled at my table, I've expended it.   105
I never eat or drink—except expensively.
But now my army of desserts has been deserting me.

---

†*festivals* . . . The Latin refers specifically to the Festival of Ceres, a holiday in April,
when public banquets were held in Rome.

I've got to have a talk with him. But wait—the door!
Behold, I see Menaechmus himself now coming out.

(Enter MENAECHMUS, *still facing indoors, berating someone.
We will soon see that he is hiding a lady's dress
under his usual garments.)*

MENAECHMUS:

(singing, in anger at his wife in the house)

If you weren't such a shrew, so uncontrolled, ungrateful too,†   110
Whatever thing your husband hated, you'd find hateful too.
And if you act up once again, the way you've acted up today,
I'll have you packed up—back to Daddy as a divorcée.
However often I try to go out you detain me, delay me,
                                        demand such details as
Where I'm going, what I'm doing, what's my business all
                                        about,   115
Deals I'm making, undertaking, what I did when I was out.
I don't have a wife, I have a customs office bureaucrat,
For I must declare the things I've done, I'm doing, and all
                                        that!
All the luxuries you've gotten spoiled you rotten. I want to
                                        live for what I give:

        Maids and aides, a pantry full,   120
Purple clothing, gold and wool:
You lack for nothing money buys.
So watch for trouble if you're wise;
A husband hates a wife who spies.

But so you won't have watched in vain, for all your diligence
                                        and care,
I'll tell you: "Wench to lunch today, lovely dinner off some-
                                        where."

PENICULUS:

The man now thinks he hurts his wife; it's me he hurts: 125
By eating dinner somewhere else, he won't give me my just
                                        desserts!

---

†*ungrateful too . . .* This is the first "lyric" in the play. There will be four more (lines
351ff.; 571ff.; 753ff.; 966ff.).

MENAECHMUS:

> *(looks into house, satisfied,*
> *then turns to audience with a big grin)*

My word barrage has put the wife in full retreat. It's victory!
Now where are all the married "lovers"? Pin your medals
                                        right on me.
Come honor me en masse. Look how I've battled with such
                                                    guts,
And look, this dress I stole inside—it soon will be my little
                                                slut's.   130
I've shown the way: to fool a guard both hard and shrewd
                                        takes aptitude.
Oh, what a shining piece of work! What brilliance, glitter,
                                            glow and gloss!
I've robbed a rat—but lose at that, for my own gain is my
                                            own loss!

> *(indicates the dress)*

Well, here's the booty—there's my foes, and to my ally—
                                        now it goes.

PENICULUS:

Hey, young man! Does any of that stolen booty go to me?   135

MENAECHMUS:

Lost—I'm lost—and caught in crime!

PENICULUS:

> Oh, no, you're found
> —and found in time.

MENAECHMUS:

Who is that?

PENICULUS:

> It's me.

MENAECHMUS:

> Oh, *you*—my Lucky Charm, my Nick-
> of-Time!

Greetings.   *(Rushes to him; they shake hands vigorously.)*

PENICULUS:

> Greetings.

MENAECHMUS:

Whatcha doing?

PENICULUS:

Shaking hands with my
good-luck charm.

MENAECHMUS:

Say—you couldn't come more rightly right on time than
you've just come.

PENICULUS:

That's my style: I know exactly how to pick the nick of time.   140

MENAECHMUS:

Want to see a brilliant piece of work?

PENICULUS:

What cook concocted it?
Show me just a tidbit and I'll know if someone bungled it.

MENAECHMUS:

Tell me, have you ever seen those frescoes painted on the
wall—
Ganymede snatched by the eagle, Venus . . . likewise . . .
with Adonis?

PENICULUS:

Sure, but what do those damn pictures have to do with me?

MENAECHMUS:

Just look.   145

(He strikes a pose, showing off his dress.)

Notice something similar?

PENICULUS:

What kind of crazy dress is that?

MENAECHMUS:

(very fey)

Tell me that I'm so attractive.

PENICULUS:

Tell me when we're going to eat.

MENAECHMUS:

First you tell me—

PENICULUS:

Fine, I'll tell you: you're attractive. So
attractive.

MENAECHMUS:

Don't you care to add a comment?

PENICULUS:

(a breath)   Also witty. Very witty.

MENAECHMUS:

More!

PENICULUS:

No more, by Hercules, until I know what's in it for me.
Since you're warring with your wife, I must be wary and
                                        beware.

MENAECHMUS:

Hidden from my wife we'll live it up and burn this day to 152–
                                        ashes.   153

PENICULUS:

Now you're really talking sense. How soon do I ignite the
                                        pyre?
Look—the day's half dead already, right to near its belly
                                        button.

MENAECHMUS:

You delay me by interrupting—

PENICULUS:

                         Knock my eyeball through
                                    my ankle,
Mangle me, Menaechmus, if I fail to heed a single word.

MENAECHMUS:

Move—we're much too near my house.

(tiptoes to center stage, motions to PENICULUS*)*

PENICULUS:

(follows MENAECHMUS*)*   Okay.

MENAECHMUS:

(moves more, motions)   We're still too
                                    near.

PENICULUS:

                    (follows)   How's this?

MENAECHMUS:

Bolder, let's go farther from the bloody mountain lion's cave.

PENICULUS:

Pollux! You'd be perfect racing chariots—the way you act.   160

MENAECHMUS:

Why?

PENICULUS:

You're glancing back to see if *she's* there, riding after
you.

MENAECHMUS:

All right, speak your piece.

PENICULUS:

My piece? Whatever piece you
say is fine.

MENAECHMUS:

How are you at smells? Can you conjecture from a simple sniff?

PENICULUS:

Sir, my nose knows more than all the city prophets.†   165

MENAECHMUS:

Here now, sniff this dress I hold. What do you smell? You
shrink?

PENICULUS:

When it comes to women's garments, prudence bids us smell
the *top*.
Way down there, the nose recoils at certain odors quite
unwashable.‡

MENAECHMUS:

All right, smell up here, you're such a fussy one.

PENICULUS:

All right, I
sniff.

MENAECHMUS:

Well? What do you smell? Well—

PENICULUS:

(quickly)   Grabbing, grubbing,
rub-a-dub-dubbing.*   170

---

†*the city prophets* . . . The text is fragmentary. Peniculus seems to be referring to the
College of Augurs, official prophets of Rome.

‡*odors quite unwashable* . . . Never a praiser of women, Plautus nonetheless stoops
very, very rarely to jokes this unsavory.

*rub-a-dub-dubbing . . . The Latin is *furtum scortum prandium*. This triad has never
been rendered into English with all its assonantal splendor. Harry Levin has offered
"pinching, wenching, and lunching." Still another attractive suggestion is "purloin,
sirloin, her loin," although the reference to the steak seemed anachronistic. Perhaps the
reader himself can concoct a thrilling threesome.

Hope I'm right.

MENAECHMUS:

        I hope so too. . . .
Now I'll take this dress to my beloved wench, Erotium,
With the order to prepare a banquet for us both.

PENICULUS:

                Oh, good!

MENAECHMUS:

Then we'll drink, we'll toast until tomorrow's morning star
                appears.   175

PENICULUS:

Good, a perfect plan! May I proceed to pound the portals?

MENAECHMUS:

                Pound.

No no—wait!

PENICULUS:

      Why wait? The flowing bowl's more than a
           mile away!

MENAECHMUS:

Pound politely.

PENICULUS:

      Why? You think the door is made of pottery?

MENAECHMUS:

Wait wait wait, by Hercules. She's coming out. Oh, see the 179–
           sun!   180
How the sun's eclipsed by all the blazing beauty from her
           body.

    (*grand entrance of* EROTIUM *from her house*)

EROTIUM:

      (*to* MENAECHMUS)

Greetings, O my only soul!

PENICULUS:

        And me?

EROTIUM:

      (*to* PENICULUS)   Not on my list at all.

PENICULUS:

Such is life for us unlisted men—in every kind of war.

MENAECHMUS:

(to EROTIUM*)*

Darling, at your house today, prepare a little battleground.   184–
185

EROTIUM:

So I will.

MENAECHMUS:

We'll hold a little drinking duel, *(indicating* PEN-
ICULUS*)* the two of us.
Then the one who proves the better fighter with the flowing
bowl,
He's the one who'll get to join your company for night
maneuvers.

(getting more enthusiastic)

Oh, my joy! My wife, my wife! When I see *you*—how I hate
her!

EROTIUM:

(sarcastically)

Meanwhile, since you hate your wife, you wear her clothing,
is that it?   190
What have you got on?

MENAECHMUS:

It's just a dress addressed to you,
sweet rose.

EROTIUM:

You're on top, you outtop† all the other men who try for me.

PENICULUS:

(aside)

Sluts can talk so sweet, while they see something they can
snatch from you.

---

†*outtop* . . . Erotium's sexual innuendo that Menaechmus will always be *superior* as far
as she is concerned, recalls Martial's wry epigram advising that a wife should always be
inferior:

Inferior matrona suo sit, Prisce, marito
non aliter fiunt femina virque pares.
(8.12.3–4)
Priscus, a woman should always be beneath her husband,
Otherwise they won't be equal in relationship.

(to EROTIUM*)*

If you really loved him, you'd have smooched his nose right   194—
                                                    off his face.   195

MENAECHMUS:

Hold this now, Peniculus; religion bids me make redress.

PENICULUS:

Fine, but while you've got a skirt on, why not pirouette a bit?

MENAECHMUS:

Pirouette? By Hercules, you've lost your mind!

PENICULUS:

                                        Not more than
                                                you.

Take it off—if you won't dance.

MENAECHMUS:

            (to EROTIUM*)*   What risks I ran in stealing
                                                    this!
Hercules in labor number nine was not as brave as I,   200
When he stole the girdle from that Amazon Hippolyta.
Take it, darling, since you do your duties with such diligence.†

EROTIUM:

That's the spirit. Lovers ought to learn from you the way to
                                                    love.

PENICULUS:

                        (to the audience)

Sure, that way to love's the perfect short cut to a bankruptcy.

MENAECHMUS:

Just last year I bought my wife this dress. It cost two hundred
                                            drachmae.   205

PENICULUS:

                        (to the audience)

Well, there goes two hundred drachmae down the drain, by
                                            my accounts.

MENAECHMUS:

                        (to EROTIUM*)*

Want to know what I would like prepared?

---

†*duties . . . diligence . . .* Menaechmus calls his mistress *morigera,* "dutiful," an
epithet usually reserved for Roman wives. Cf. *Mostellaria,* line 189.

EROTIUM:

> I know, and I'll
> prepare it.

MENAECHMUS:

Please arrange a feast at your house; have it cooked for three
> of us.
Also have some very special party foods bought in the
> forum:
Glandiose, whole-hog and a descendant of the lardly ham.　210
Or perhaps some pork chopettes, or anything along those
> lines.†
Let whatever's served be *stewed*, to make me hungry as a
> hawk.
Also hurry up.

EROTIUM:

> I will.

MENAECHMUS:

> Now we'll be heading to the forum.
We'll return at once and, while the dinner's cooking, we'll be
> drinking.

EROTIUM:

When you feel like it, come. It will be all prepared.

MENAECHMUS:

> And
> quickly too.　215

> *(to* PENICULUS*)*

Follow me—

PENICULUS:

> By Hercules, I'll follow you in every way.
No, I'd lose the gods' own gold before I lose your track today.

> (MENAECHMUS *and* PENICULUS *exit toward the forum.*)

EROTIUM:

Someone call inside and tell my cook Cylindrus to come out.

---

†*along those lines* . . . All foods "along those lines" were forbidden to Romans by
various censorship rulings, especially the puritanical food prohibitions put forth by the
Elder Cato. See Introduction, p. 119.

(CYLINDRUS enters from EROTIUM's house.)

Take a basket and some money. Here are several coins for
you.

CYLINDRUS:

Got 'em.

EROTIUM:

Do your shopping. See that there's enough for three
of us,   220

Not a surplus or a deficit.

CYLINDRUS:

What sort of guests, madam?

EROTIUM:

I, Menaechmus and his parasite.

CYLINDRUS:

That means I cook for *ten*:

By himself that parasite can eat for eight with greatest ease.

EROTIUM:

That's the list. The rest is up to you.

CYLINDRUS:

Consider it as cooked
already.

Set yourself at table.

EROTIUM:

Come back quickly.

CYLINDRUS:

(starting to trot off)   I'm as good as back.   225

(He exits.)

*(From the exit nearer the harbor
enters the boy from Syracuse—MENAECHMUS II—
accompanied by his slave MESSENIO.
As chance [i.e., the playwright]
would have it,
the twin is also wearing the exact same outfit
as his long-lost brother.
Several sailor types carry their luggage.)*

MENAECHMUS II:

Oh, joy, no greater joy, my dear Messenio,

Than for a sailor when he's on the deep to see
Dry land.

MESSENIO:

It's greater still, if I may speak my mind,
To see and then arrive at some dry land that's *home*.
But tell me, please†—why have we come to Epidamnus?   230
Why have we circled every island like the sea?

MENAECHMUS II:

(pointedly, melodramatically)

We are in search of my beloved long-lost twin.

MESSENIO:

But will there ever be a limit to this searching?
It's six entire years since we began this job.
Through Istria, Iberia, Illyria,   235
The Adriatic, up and down, exotic Greece,‡
And all Italian towns. Wherever sea went, *we* went!
I frankly think if you were searching for a needle,
You would have found it long ago, if it existed.
We seek and search among the living for a dead man.   240
We would have found him long ago if he were living.

MENAECHMUS II:

But therefore I search on till I can prove the fact;
If someone says he knows for sure my brother's dead,
I'll stop my search and never try an instant further.
But otherwise, I'll never quit while I'm alive,   245
For I alone can feel how much he means to me.

MESSENIO:

You seek a pin in haystacks. Let's go home—
Unless we're doing this to write a travel book.

MENAECHMUS II:

(losing his temper)

Obey your orders, eat what's served you, keep from mischief!
And don't annoy me. Do things *my* way.

---

†*tell me, please* . . . One of the all-time obvious cue lines.
‡*exotic Greece* . . . Greek beyond the mainland. Most specifically, Magna Graecia, the
Greek settlements in Southern Italy. The precise area is hard to define. According to
some, "Exotic Greece" might extend as far north as Naples.

MESSENIO:

Yessir, yessir.   250
  I get the word. The word is simple: I'm a slave.
  Concise communication, couldn't be much clearer.

(a chastened pause, then back to harping at his master)

  But still and all, I just can't keep from saying this:
  Menaechmus, when I inspect our purse, it seems
  We're traveling for summer—very, very light.   255
  By Hercules, unless you go home right away,
  While you search on still finding *no* kin . . . you'll be
                             "bro-kin."†
  Now here's the race of men you'll find in Epidamnus:
  The greatest libertines, the greatest drinkers too,
  The most bamboozlers and charming flatterers   260
  Live in this city. And as for wanton women, well—
  Nowhere in the world, I'm told, are they more dazzling.
  Because of this, they call the city Epidamnus,
  For no one leaves unscathed, "undamaged,"‡ as it were.

MENAECHMUS II:
  Oh, I'll have to watch for that. Give me the purse.   265

MESSENIO:
  What for?

MENAECHMUS II:
          Because your words make me afraid of you.

MESSENIO:
  Of me?

MENAECHMUS II:
        That you might cause . . . Epidamnation for me.
  You love the ladies quite a lot, Messenio.
  And I'm a temperamental man, extremely wild.
  If I can hold the cash, it's best for both of us.   270
  Then you can do no wrong, and I can't yell at you.

MESSENIO:

(giving the purse)

  Take it, sir, and guard it; you'll be doing me a favor.

---

† *no kin . . . bro-kin . . .* This pun renders Plautus' play on *geminum*, "twin brother,"
. . . *gemes*, "you'll groan."
‡ *"undamaged"* . . . Plautus puns on the name of the town, Epidamnus, and *damnum*,
which means "financial ruin."

(Re-enter cook CYLINDRUS, *his basket full of goodies.)*

CYLINDRUS:

    I've shopped quite well, and just the sort of things I like.
    I know I'll serve a lovely dinner to the diners.
    But look—I see Menaechmus. Now my back is dead!†   275
    The dinner guests are strolling right outside our door
    Before I even finish shopping. Well, I'll speak.

(going up to MENAECHMUS II)

    Menaechmus, sir . . .

MENAECHMUS II:

                God love you—God knows who you
                                      are.

CYLINDRUS:

(thinks it's a joke)

    Who am I? Did you really say you don't know me?

MENAECHMUS II:

    By Hercules, I don't.

CYLINDRUS:

                Where are the other guests?   280

MENAECHMUS II:

    What kind of other guests?

CYLINDRUS:

                    Your parasite, that is.

MENAECHMUS II:

    My parasite? *(to* MESSENIO) The man is simply raving mad.

MESSENIO:

    I *told* you there were great bamboozlers in this town.

MENAECHMUS II:

(to CYLINDRUS, *playing it cool)*

    Which parasite of mine do you intend, young man?   285

CYLINDRUS:

    The Sponge.

---

†*my back is dead* . . . Nonclever slaves in comedy (especially Plautine comedy) are
always worried about whip lashes on their backs—the reward for misbehavior. Cf.
Braggart Soldier, line 447; *Mostellaria*, line 991.

MENAECHMUS II:

(jocular, points to luggage)

       Indeed, my sponge is here inside my bag.

CYLINDRUS:

Menaechmus, you've arrived too early for the dinner.
Look, I've just returned from shopping.

MENAECHMUS II:

                Please, young man,
What kind of prices do you pay for sacred pigs,†
The sacrificial kind?

CYLINDRUS:

      Not much.

MENAECHMUS II:

            Then take this coin,   290
And sacrifice to purify your mind at my expense.
Because I'm quite convinced you're absolutely raving mad
To bother me, an unknown man who doesn't know you.

CYLINDRUS:

You don't recall my name? Cylindrus, sir, Cylindrus!

MENAECHMUS II:

Cylindrical or Cubical, just go away.   295
Not only don't I know you, I don't *want* to know you.

CYLINDRUS:

Your name's Menaechmus, sir, correct?

MENAECHMUS II:

             As far as *I* know.
You're sane enough to call me by my rightful name.
But tell me how you know me.

CYLINDRUS:

          How I know you? . . . *Sir—*

(discreetly, but pointedly)

You have a mistress . . . she owns me . . . Erotium?   300

MENAECHMUS II:

By Hercules, I haven't—and I don't know you.

---

†*for sacred pigs* . . . As the context suggests, pigs were used as expiatory animals,
offered up to cure diseases, especially mental ones.

CYLINDRUS:

You don't know me, a man who many countless times
Refilled your bowl when you were at our house?

MESSENIO:

Bad luck!

I haven't got a single thing to break the fellow's skull with.

(to CYLINDRUS*)*

Refilled the bowl? The bowl of one who till this day   305
Had never been in Epidamnus?

CYLINDRUS:

(to MENAECHMUS II*)*   You deny it?

MENAECHMUS II:

By Hercules, I do.

CYLINDRUS:

(points across stage)

And I suppose that house
Is not your house?

MENAECHMUS II:

God damn the people living there!

CYLINDRUS:

(to audience)

Why, *he's* the raving lunatic—he cursed himself!   310
Menaechmus—

MENAECHMUS II:

Yes, what is it?

CYLINDRUS:

Do take my advice,
And use that coin you promised me a while ago,
And since, by Hercules, you're certainly not sane,
I mean, Menaechmus, since you just now cursed yourself—
Go sacrifice that sacred pig to cure yourself.   314–315

MENAECHMUS II:

By Hercules, you talk a lot—and you annoy me.

CYLINDRUS:

(embarrassed, to audience)

He acts this way a lot with me—he jokes around.
He can be very funny if his wife is gone.

(to MENAECHMUS*)*

But now, what do you say?

MENAECHMUS II:

To what?

CYLINDRUS:

(showing basket)   Is this enough?
I think I've shopped for three of you. Do I need more   320
For you, your parasite, your girl?

MENAECHMUS II:

What girls? What girls?
What parasites are you discussing?

MESSENIO:

(to CYLINDRUS*)*   And what madness
Has caused you to be such a nuisance?

CYLINDRUS:

(to MESSENIO*)*   What do *you* want
now?

I don't know you. I'm chatting with a man I know.

MESSENIO:

(to CYLINDRUS*)*

By Pollux, it's for sure you're not exactly sane.   325

CYLINDRUS:

(abandons the discussion)

Well then, I guess I'll stew these up. No more delay.
Now don't you wander off too far from here.

(bowing to MENAECHMUS*)*

Your humble servant.

MENAECHMUS II:

(half aside)   If you *were,* I'd crucify you!

CYLINDRUS:

Oh, take a cross yourself—cross over and come in—
Whilst I apply Vulcanic arts to all the party's parts.†   330

---

†*the party's parts* . . . Cylindrus talks grandiloquently, as comic cooks were wont to.
The Latin states, in stately fashion, that he is about to bring his delicacies to Vulcan, the
fire god. A fancy way of saying "stove."

I'll go inside and tell Erotium you're here.
Then she'll convince you you'll be comfier inside.

(Exit.)

MENAECHMUS II:

(stage whisper to MESSENIO*)*

Well—has he gone?

MESSENIO:

He has.

MENAECHMUS II:

Those weren't lies you told.
There's truth in every word of yours.

MESSENIO:

(his shrewd conclusion)

Here's what I think:
I think the woman living here's some sort of slut.   335
That's what I gathered from that maniac who left.

MENAECHMUS II:

And yet I wonder how that fellow knew my name.

MESSENIO:

Well, I don't wonder. Wanton women have this way:
They send their servants or their maids to port   340
To see if some new foreign ship's arrived in port.
To ask around, "Where are they from? What are their
                                                    names?"
Right afterward, they fasten on you hard and fast.
They tease you, then they squeeze you dry and send you
                                                    home.
Right now, I'd say a pirate ship is in *this* port
And I would say we'd better both beware of it.   345

MENAECHMUS II:

By Hercules, you warn me well.

MESSENIO:

I'll know I have
If you stay well aware and *show* I've warned you well.

MENAECHMUS II:

Be quiet for a minute now; the door just creaked.

Let's see who comes out now.

MESSENIO:

                        I'll put the luggage down.

        (to the sailors)

Me hearties, if you please, please guard this stuff for us.

    (EROTIUM appears, in a romantic mood, singing.)

EROTIUM:

        Open my doors, let my welcome be wide,
           Then hurry and scurry—get ready inside.
  See that the incense is burning, the couches have covers.
        Alluring decor is exciting for lovers.   354–355
Lovers love loveliness, we don't complain; their loss is our gain.
    But the cook says someone was out here—*(looks)* I see!
    It's that man of great worth—who's worth so much to me.
    I ought to greet him richly—as he well deserves to be.

Now I'll go near, and let him know I'm here.   360

      (to MENAECHMUS)

My darling-darling, it's a mite amazing
To see you standing out-of-doors by open doors.
You know full well how very much my house is yours.
All you ordered we're supplied with,
All your wishes are complied with.   365
So why stay here, why delay here? Come inside with . . . me.
Since dinner's ready, come and dine,   367
As soon as suits you, come . . . recline.   368

MENAECHMUS II:

    (To say the very least, MENAECHMUS II is stunned.
    After a slight pause, he regains his powers of speech.
       To MESSENIO)

Who's this woman talking to?

EROTIUM:

                To you.

MENAECHMUS II:

                    To me?

What have we—?

EROTIUM:

>   By Pollux, you're the only one of all my
>   lovers   370
>   Venus wants me to arouse to greatness. You deserve it, too.
>   For, by Castor, thanks to all your gifts, I've flourished like a
>   flower.

MENAECHMUS II:

>   *(aside to* MESSENIO)

>   She is surely very mad or very drunk, Messenio.
>   Speaking to a total stranger like myself so . . . sociably.

MESSENIO:

>   Didn't I predict all this? Why, these are only falling leaves.   375
>   Wait three days and I predict the trees themselves will fall
>   on you.
>   Wanton women are this way, whenever they can sniff some
>   silver.
>   Anyway, I'll speak to her. *(to* EROTIUM)   Hey, woman—
>   there.

EROTIUM:

>   *(with hauteur)*

>   Yes, can I help you?

MESSENIO:

>   Tell me where you know this man from.

EROTIUM:

>   Where? Where he
>   knows *me* for years.
>   Epidamnus.

MESSENIO:

>   Epidamnus, where he's never set a foot,   380
>   Never been until today?

EROTIUM:

>   *(laughing)*   Aha—you're making jokes with me.
>   Dear Menaechmus, come inside, you'll see that things . . .
>   will pick up right.

MENAECHMUS II:

>   *(to* MESSENIO)

>   Pollux, look, the creature called me by my rightful name as
>   well.

How I wonder what it's all about.

MESSENIO:

> The perfume from your
> purse.

That's the answer.

MENAECHMUS II:

> And, by Pollux, you did warn me right-
> fully.   385

(Gives purse back to MESSENIO.*)*

Take it then. I'll find out if she loves my person or my purse.

EROTIUM:

Let's go in, let's dine.

MENAECHMUS II:

(declining)   That's very nice of you. Thanks just
> the same.

EROTIUM:

Why on earth did you command a dinner just a while ago?

MENAECHMUS II:

I commanded dinner?

EROTIUM:

> Yes. For you, and for your parasite.

MENAECHMUS II:

What the devil parasite? *(aside)* This woman's certainly in-
> sane.   390

EROTIUM:

Your old sponge, Peniculus.

MENAECHMUS II:

> A sponge—to clean your shoes,
> perhaps?

EROTIUM:

No, of course—the one that came along with you a while ago.
When you brought the dress you'd stolen from your wife to
> give to me.

MENAECHMUS II:

Are you sane? I gave a dress I'd stolen from my wife to you?

(to MESSENIO*)*

Like some kind of horse this woman's fast asleep still stand-
                            ing up.   395

EROTIUM:

Do you get some pleasure making fun of me, denying things,
Things completely true?

MENAECHMUS II:

                     What do you claim I've done that I
                           deny?

EROTIUM:

Robbed your wife and gave the dress to me.

MENAECHMUS II:

                           That I'll deny
                           again!
Never have I had or do I have a wife, and never have I
Ever set a single foot inside that door, since I was born.   400
I had dinner on my ship, then disembarked and met you—

EROTIUM:

                           Oooh!
Pity me—what shall I do? What ship is this?

MENAECHMUS II:

                        A wooden one,
Much repaired, re-sailed, re-beamed, re-hammered and re-
                       nailed and such.
Never did a navy have so numerous a nail supply.

EROTIUM:

Please, my sweet, let's stop the jokes and go inside together
                        . . . mmmm?   405

MENAECHMUS II:

Woman, you want someone else. I mean . . . I'm sure you
                       don't want me.

EROTIUM:

Don't I know you well, Menaechmus, know your father's
                     name was Moschus?
You were born, or so they say, in Syracuse, in Sicily,
Where Agathocles was king, and then in turn, King Phintia,† 409–
                                  410

---

†*King Phintia* . . . There is enough historical accuracy here to suggest that Plautus
might have found these names in his Greek model. On the other hand, these names
would be well known to the Romans who had fought in Sicily during the Punic Wars.

Thirdly, King Liparo, after whom King Hiero got the crown.
Now it's still King Hiero.

MENAECHMUS II:

    (to MESSENIO*)*   Say, that's not inaccurate.

MESSENIO:

                     By Jove—
If she's not from Syracuse, how does she know the facts so
                                well?

MENAECHMUS II:

                (getting excited)

Hercules, I shouldn't keep refusing her.

MESSENIO:

                  Oh, don't you dare! 414–415
Go inside that door and you're a goner, sir.

MENAECHMUS II:

                  Now you shut up!
Things are going well. Whatever she suggests—I'll just agree.
Why not get a little . . . hospitality? *(to* EROTIUM*)* Dear
                  lady, please—
I was impolite a while ago. I was a bit afraid that   419–420

      (indicating MESSENIO*)*

He might go and tell my wife . . . about the dress . . . about
                  the dinner.
Now, when you would like, we'll go inside.

EROTIUM:

                  But where's the
                  parasite?

MENAECHMUS II:

I don't give a damn. Why should we wait for him? Now if he
                  comes,
Don't let him inside at all.

EROTIUM:

            By Castor, I'll be happy not to.
Yet *(playfully)* there's something I would like from you.

MENAECHMUS II:

              Your wish is my command. 425

EROTIUM:

Bring the dress you gave me to the Phrygian embroiderer.
Have him redesign it, add some other frills I'd like him to.

MENAECHMUS II:

Hercules, a good idea. Because of all the decoration,
When my wife observes you in the street, she won't know
                                        what you're wearing.

EROTIUM:

Therefore take it with you when you leave.

MENAECHMUS II:

                                Of course, of
                        course, of course.   430

EROTIUM:

Let's go in.

MENAECHMUS II:

                I'll follow you. *(indicates* MESSENIO*)* I want a
                        little chat with him.

                (Exit EROTIUM*)*

Hey, Messenio, come here!

MESSENIO:

                                What's up?

MENAECHMUS II:

                                Just hop to my com-
                                        mand.

MESSENIO:

Can I help?

MENAECHMUS II:

                You can. *(apologetically)* I know you'll criticize—

MESSENIO:

                                Then all the worse.

MENAECHMUS II:

Booty's in my hands. A fine beginning. You continue, fast—   435
Take these guys *(indicating sailors)* back to our lodging
                        tavern, quicker than a wink,
Then be sure you come to pick me up before the sun goes
                                        down.

MESSENIO:

(protesting)

Master, you don't know about these sluts—

MENAECHMUS II:

Be quiet! Just obey.

If I do a stupid thing, then I'll be hurting, not yourself.

Here's a woman stupid and unwitting, from what I've just
seen.   440

Here's some booty we can keep.

MESSENIO:

I'm lost. *(looks)* Oh, has he
gone? He's lost!

Now a mighty pirate ship is towing off a shipwrecked skiff.

I'm the fool as well. I tried to argue down the man who owns
me.

But he bought me only as a sounding board, not to sound off.

Follow me, you men *(to the sailors)*, so I can come on time—
as I've been ordered.   445

(They exit.

*Stage empty for a moment
[musical interlude?].
Enter* PENICULUS—*all upset.)*

PENICULUS:

More than thirty years I'm on this earth and during all that
time

Never till today have I done such a damned and dopey deed!

Here I had immersed my whole attention in a public meeting.

While I stood there gaping, that Menaechmus simply stole
away,

Went off to his mistress, I suppose, and didn't want me there.   450

Curse the man who was the first to manufacture public
meetings,

All designed to busy men already busy with their business.

They should choose the men who have no occupation for
these things,

Who, if absent when they're called, would face fantastic fines
—and fast.

Why, there's simply gobs of men who only eat just once a
                                                    day,   456
Who have nothing else to do; they don't invite, they're not
                                                    invited.
Make *these* people spend their time at public meetings and
                                                    assemblies.
If this were the case today, I'd not have lost my lovely feast.   460
Sure as I'm alive, that man had really wished to feed me well.
Anyhow, I'll go. The thought of scraps left over lights my
                                                    soul.
But—what's this? Menaechmus with a garland, coming from
                                                    the house?
Party's over, I'm arriving just in time to be too late!
First, I'll spy how he behaves and then I'll go accost the man.   465

(MENAECHMUS II *wobbles happily out of* EROTIUM's *house,*
wearing a garland, and carrying the dress
earlier delivered by his brother.)

MENAECHMUS II:

(*to* EROTIUM)

Now, now, relax, you'll get this dress today for sure,
Returned on time, with lovely new embroidery.
I'll make the old dress vanish—it just won't be seen.
PENICULUS:

(*indignant, to the audience*)

He'll decorate the dress now that the dinner's done,
The wine's been drunk, the parasite left in the cold.   470
No, Hercules, I'm not myself, if not revenged,
If I don't curse him out in style. Just watch me now.
MENAECHMUS II:

(*drunk with joy—and a few other things*)

By all the gods, what man in just a single day   473–474
Received more pleasures, though expecting none at all: 475
I've wined, I've dined, I've concubined, and robbed her blind—
No one but me will own this dress after today!

PENICULUS:

> I just can't bear to hide and hear him prate like this.
> Smug and satisfied, he prates about *my* party.

MENAECHMUS II:

> She says I gave her this—and tells me that I stole it.   480
> I stole it from my *wife*! *(confidentially)* I knew the girl was
> wrong,
> Yet I pretended there was some affair between us two.
> Whatever she proposed, I simply said, "Yes, yes,
> Exactly, what you say." What need of many words?
> I've never had more fun at less expense to me.   485

PENICULUS:

> Now I'll accost the man, and make an awful fuss.

MENAECHMUS II:

> Now who's this fellow coming toward me?

PENICULUS:

> *(in a fury)*   Well, speak up!
> You lighter than a feather, dirty, rotten person,
> You evil man, you tricky, worthless individual!
> What did I ever do to you that you'd destroy me?   490
> You stole away from me, when we were in the forum;
> You dealt a death blow to the dinner in my absence!
> How could you dare? Why, I deserved an equal part!

MENAECHMUS II:

> Young man, please indicate precisely what you want from me.
> And why you're cursing someone you don't know at all.   495
> Your dressing-down of me deserves a beating-up!

PENICULUS:

> By Pollux, you're the one who beat me out, just now.

MENAECHMUS II:

> Now please, young man, do introduce yourself at least.

PENICULUS:

> And now insult to injury! You don't know *me*?

MENAECHMUS II:

> By Pollux, no, I don't, as far as I can tell.   500
> I've never seen you, never met you. Whoever you are—
> At least behave, and don't be such a nuisance to me.

PENICULUS:

> Wake up, Menaechmus!

MENAECHMUS II:

I'm awake—it seems to me.

PENICULUS:

And you don't recognize me?

MENAECHMUS II:

Why should I deny it?

PENICULUS:

Don't recognize your parasite?

MENAECHMUS II:

My dear young man,   505

It seems to me your brain is not so very sane.

PENICULUS:

Just answer this: did you not steal that dress today?

It was your wife's. You gave it to Erotium.

MENAECHMUS II:

By Hercules, I have no wife. Erotium?

I gave her nothing, didn't steal this dress. You're mad.   510

PENICULUS:

(to audience)

Total disaster! *(to* MENAECHMUS II*)* But I saw you wear

that dress

And, wearing it, I saw you leave your house.

MENAECHMUS II:

Drop dead!

You think all men are fags because *you* are?

You claim I actually put on a woman's dress!   514–515

PENICULUS:

By Hercules, I do.

MENAECHMUS II:

Oh, go where you belong!

Get purified or something, raving lunatic!

PENICULUS:

By Pollux, all the begging in the world won't keep me

From telling every single detail to your wife.

Then all these present insults will rebound on you.   520

You've gobbled up my dinner—and I'll be revenged!

(He storms into MENAECHMUS' *house.)*

MENAECHMUS II:

What's going on? Everyone I run across
Makes fun of me . . . but why? Oh, wait, the door just
                                                    creaked.

(Enter EROTIUM'S MAID, *a sexy little thing.*
She carries a bracelet.)

MAID:

Menaechmus, your Erotium would love a favor—
Please, while you're at it, take this to the goldsmith for her   525
And have him add about an extra . . . ounce . . . of gold,
So that the bracelet is remodeled, shining new.

MENAECHMUS II:

(ironically)

I'm happy to take care of both these things for her,
And any other thing that she'd like taken care of.

MAID:

You recognize the bracelet?

MENAECHMUS II:

Uh—I know it's gold.   530

MAID:

This very bracelet long ago was once your wife's,
And secretly you snatched it from her jewel box.

MENAECHMUS II:

By Hercules, I never did.

MAID:

You don't recall?
Return the bracelet, if you don't remember.

MENAECHMUS II:

Wait!
I'm starting to remember. Why, of course I gave it.   535
Now where are those two armlets that I gave as well?

MAID:

You never did.

MENAECHMUS II:

Of course, by Pollux—this was all.

MAID:

Will you take care of things?

MENAECHMUS II:

     (ironically)   I said I'd take good care.
I'll see that dress and bracelet are both carried back together. 539–540

MAID:

     (the total coquette)

And, dear Menaechmus, how about a gift for me?
Let's say four drachmae's worth of jingly earrings?
Then when you visit us, I'll really welcome you.

MENAECHMUS II:

Of course. Give me the gold, I'll pay the labor costs.

MAID:

Advance it for me, afterwards I'll pay you back.   545

MENAECHMUS II:

No, you advance it, afterwards I'll double it.

MAID:

I haven't got it.

MENAECHMUS II:

     If you ever get it—give it.

MAID:

     (frustrated, she bows)

I'm at your service.

     (Exit.)

MENAECHMUS II:

     I'll take care of all of this
As soon as possible, at any cost—I'll sell them.
Now has she gone? She's gone and closed the door behind
                            her.   550
The gods have fully fostered me and favored me unfailingly!
But why do I delay? Now is the perfect chance,
The perfect time to flee this prostitutish place.
Now rush, Menaechmus, lift your foot and lift the pace!
I'll take this garland off, and toss it to the left,   555
So anyone who follows me will think I'm thataway.
I'll go at once and find my slave, if possible,
And tell him everything the gods have given me today.†

---

†*given me today* . . . In a modern production, this would seem an ideal moment for the intermission.

(Exit.)

From MENAECHMUS' *house enter* PENICULUS
and MENAECHMUS' WIFE.*)*

WIFE:

(melodramatic, a big sufferer)

Must I keep suffering this mischief in my marriage?
Where husband sneaks and steals whatever's in the house   560
And takes it to his mistress?

PENICULUS:

Can't you quiet down?
You'll catch him in the act, if you just follow me.
He's drunk and garlanded—at the embroiderer's,
Conveying that same dress he stole from you today.
Look—there's the garland. Do I tell you lies or truth?   565
He's gone in that direction; you can follow clues.
But wait—what perfect luck—he's come back right now!
Without the dress.

WIFE:

What should I do? How should I act with
him?

PENICULUS:

The very same as always: make him miserable.
But let's step over here—and spread a net for him.   570

(Enter MENAECHMUS I.*)*

MENAECHMUS:

(singing)

We have this tradition, we have this tradition,†
An irksome tradition, and yet it's the best
Who love this tradition much more than the rest.
They want lots of clients, all want lots of clients.
Who cares if they're honest or not—are they rich?   575

---

†*this tradition* . . . Menaechmus talks a great deal about "tradition," *mos* in the Latin,
leading many scholars to believe that this is a "Roman song," for the benefit of the
patroni and *clientes* in the house (i.e., almost everybody). This is likely, for the word
mos was a very important one. The Romans, as anyone who has read Cicero will know,
constantly harped upon *mos maiorum*, their forefathers' tradition.

Who cares if they're honest, we'll take them with zest—
   If they're rich.

If he's poor but he's honest—who cares for him?
He's dishonest but rich? Then we all say our prayers for him.
So it happens that lawless, corrupting destroyers   580
   Have overworked lawyers.
Denying what's done and delivered, this grasping and fraudu-
                              lent sort
Though their fortunes arise from exorbitant lies
   They're all anxious to step into court.†   584a
When the day comes, it's hell for their lawyer as well,   585
For we have to defend things unjust and unpretty
To jury, to judge, or judicial committee.

So I just was delayed, forced to give legal aid, no evading
                   this client of mine who had found me.
I wanted to do you know what—and with whom—but he
                  bound me and tied ropes around me.
Facing the judges just now, I had countless despicable deeds
                     to defend.   590
Twisting torts with contortions of massive proportions,
I pleaded and pleaded right down to the end.
But just when an out-of-court settlement seemed to be sealed
               —my client appealed!
I never had seen someone more clearly caught in the act:
For each of his crimes there were three who could speak to
                  the fact!   595

      By all the heavens, cursed be he
      Who just destroyed this day for me.   596
      And curse me too, a fool today,
      For ever heading forum's way.   597
      The greatest day of all—destroyed.
      The feast prepared, but not enjoyed.   598

---

†*step into court . . .* To make all this litigation intelligible to the modern reader, the translator has merely given the gist of Menaechmus' legal maneuvering, which involves a procedure *per sponsionem*, a type of out-of-court arbitration. For a full explanation, see the edition of Moseley and Hammond, pp. 90–91. The important points are that Menaechmus (a) was forced to defend a client, (b) the client was clearly guilty, and (c) notwithstanding his guilt, the client was an idiot, who spoiled all of Menaechmus' efforts on his behalf.

The wench was waiting too, indeed.
The very moment I was freed   599
I left the forum with great speed.
She's angry now, I'm sure of it.   600
The dress I gave will help a bit,

Taken from my wife today . . . a token for Erotium.

(A pause. MENAECHMUS *catches his breath,
still not noticing his* WIFE *or the* PARASITE,
who now speaks.)

PENICULUS:
Well, what say you to that?

WIFE:

That I've married a rat.

PENICULUS:

Have you
heard quite enough to complain to him?

WIFE:
Quite enough.

MENAECHMUS:
Now I'll go where the pleasures will flow.

PENICULUS:
No, remain. Let's be flowing some *pain* to him.

WIFE:
You'll be paying off at quite a rate for this!

PENICULUS:

(to wife)   Good, good attack!

WIFE:
Do you have the nerve to think you'd get away with secret
smuggling?   605

MENAECHMUS:
What's the matter, Wife?

WIFE:

You're asking me?

MENAECHMUS:

(indicating PENICULUS)   Should I ask
him instead?

WIFE:
Don't turn on the charm.

PENICULUS:

That's it!

MENAECHMUS:

But tell me what I've done
to you.

Why are you so angry?

WIFE:

You should know.

PENICULUS:

He knows—and can't
disguise it.

MENAECHMUS:

What's the matter?

WIFE:

Just a dress.

MENAECHMUS:

A dress?

WIFE:

A dress.

PENICULUS:

(to MENAECHMUS*)*   Aha, you're
scared.

MENAECHMUS:

What could I be scared of?

PENICULUS:

Of a dress—and of a dressing-
down.   610

You'll be sorry for that secret feast. *(to* WIFE*)* Go on, attack
again!

MENAECHMUS:

You be quiet.

PENICULUS:

No, I won't. He's nodding to me not to speak.

MENAECHMUS:

Hercules, I've never nodded to you, never winked at you!   613

PENICULUS:

Nothing could be bolder: he denies it while he's doing it!   615

MENAECHMUS:

By Jove and all the gods I swear—is that enough for you,
dear Wife?—

Never did I nod to him.

PENICULUS:

    (sarcastically)   Oh, she believes you. Now go back!

MENAECHMUS:

Go back to what?

PENICULUS:

          Go back to the embroiderers—and get the
                                dress!!

MENAECHMUS:

Get what dress?

PENICULUS:

        I won't explain, since he forgets his own . . .
                         affairs.   619

WIFE:

What a woeful wife I am.

MENAECHMUS:

    (playing very naïve)   Woeful wife? Do tell me why?   614
Has a servant misbehaved, or has a maid talked back to you?   620
Tell me, dear, we'll punish misbehavers.

WIFE:

                       Oh, is *that* a joke.

MENAECHMUS:

You're so angry. I don't like to see you angry.

WIFE:

                       That's a joke!

MENAECHMUS:

Someone from the household staff has angered you.

WIFE:

                     Another joke!

MENAECHMUS:

Well, of course, it isn't me.

WIFE:

              Aha! At last he's stopped the jokes!

MENAECHMUS:

Certainly I haven't misbehaved.

WIFE:

              He's making jokes again!   625

MENAECHMUS:

Tell me, dear, what's ailing you?

PENICULUS:

He's giving you a lovely
line.

MENAECHMUS:

Why do you annoy me? Did I talk to you?

(throws a punch at PENICULUS*)*

WIFE:

(to MENAECHMUS*)* Don't raise your
hand!

PENICULUS:

(to WIFE*)*

Let him have it! *(to* MENAECHMUS*)* Now go eat your little
feast while I'm not there.
Go get drunk, put on a garland, stand outside, and mock me
now!

MENAECHMUS:

Pollux! I've not eaten any feast today—or been in there.   630

PENICULUS:

You deny it?

MENAECHMUS:

I deny it all.

PENICULUS:

No man could be more brazen.
Didn't I just see you here, all garlanded, a while ago?
Standing here and shouting that my brain was not exactly sane?
And you didn't know me—you were just a stranger here in
town!

MENAECHMUS:

I've been absolutely absent, since the second we set out.   635

PENICULUS:

I know you. You didn't think that I could get revenge on you.
All has been recounted to your wife.

MENAECHMUS:

What "all"?

PENICULUS:

Oh, I don't
know.

Ask her for yourself.

MENAECHMUS:

> Dear Wife, what fables has this man
> been telling?

What's the matter? Why are you so silent? Tell me.

WIFE:

> You're
> pretending,†

Asking what you know.

MENAECHMUS:

> Why do I ask, then?

PENICULUS:

> What an evil man!   640

How he fakes. But you can't hide it, now the whole affair is
> out.

Everything's been publicized by me.

MENAECHMUS:

> But *what*?

WIFE:

> Have you no
> shame?

Can't you tell the truth yourself? Attend me and please pay
> attention:

I will now inform you what he told, and why I'm angry at
> you.

There's a dress been snatched from me.

MENAECHMUS:

> There's a dress been
> snatched from me?   645

PENICULUS:

Not from *you,* from *her.* (to WIFE) The evil man resorts to
> every dodge.

> *(to* MENAECHMUS*)*

If the dress were snatched from you, it *really* would be lost
> to us.

MENAECHMUS:

You're not anything to me. (to WIFE) Go on, my dear.

---

†Line 639a omitted.

WIFE:

           A dress
          is gone.

MENAECHMUS:

  Oh—who snatched it?

WIFE:

        Pollux; who'd know better than the
            man himself?

MENAECHMUS:

  Who is this?

WIFE:

     His name's Menaechmus.

MENAECHMUS:

           Pollux, what an evil
               deed!   650
  What Menaechmus could it be?

WIFE:

        Yourself.

MENAECHMUS:

          Myself?

WIFE:

           Yourself.

MENAECHMUS:

            Who says?

WIFE:

  I do.

PENICULUS:

    I do, too. And then you gave it to Erotium.

MENAECHMUS:

  I did?

WIFE:

    You, you, you!

PENICULUS:

        Say, would you like an owl for a pet—
Just to parrot "you you you"? The both of us are all worn
               out.

MENAECHMUS:

  By Jove and all the gods, I swear—is that enough for you,
          dear Wife?—   655

No, I didn't give it to her.†

PENICULUS:

> No, we know *we* tell the truth.

MENAECHMUS:

(backing down)

Well . . . that is to say . . . I didn't *give* the dress. I
loaned it to her.

WIFE:

Oh, by Castor, do I give your tunics or your clothes away—
Even as a loan? A woman can give women's clothes away.
Men can give their own. *Now will you get that dress
back home to me?*   660

MENAECHMUS:

(cowed)

Yes, I'll . . . get it back.

WIFE:

> I'd say you'd better get it back, or
else.

Only with that dress in hand will you re-enter your own
house.

Now I'm going in.

PENICULUS:

(to WIFE*)*   But what of me—what thanks for all my
help?

WIFE:

(sweet-bitchy)

I'll be glad to help you out—when someone steals a dress
from you.

PENICULUS:

That'll never happen. I don't own a single thing to steal.   665

---

†*I didn't give it to her . . .* The emphatic *non dedisse* in the Latin has much the same
double entendre of the English phrase. We recall Ovid's plea to his mistress, urging her
to reject her husband's amorous advances:

> *Sed quaecumque tamen noctem fortuna sequetur
> cras mihi constanti voce* dedisse nega!
> *(Amores,* 1.4. 69–70)
> And yet, whatever chances to happen this night, tomorrow—
> In unshaking tones, deny you gave him anything!

Wife and husband—curse you both. I'll hurry to the forum
                                                        now.
I can very clearly see I've been expelled from this whole
                                                      house.

(He storms off.)

MENAECHMUS:

Hah—my wife thinks that she hurts me, when she shuts the
                                                  door on me.
But, as far as entering, I've got another, better place.

(to WIFE'*s door)*

You don't like me. I'll live through it since Erotium here does.   670
She won't close me out, she'll close me tightly in her arms,
                                                        she will.
I'll go beg the wench to give me back the dress I just now
                                                          gave,
Promising another, better one. *(knocks)* Is there a doorman
                                                          here?
Open up! And someone ask Erotium to step outside.

*(*EROTIUM *steps outside her house.)*

EROTIUM:

Who has asked for me?

MENAECHMUS:

                          A man who loves you more than
                                          his own self.   675

EROTIUM:

Dear Menaechmus, why stand here outside? Come in.

MENAECHMUS:

                                            Wait just
                                          a minute.
Can you guess what brings me here?

EROTIUM:

                              I know—you'd like some
                                . . . joy with me.

MENAECHMUS:

Well . . . indeed, by Pollux. But—that dress I gave to you
                                            just now.

Please return it, since my wife's discovered all in full detail.
I'll replace it with a dress that's twice the price, and as you
like it.   680

EROTIUM:

But I gave it to you for embroidery a moment back,
With a bracelet you would bring the goldsmith for re-
modeling.

MENAECHMUS:

What—you gave me dress and bracelet? No, you'll find that
isn't true.
No—I first gave *you* the dress, then went directly to the
forum.

Now's the very second I've returned.

EROTIUM:

Aha—I see what's up.   685
Just because I put them in your hands—you're out to swindle
me.

MENAECHMUS:

Swindle you? By Pollux, no! Why, didn't I just tell you why?
Everything's discovered by my wife!

EROTIUM:

(exasperated)   I didn't ask you for it.
No, you brought it to me of your own free will—and as a
gift.
Now you want the dress right back. Well, have it, take it,
wear it!   690
You can wear it, or your wife—or lock it in your money box.
But from this day on you'll never set a foot inside my house.
After all my loyal service, suddenly you find me hateful,
So you'll only have me now by laying cash right on the line.
Find yourself some other girl to cheat the way you've cheated
me!   695

MENAECHMUS:

Hercules, the woman's angry! Hey—please wait, please listen
to me—

(EROTIUM *exits, slamming her door.*)

Please come back! Please stay—oh, won't you do this favor
for me?

Well, she's gone—and closed the door. I'm universally kicked
                                    out.†
Neither wife nor mistress will believe a single thing I say.
What to do? I'd better go consult some friends on what they
                                    think.   700

(*Exit* MENAECHMUS.
A slight pause [musical interlude?]. Then enter MENAECHMUS II
from the opposite side of the stage.
He still carries the dress.)

MENAECHMUS II:

I was a fool a while ago to give that purse
With all that cash to someone like Messenio.
I'm sure by now the fellow's "oozing" in some dive.

(WIFE *enters from her house*).

WIFE:

I'll stand on watch to see how soon my husband comes.
Why, here he is—I'm saved! He's bringing back the dress.   705

MENAECHMUS II:

I wonder where Messenio has wandered to. . . .

WIFE:

I'll go and greet the man with words that he deserves.

(*to* MENAECHMUS II)

Tell me—are you not ashamed to show your face,
Atrocious man—and with that dress?

MENAECHMUS II:

                                    I beg your pardon,
What seems to be the trouble, madam?

WIFE:

                                    Shame on you!   710
You dare to mutter, dare to speak a word to me?

MENAECHMUS II:

Whatever have I done that would forbid my talking?

---

†*universally kicked out* . . . Perhaps not an adequate rendering of *exclusissumus*,
a Plautine coinage based on the adjective *exclusus*, "kicked out." Most literally,
I suppose, we could say "kickedest-out," but the word does not play very well.

WIFE:

You're asking me? Oh, shameless, brazen, wicked man!

MENAECHMUS II:

(with quiet sarcasm)

Madam, do you have any notion why the Greeks
Referred to Hecuba as . . . female dog?

WIFE:

                                     I don't.   715

MENAECHMUS II:

Because she acted just the way you're acting now.
She barked and cursed at everyone who came in sight,
And thus the people rightly called her . . . female dog.

WIFE:

I simply can't endure all this disgracefulness—
I'd even rather live my life . . . a divorcée   720
Than bear the brunt of this disgracefulness of yours.

MENAECHMUS II:

What's it to me if you can't stand your married life—
Or ask for a divorce? Is it a custom here
To babble to all foreigners who come to town?

WIFE:

"To babble"? I won't stand for that. I won't! I won't!   725
I'll die a divorcée before I'd live with you.

MENAECHMUS II:

As far as I'm concerned you can divorce yourself,
And stay a divorcée till Jupiter resigns his throne.

WIFE:

Look—you denied you stole that dress a while ago,
And now you wave it at me. Aren't you ashamed?   730

MENAECHMUS II:

By Hercules, you are a wild and wicked woman!
You dare to claim this dress I hold was stolen from you?
Another woman gave it to me for . . . repairs.

WIFE:

By Castor—no, I'd better have my father come,
So I can tell him all of your disgracefulness.   735

(calls in to one of her slaves)

Oh, Decio—go find my father, bring him here.
And tell my father the entire situation.

(to MENAECHMUS II*)*

I'll now expose all your disgracefulness.

MENAECHMUS II:

You're sick!

All what disgracefulness?

WIFE:

A dress—and golden bracelet.
You rob your legal wife at home and then you go   740
Bestow it on your mistress. Do I "babble" truth?

MENAECHMUS II:

Dear Madam, can you tell me please what I might drink
To make your bitchy boorishness more bearable?
I've not the slightest notion who you think I am.
I know you like I know the father-in-law of Hercules!†   745

WIFE:

You may mock me, by Pollux, but you can't mock *him*.
My father's coming. *(to* MENAECHMUS II*)* Look who's
coming, look who's coming;
You do know *him*.

MENAECHMUS II:

(ironically)   Of course, a friend of Agamemnon.‡
I first met him the day I first met you—*today*.

WIFE:

You claim that you don't know me, or my father?   750

MENAECHMUS II:

And how about your grandpa—I don't know him either.

WIFE:

By Castor, you just never change, *you never change!*

(Enter the OLD MAN, MENAECHMUS' *father-in-law,
a groaning wheezer-geezer.)*

---

†*father-in-law of Hercules* . . . Plautus, showing off his erudition, refers to Porthaon.
grandfather of Deianira, wife of Hercules. The aim, of course, is mytho-hyperbolic: "I
don't know you from Adam," or some such.
‡*friend of Agamemnon* . . . Plautus uses Calchas, prophet of the Greek army at Troy.
The translator substituted Calchas' employer, King Agamemnon, to avoid boring
footnotes like the one preceding.

OLD MAN:

(to the audience, in halting song)

Oh, my old age, my old age, I lack what I need,
I'm stepping unlively, unfast is my speed,
But it isn't so easy, I tell you, not easy indeed.   755
For I've lost all my quickness, old age is a sickness.
My body's a big heavy trunk, I've no strength.
Oh oh, old age is bad—no more vigor remains.
Oh, when old age arrives, it brings plenty of pains.
I could mention them all but I won't talk at length.   760
But deep in my heart is this worry:
My daughter has sent for me now in a hurry.
She won't say what it is,
What it is I've not heard.
She just asked me to come, not explaining a word.

And yet I've a pretty good notion at that:
That her husband and she are involved in a spat.   765
Well, that's how it is always with big-dowry wives,†
They're fierce to their husbands, they order their lives.
But then sometimes the man is . . . let's say . . . not so
                                                    pure.
There's limits to what a good wife can endure.
And, by Pollux, a daughter won't send for her dad.   770
Unless there's some cause, and her husband's been bad.
Well, anyway I can find out since my daughter is here.
Her husband looks angry. Just what I suspected, it's clear. 773–774

(The song ends. A brief pause.)

I'll address her.

WIFE:

                I'll go meet him. Many greetings, Father dear.   775

OLD MAN:

Same to you. I only hope I've come when all is fine and
                                                    dandy.

---

† *big-dowry wives* . . . Plautus abounds in jokes about the pains which accompany
dowried wives. Here even the woman's own father complains of the convention. Cf.
Braggart Soldier, line 766; *Mostellaria*, line 280 (and note).

Why are you so gloomy, why does he stand off there, looking
                                                                    angry?
Has there been some little skirmishing between the two of
                                                                    you?
Tell me who's at fault, be brief. No lengthy arguments at
                                                                    length.

WIFE:

I've done nothing wrong, dear Father, you can be assured of
                                                    that.   780
But I simply can't go on and live with him in any way.
Consequently—take me home.

OLD MAN:

                                        What's wrong?

WIFE:

                                                    I'm made a total
                                                    fool of.

OLD MAN:

How and who?

WIFE:

                        By him, the man you signed and sealed to me
                                                    as husband.

OLD MAN:

Oh, I see, disputing, eh? And yet I've told you countless
                                                                    times
Both of you beware, don't either one approach me with com-
                                                    plaints.   785

WIFE:

How can I beware, when he's as bad as this?

OLD MAN:

                                        You're asking me?

WIFE:

Tell me.

OLD MAN:

            Oh, the countless times I've preached on duty to your
                                                    husband:
Don't check what he's doing, where he's going, what his
                                                    business is.†

---

†*what his business is* . . . The old man advises her to be *morigera*, as the ideal
Roman wife should be.

WIFE:

But he loves a fancy woman right next door.

OLD MAN:

He's very wise! 790

Thanks to all your diligence, I promise you, he'll love her
more.

WIFE:

But he also boozes there.

OLD MAN:

You think you'll make him booze the
less,

If he wants to, anywhere he wants? Why must you be so
rash?

Might as well go veto his inviting visitors to dine,

Say he can't have guests at home. What do you women want
from husbands? 795

Servitude? Why, next you'll want him to do chores around
the house!

Next you'll order him to sit down with the maids and card
the wool!

WIFE:

Father dear, I called you to support my cause, not help my
husband.

You're a lawyer prosecuting your own client.

OLD MAN:

If *he's* wrong,

I'll attack him ten times harder than I'm now attacking you. 800

Look, you're quite well dressed, well jeweled and well supplied
with food and maids.

Being well off, woman, why, be wise, leave well enough alone.

WIFE:

But he filches all the jewels and all the dresses from the house.

Stealing on the sly, he then bestows the stuff on fancy women.

OLD MAN:

Oh, he's wrong if he does that, but if he doesn't, then you're
wrong, 805

Blaming blameless men.

WIFE:

He has a dress this very moment,
Father,

And a bracelet he's brought from her because I've found him
out.

OLD MAN:

Well, I'll get the facts, I'll go accost the man, and speak to
him.

(He puffs over to MENAECHMUS II.*)*

Say, Menaechmus, tell me why you're muttering. I'll understand.

Why are you so gloomy? Why is she so angry over there?   810

MENAECHMUS II:

Whatever your name is, old man, and whoever you are, I
swear by Jove supreme,

Calling all the gods to witness—

OLD MAN:

Witness for what, about
what in the world?

MENAECHMUS II:

Never ever did I hurt this woman now accusing me of
Having sneaked into her house and filched this dress.

WIFE:

He's telling lies!

MENAECHMUS II:

If I've ever set a single foot inside that house of hers,   815–816
Anxiously I long to be the very saddest man on earth.

OLD MAN:

No, you can't be sane too long for that, to claim you've not
set foot
In the house you live in. Why, you're the very *maddest* man
on earth!

MENAECHMUS II:

What was that, old man? You claim I live right here and in
this house?   820

OLD MAN:

You deny it?

MENAECHMUS II:

I deny it.

OLD MAN:

Your denial isn't true.

That's unless you moved away last night. Daughter, come
over here.

(Father and daughter walk aside;
OLD MAN *whispers confidentially.)*

Tell me—did you move away from here last night?

WIFE:

Where to?
What for?

OLD MAN:

I don't know, by Pollux.

WIFE:

He's just mocking you—or don't
you get it?

OLD MAN:

That's enough, Menaechmus, no more joking, now let's tend
to business.   825

MENAECHMUS II:

Tell me, sir, what business do you have with me? Just who
are you?
What have I to do with you or—*(points to* WIFE*)* that one,
who is such a bother?

WIFE:

Look—his eyes are getting green, a greenish color's now
appearing
From his temples and his forehead. Look, his eyes are 829–
flickering!   830

MENAECHMUS II:

(aside, to the audience)

Nothing could be better. Since they both declare that I'm
raving mad
I'll pretend I am insane, and scare them both away from me.

*(*MENAECHMUS *begins to "go berserk.")*

WIFE:

What a gaping mouth, wide open. Tell me what to do, dear
Father.

OLD MAN:

Over here, dear Daughter, get as far as possible from him.

MENAECHMUS II:

(caught up in his own act, "hearing" divine words)

Bacchus! Yo-ho, Bacchus, in what forest do you bid me hunt?   835
Yes, I hear you, but I can't escape from where I am just now:
On my left I'm guarded by a very rabid female dog.
Right behind her is a goat who reeks of garlic, and this goat
                                                         has
Countless times accused a blameless citizen with perjury.†

OLD MAN:

(enraged)

You you you, I'll—

MENAECHMUS II:

("hearing")   What, Apollo? Now your oracle com-
                                            mands me: 840
   Take some hotly blazing torches, set this woman's eyes on
                                                        fire.

WIFE:

Father, Father—what a threat! He wants to set my eyes on
                                                        fire!

MENAECHMUS II:

(aside, to audience)

They both say I'm crazy; I know they're the really crazy ones!

OLD MAN:

Daughter—

WIFE:

            Yes?

OLD MAN:

                  Suppose I go, and send some servants here
                                                   at once.
   Let them come and take him off, and tie him up with ropes
                                                at home.   845

---

†*with perjury* . . . It may seem odd to the modern reader that, after calling your
antagonist a smelly goat, you then call him (merely) a perjurer. But we must remember
how the Romans praised plain-dealing and honesty; by their standards, how you reek
was less important than how you speak.

Now—before he makes a bigger hurricane!

MENAECHMUS II:

I'm caught!
I'll be taken off unless I find myself a plan right now.

("hearing oracle," aloud)

Yes, Apollo, "Do not spare thy fists in punching in her face?
That's unless she hurries out of sight and quickly goes to
hell!"

Yes, Apollo, I'll obey you.

OLD MAN:

Run, dear Daughter—quickly home!   850
Otherwise, he'll pound you.

WIFE:

While I run, please keep an eye
on him.
See he doesn't get away. (a final groan) What wifely woe to
hear such things!

(Exit.)

MENAECHMUS II:

Hah, not bad, I got her off. And now I'll get this—poisoned
person,
White-beard, palsied wreck. Tithonus was a youth compared
to him.†
Yes, I'll do thy bidding: take a double ax and this old fogey,
Chop his innards into little pieces, till I reach the bone?

(to "Apollo")

What's my orders? Beat the fellow limb from limb and bone
from bone?   855
Use the very stick he carries for the job?

OLD MAN:

I'll punish you—
If you try to touch me, if you try to get much closer to me!

MENAECHMUS II:

(to "Apollo")

Yes, I'll do thy bidding: take a double ax and this old fogey,
Chop his innards into little pieces, till I reach the bone?

---

†compared to him . . . Reading Tithonus for Lindsay's Titanus. Tithonus was Aurora's
lover, immortal but not immutable. With time he became a mere wrinkle.

OLD MAN:

(panicked)

Goodness, now's the time for me to be on guard and very
wary.   860
I'm afraid he'll carry out his threats and cause some harm to
me.

MENAECHMUS II:

(to "Apollo" again)

Dear Apollo, you command so much. I now must hitch up
horses,
Wild, ferocious horses, and then mount up in my chariot,
Then to trample on this lion—creaking, stinking, toothless
lion?
Now I'm in the chariot, I've got the reins, I've got the whip.   865
Up up up, ye steeds, now let us see the sound of horses'
hoofbeats.†
Quickly curve your course with splendid speed and swifty
swoop of steps.

OLD MAN:
Threatening me with hitched-up horses?

MENAECHMUS II:

Yea, Apollo, once
again,
Now you bid me charge and overwhelm the man who's
standing here.

(fakes another bit—Homeric divine intervention)

But what's this? Who takes me by the hair and hauls me from
the car?‡   870

---

†*horses' hoofbeats* . . . In "*see* the sound of horses' hoofbeats," Menaechmus antici-
pates the nonsensical outburst of Shakespeare's Pyramus: "I see a voice!" (*Midsummer
Night's Dream*, V, i, 194).
‡*hauls me from the car?* . . . Needless to say, Menaechmus II is making all this up as he
goes along. But Moseley and Hammond, in their note to this line, point out that
Menaechmus has improvised this "staying hand," to keep him from attacking an old
man. The Romans revered their elders; any assault on an oldster, even on the comic
stage, was unthinkable.

Look, Apollo, someone's changing your command as spoke
                                                to me!

OLD MAN:

By Hercules, he's sick, he's very sick. Ye gods!
And just a while ago, the man was very sane,
But suddenly this awful sickness fell on him.
I'll go and get a doctor—fast as possible.   875

(Exit at a senile sprint.)

MENAECHMUS II:

Well, have they disappeared from sight, the two of them,
Who forced a normal, healthy man to act insane?
I shouldn't wait to reach my ship while things are safe.

(to the audience)

But, everybody, please—if that old man returns,   879–880
Don't tell him, please, which street I took to get away.

*(He dashes offstage, toward the harbor.
Enter* OLD MAN,† *tired, annoyed, complaining.)*

OLD MAN:

My limbs just ache from sitting and my eyes from looking,
While waiting for that doctor to leave office hours.
At last, unwillingly, he left his patients. What a bore!
He claims he'd set Asclepius' broken leg,   885
And then Apollo's broken arm. I wonder if
The man I bring's a doctor or a carpenter!
But here he's strutting now. *(calling off)* Why can't you
                                                hurry up?

(Enter DOCTOR, *the superprofessional.)*

DOCTOR:

(right to the point)

What sort of illness does he have? Speak up, old man.
Is he depressed, or is he frantic?‡ Give the facts.   890

---

†*Enter* OLD MAN . . . The old man does get back with the doctor rather quickly. And
he complains of having had to wait, at that. Perhaps there was a musical interlude. Or
perhaps, counter to the comic spirit, we are being too literal in noticing.
‡*or is he frantic? . . .* "Depressed" and "frantic" in the Latin are *larvatus*, literally,
"haunted by ghosts," and *cerritus*, "out of his head."

Or is he in a coma? Has he liquid dropsy?

OLD MAN:

But that's precisely why I've brought you—to tell *me*—
And make him well again.

DOCTOR:

Of course. A snap.
He shall be well again. You have my word on that.

OLD MAN:

I want him to be cared for with the greatest care.   895

DOCTOR:

I'll sigh a thousand sighs, I'll take great pains with him.
For you—I'll care for him with all the greatest care.
But here's the man himself; let's see how he behaves.

(They step aside to eavesdrop.
From the forum side enter MENAECHMUS,
addressing himself in soliloquy.)

MENAECHMUS:

Pollux, what a day for me: perverted and inverted too.
Everything I plotted to be private's now completely public.   900
My own parasite has filled me full of fearful accusations!
My Ulysses, causing so much trouble for his royal patron!†
If I live, I'll skin him live. I'll cut off all his livelihood.
What a foolish thing to say. What I call his is really mine.
My own food and fancy living nurtured him. I'll starve him
                                                            now.   905
And my slut has been disgraceful. Typical of slutitude.
All I did was ask her to return the dress to give my wife.
She pretends she gave it to me. Pollux, I'm in awful shape!

OLD MAN:

(to DOCTOR*)*

Did you hear his words?

DOCTOR:

(nods)   Admits his "awful shape."

OLD MAN:

Go up to
him.

---

†*this royal patron* . . . The Latin is *rex*, "king," the title by which a parasite would
refer to his benefactor.

DOCTOR:

(aloud)

Greetings, dear Menaechmus. Do you realize that your cloak
has slipped910

Don't you know how dangerous that sort of thing is for your
health?

MENAECHMUS:

Why not hang yourself?

OLD MAN:

(whispers to DOCTOR*)*   You notice anything?

DOCTOR:

Of course I do!

This condition couldn't be relieved with tons of hellebore.

(to MENAECHMUS, *again)*

Tell me now, Menaechmus.

MENAECHMUS:

Tell what?

DOCTOR:

Just answer what I ask.

Do you drink white wine or red?

MENAECHMUS:

And why don't you go
straight to hell?   915

DOCTOR:

Hercules, I notice teeny traces of insanity.

MENAECHMUS:

Why not ask

Do I favor purple bread, or pink or maybe even mauve?

Do I eat the gills of birds, the wings of fishes—?

OLD MAN:

Oh, good
grief!

Listen to his ravings, you can hear the words. Why wait at 919–
all?   920

Give the man some remedy before the madness takes him
fully.

DOCTOR:

Wait—I have more questions.

OLD MAN:

But you're killing him with all
this blab!

DOCTOR:

(to MENAECHMUS*)*

Tell me this about your eyes: at times do they get glazed at
all?

MENAECHMUS:

What? You think you're talking to a lobster, do you, rotten
man!

DOCTOR:

(unfazed)

Tell me, have you ever noticed your intestines making noise?   925

MENAECHMUS:

When I've eaten well, they're silent; when I'm hungry, they
make noise.

DOCTOR:

Pollux, that's a pretty healthy answer he just gave to me.

(to MENAECHMUS*)*

Do you sleep right through till dawn, sleep easily when you're
in bed?

MENAECHMUS:

I sleep through if all the debts I owe are paid. But listen you,   929–
you   930
Question-asker, you be damned by Jupiter and all the   931–
gods!   933

DOCTOR:

Now I know the man's insane, those final words are proof.
(to OLD MAN)   Take care!

OLD MAN:

He speaks like a Nestor now,† compared to just a while ago.   935

---

†*like a Nestor now . . .* Nestor, elder statesman of the Greeks at Troy. Homeric legends
were just becoming fashionable at Rome, which may explain Plautus' frequent references to them.

Just a while ago he called his wife a rabid female dog.

MENAECHMUS:

I said that?

OLD MAN:

You're mad, I say.

MENAECHMUS:

I'm mad?

OLD MAN:

And do you know
what else? You
Also threatened that you'd trample over me with teams of
horses!
Yes, I saw you do it. Yes, and I insist you did it, too.   939–940

MENAECHMUS:

(to OLD MAN*)*

You, of course, have snatched the sacred crown of Jove, that's
what I know.
Afterwards, they tossed you into prison for this awful crime.
When they let you out, while you were manacled, they beat
you up.
Then you killed your father. Then you sold your mother as a
slave.
Have you heard enough to know I'm sane enough to curse
you back?   945

OLD MAN:

Doctor, please be quick and do whatever must be done for
him.

Don't you see the man's insane?

DOCTOR:

I think the wisest thing
for you's to
Have the man delivered to my office.

OLD MAN:

Do you think?

DOCTOR:

Of course.

There I'll treat him pursuant to diagnosis.

OLD MAN:

As you say.

DOCTOR:

(to MENAECHMUS*)*

Yes, I'll have you drinking hellebore for twenty days or so.   950
MENAECHMUS:

Then I'll have *you* beaten hanging upside down for thirty
days.

DOCTOR:

(to OLD MAN*)*

Go and call for men who can deliver him.
OLD MAN:

How many men?

DOCTOR:

From the way he's acting, I'd say four, none less could do
the job.

OLD MAN:

(exiting)

They'll be here. You watch him, Doctor.
DOCTOR:

(anxious to retreat)   No, I think I'd best
go home.
Preparations are in order for the case. You get the slaves.   955
Have them carry him to me.
OLD MAN:

I will.

DOCTOR:

I'm going now.

OLD MAN:

Goodbye.

MENAECHMUS:

Doctor's gone, father-in-law's gone. I'm now alone. By
Jupiter!—
What does all this mean? Why do these men insist that I'm
insane?
Really, I have not been sick a single day since I've been born.

Nor am I insane, nor have I punched or fought with anyone. 960
Healthy, I see healthy people, only talk with folks I know.
Maybe those who wrongly say I'm mad are really mad
                                themselves.
What should I do now? My wife won't let me home, as I
                                would like.

(pointing to EROTIUM's *house)*

No one will admit me there. All's well—well out of hand,
                                that is.† 965
Here I'm stuck. At least by night—I think—they'll let me in
                                my house.

*(*MENAECHMUS *sits dejectedly in front of his house,
all wrapped up in his troubles.
From the other side of the stage, enter* MESSENIO
singing about How to Succeed in Slavery.)

MESSENIO:

If you should seek the proof of whether someone's slave is
                                good,
See, does he guard his master's interest, serve right to the
                                letter
When Master is away—the way he should
If Master were at hand—or even better.
For if the slave is worthy, and he's well brought up, 971
He'll care to keep his shoulders empty—not to fill his cup. 970

His master will reward him. Let the worthless slave be told
The lowly, lazy louts get whips and chains,
And millstones, great starvation, freezing cold. 975
The price for all their misbehaviors: pains.
I therefore fully fear this fate and very gladly
Remain determined to be good—so I won't turn out badly.
I'd so much rather be bawled out than sprawled out on a
                                pillory,
I'd so much rather eat what's cooked than have some work
                                cooked up for me.
So I follow Master's orders, never argue or protest. 980

---

†*All's well* . . . Plautus too is tampering with a proverb.

Let the others do it their way; I obey; for me, that's best. . . .†

But I haven't much to fear; the time is near for something
nice.‡

My master will reward his slave for "thinking with his back"
—and thinking twice.   985

(Enter OLD MAN, *leading four burly servants.)*

OLD MAN:

Now, by all the gods and men, I bid you all obey my orders.   990

Be most careful so you'll follow what I've ordered and will
order.

Have that man picked up aloft, and carried to the doctor's
office.

That's unless you're not a bit concerned about *your* back and
limbs.

Every man beware. Don't pay attention to his threats of
violence.

But why just stand? Why hesitate? It's time to lift the man
aloft!   995

(not very brave himself)

And I'll head for the doctor's office. I'll be there when you
arrive.

MENAECHMUS:

(notices the charging mob)

I'm dead! What's this? I wonder why these men are rushing
swiftly toward me?

Hey, men, what do you want? What are you after? Why sur-
round me now?

(They snatch up MENAECHMUS.*)*

Where are you snatching me and taking me? Won't someone
help me, please?

O citizens of Epidamnus, rescue me! *(to slaves)* Please let me
go!   1000

---

†*for me, that's best* . . . A few lines of dubious authenticity have been omitted here.
‡*for something nice* . . . The meaning of this line is unsure. I have made a conjecture.

MESSENIO:

By the immortal gods, what am I seeing with my very eyes?
Some unknown men are lifting Master in the air. Out-
rageously!

MENAECHMUS:

Won't someone dare to help?

MESSENIO:

Me, me! I'll dare to help with
derring-do!
O citizens of Epidamnus, what a dirty deed to Master!
Do peaceful towns allow a freeborn tourist to be seized in
daylight?   1005

(to slaves)

You let him go!

MENAECHMUS:

(to MESSENIO)

Whoever you may be, please help me out!
Don't allow this awful outrage to be perpetrated on me.

MESSENIO:

Why, of course I'll help, and hustle hurriedly to your defense.
Never would I let you down. I'd rather let myself down first.   1010

(to MENAECHMUS)

Grab that fellow's eye—the one who's got you by the
shoulder now.
I can plow the other guys and plant a row of fists in them.

(to slaves)

Hercules, you'll lose an awful lot by taking him. Let go!

(A wild melee ensues.)

MENAECHMUS:

(while fighting, to MESSENIO)

Hey, I've got his eye.

MESSENIO:

Then make the socket in his head appear!

Evil people! People snatchers! Bunch of pirates!

SLAVES:

                         (together)   Woe is us! 1015

Hercules! No—please!

MESSENIO:

           Let go!

MENAECHMUS:

                  What sort of handiwork is this?

Face a festival of fists.

MESSENIO:

              Go on, be gone, and go to hell!

          (kicking the slowest slave)

You take that as your reward for being last to get away.

         (They are all gone.
    MESSENIO *takes a deep breath of satisfaction.)*

Well, I've really made my mark—on every face I've faced
                              today.

Pollux, Master, didn't I come just in time to bring you aid! 1020

MENAECHMUS:

Whoever you are, young man, I hope the gods will always
                           bring you blessings.

If it hadn't been for you, I'd not have lived to see the sunset.

MESSENIO:

If that's true, by Pollux, then do right by me and free me,
                            Master.

MENAECHMUS:

Free you? I?

MESSENIO:

          Of course. Because I saved you, Master.

MENAECHMUS:

                         Listen
                    here, you're

Wand'ring from the truth—

MESSENIO:

           I wander?

MENAECHMUS:

                  Yes, I swear by Father
                     Jove   1025

I am not your master.

MESSENIO:

(stunned) Why proclaim such things?

MENAECHMUS:

But it's no
lie.

Never did a slave of mine serve me as well as you just did.

MESSENIO:

If you're so insistent and deny I'm yours, then I'll go free.

MENAECHMUS:

Hercules, as far as I'm concerned, be free. Go where you'd
like.

MESSENIO:

Am I really authorized?

MENAECHMUS:

If I've authority for you. 1030

MESSENIO:

(dialogue with himself)

"Greetings, patron."—"Ah, Messenio, the fact that you're
now free
Makes me very glad."—"Well, I believe that's true." (to
MENAECHMUS) But, patron dear,
You can have authority no less than when I was a slave.
I'll be glad to live with you, and when you go, go home with
you.

MENAECHMUS:

(doesn't want some strange person in his house)

Not at all, no thank you.

MESSENIO:

(jubilant) Now I'll get our baggage at the
inn— 1035
And, of course, the purse with all our money's sealed up in
the trunk
With our travel cash. I'll bring it to you.

MENAECHMUS:

(eyes lighting up at this) Yes! Go quickly,
quickly!

MESSENIO:

I'll return it just exactly as you gave it to me. Wait right here.

(MESSENIO *dashes off toward the harbor*.)

MENAECHMUS:

(soliloquizing)

What unworldly wonders have occurred today in wondrous
ways:
People claim I'm not the man I am and keep me from their
houses.   1040
Then this fellow said he was my slave—and that I set him
free!   1041
Then he says he'll go and bring a wallet full of money to me.   1043
If he does, I'll tell him he can go quite freely where he'd like—
That's so when he's sane again he won't demand the money
back.   1045

(musing more)

Father-in-law and doctor said I was insane. How very strange.
All this business seems to me like nothing other than a dream.
Now I'll go and see this harlot, though she's in a huff with
me.
Maybe I'll convince her to return the dress, which I'll take
home.

(He enters EROTIUM's *house*.

Enter MENAECHMUS II *and* MESSENIO.)

MENAECHMUS II:

(angry with MESSENIO)

Effrontery in front of me! You dare to claim we've seen each
other   1050
Since I gave you orders that we'd meet back here?

MESSENIO:

But didn't
I just
Snatch and rescue you from those four men who carried you
aloft

Right before this house? You called on all the gods and men
for aid.

I came running, snatched you from them, though with fists
they fought me back.

For this service, since I saved your life, you made a free man
of me.   1055

(ruefully)

Now just when I said I'd get the cash and baggage, you sped
up and

Ran ahead to meet me, and deny you've done the things
you've done.

MENAECHMUS II:

Free? I said you could go free?

MESSENIO:

For sure.

MENAECHMUS II:

Now look, for *super*-
sure

I would rather make *myself* a slave than ever set you free.

(MENAECHMUS I is pushed by EROTIUM out of her house.)

MENAECHMUS I:

If you would like to swear by your two eyes, go right ahead,
but still   1060

You'll never prove that I absconded with your dress and
bracelet—*(door slams)* hussy!

MESSENIO:

(suddenly seeing double)

By the gods, what do I see?

MENAECHMUS II:

What do you see?

MESSENIO:

Why—your
reflection!

MENAECHMUS II:

What?

MESSENIO:

      Your very image just as like yourself as it could be.

MENAECHMUS II:

Pollux—he's not unlike me . . . I notice . . . similarities.

MENAECHMUS I:

(to MESSENIO*)*

Hey, young man, hello! You saved my life—whoever you
                             may be.   1065

MESSENIO:

You, young man, if you don't mind, would you please
                        tell me your name?

MENAECHMUS I:

Nothing you could ask would be too much since you have
                        helped me so.
My name is Menaechmus.

MENAECHMUS II:

             Oh, by Pollux, so is mine as well!

MENAECHMUS I:

Syracuse-Sicilian—

MENAECHMUS II:

        That's my city, that's my country too!

MENAECHMUS I:

What is this I hear?

MENAECHMUS II:

        Just what is true.

MESSENIO:

      (to MENAECHMUS II*)*   I know you—*you're* my
                        master!   1070

      (to audience)

I belong to this man though I thought that I belonged to that
                        man.

      (to MENAECHMUS I, *the wrong man)*

Please excuse me, sir, if I unknowingly spoke foolishly.
For a moment I imagined he was you—and gave him trouble.

MENAECHMUS II:

Madness, nothing but! *(to* MESSENIO*)* Don't you recall that
                  we were both together,

Both of us got off the ship today?

MESSENIO:

    (thinking, realizing)   That's right. You're very
                                 right.   1075

You're my master. (*to* MENAECHMUS I) Find another slave,
    farewell. (*to* MENAECHMUS II) And you, hello!
        (pointing to MENAECHMUS II)
Him, I say, this man's Menaechmus.

MENAECHMUS I:

                    So am I!

MENAECHMUS II:

                          What joke is this?

You're Menaechmus?

MENAECHMUS I:

          That I say I am. My father's name was
                         Moschus.

MENAECHMUS II:

You're the son of my own father?

MENAECHMUS I:

                No, the son of *my* own
                        father.
I'm not anxious to appropriate your father or to steal him
                         from you.   1080

MESSENIO:

Gods in heaven, grant me now that hope unhoped-for I
                         suspect.
For, unless my mind has failed me, these two men are both
                        twin brothers.
Each man claims the selfsame fatherland and father for his
                        own.
I'll call Master over. O Menaechmus—

MENAECHMUS I and II:

             (together)   Yes?

MESSENIO:

                        Not both of you.
Which of you two traveled with me on the ship?

MENAECHMUS I:

                        It wasn't me. 1085

MENAECHMMUS II:

Me it was.

MESSENIO:

Then you I want. Step over here. *(motioning)*

MENAECHMUS II:

(following MESSENIO *to a corner)* I've stepped. What's
up?

MESSENIO:

That man there is either one great faker or your lost twin
brother.
Never have I seen two men more similar than you two men:
Water isn't more like water, milk's not more alike to milk
Than that man is like to you. And what's more he named
your father. 1090
And your fatherland. It's best to go and question him still
further.

MENAECHMUS II:

Hercules, you do advise me well. I'm very grateful to you.
Please work on, by Hercules. I'll make you free if you
discover
That man is my brother.

MESSENIO:

Oh, I hope so.

MENAECHMUS II:

And I hope so too.

MESSENIO:

(to MENAECHMUS I*)*

Sir, I do believe you've just asserted that you're named
Menaechmus. 1095

MENAECHMUS I:

That is so.

MESSENIO:

Well, his name is Menaechmus, too. You also said
You were born in Sicily at Syracuse. Well, so was he.
Moschus was your father, so you said. That was *his* father,
too.

Both of you can do yourselves a favor—and help me as well.†

MENAECHMUS I:

Anything you ask me I'll comply with, I'm so grateful to you. 1100
Treat me just as if I were your purchased slave—although
                                                    I'm free.

MESSENIO:

It's my hope to prove you are each other's brothers, twins in
                                                      fact,
Born of the selfsame mother, selfsame father, on the selfsame
                                                       day.

MENAECHMUS I:

Wonder-laden words. Oh, would you could make all your
                                              words come true.

MESSENIO:

Well, I can. But, both of you, just give replies to what I ask
                                                    you. 1105

MENAECHMUS I:

Ask away. I'll answer. I won't hide a single thing I know.

MESSENIO:

Is your name Menaechmus?

MENAECHMUS I:

                              Absolutely.

MESSENIO:

                (to MENAECHMUS II*)*   Is it yours as well?

MENAECHMUS II:

Yes.

MESSENIO:

      You said your father's name was Moschus.

MENAECHMUS I:

                                              Yes.

MENAECHMUS II:

                                              The same
                                              for me.

---

†*and help me as well . . .* The absurdly logical process that Messenio now undertakes
has puzzled many. Why are they so hesitant? Isn't it clear that the brothers have found
each other? Why this detailed investigation? In his French edition of the play, Alfred
Ernout suggests that we here see the ''cautious attitude characteristic of the Romans.''
This may well be the case. And yet there is an even simpler explanation: Plautus never
stops until he gets the nth laugh out of his audience. And he does wring quite a few
more jokes out of this protracted recognition dialogue.

MESSENIO:
And you're Syracusan?
MENAECHMUS I:
Surely.
MESSENIO:
(to MENAECHMUS II*)*   You?
MENAECHMUS II:
You *know* I am, of course.
MESSENIO:
Well, so far the signs are good. Now turn your minds to
                                        further questions.   1110

(to MENAECHMUS I*)*

What's the final memory you carry from your native land?
MENAECHMUS I:

(reminiscing)

With my father . . . visiting Tarentum for the fair. Then after
                                        that . . .
Wandering among the people, far from Father . . . Being
                                        snatched—
MENAECHMUS II:

(bursting with joy)

Jupiter above, now help me—!
MESSENIO:
(officiously)   What's the shouting? You shut
                                        up.

(turning back to MENAECHMUS I*)*

Snatched from father and from fatherland, about how old
                                        were you?   1115
MENAECHMUS I:
Seven or so. My baby teeth had barely started to fall out.
After that, I never saw my father.
MESSENIO:
No? Well, tell me this:
At the time how many children did he have?

MENAECHMUS I:

I think just two.

MESSENIO:

Which were you, the older or the younger?

MENAECHMUS I:

Neither, we were
equal.

MESSENIO:

Do explain.

MENAECHMUS I:

We were both twins.

MENAECHMUS II:

(ecstatic)   Oh—all the gods are with me
now!   1120

MESSENIO:

(sternly, to MENAECHMUS II)

Interrupt and I'll be quiet.

MENAECHMUS II:

(obedient)   I'll be quiet.

MESSENIO:

(to MENAECHMUS I)   Tell me this:

Did you both have just one name?

MENAECHMUS I:

Oh, not at all. My name is
mine,

As it is today—Menaechmus. Brother's name was Sosicles.

MENAECHMUS II:

(mad with joy)

Yes, I recognize the signs. I can't keep from embracing you!
Brother, dear twin brother, greetings! I am he—I'm Sosicles!   1125

MENAECHMUS I:

How is it you afterward received the name Menaechmus,
then?

MENAECHMUS II:

When we got the news that you had wandered off away from
Father

And that you were kidnaped by an unknown man, and Father
                                                            died,
Grandpa changed my name. The name you used to have he
                                                    gave to me.

MENAECHMUS I:
  Yes, I do believe it's as you say.

          (goes to embrace him, suddenly stops)

                            But tell me this.
MENAECHMUS II: 1129–
                            Just ask. 1130

MENAECHMUS I:
  What was Mother's name?
MENAECHMUS II:
                            Why, Teuximarcha.

MENAECHMUS I:
                                      That's correct, it
                                              fits.
  Unexpectedly I greet you, see you after so much time!
MENAECHMUS II:
  Brother, now I find you after so much suffering and toil,
  Searching for you, now you're found, and I'm so very, very
                                                        glad.

              (They embrace.)

MESSENIO:

              (to MENAECHMUS II*)*

  That's the reason why the slut could call you by your rightful
                                              name,   1135
  Thinking you were he, I think, when she invited you to
                                              dinner.
MENAECHMUS I:
  Yes, by Pollux, I had ordered dinner for myself today,
  Hidden from my wife—from whom I filched a dress a while
                                              ago—and
  Gave it to her.

              (indicates EROTIUM*'s house)*

MENAECHMUS II:

> Could you mean this dress I'm holding,
> > Brother dear?

MENAECHMUS I:

That's the one. How did you get it?

MENAECHMUS II:

> > Well, the slut led me to
> > > dinner.   1140
> There she claimed I gave it to her. *Wonderfully* have I just
> > > dined,
> Wined as well as concubined, of dress and gold I robbed her
> > > blind.

MENAECHMUS I:

O by Pollux, I rejoice if you had fun because of me!
When she asked you in to dinner, she believed that you   1144–
> > > were me.   1145

MESSENIO:

> *(impatient for himself)*

Is there any reason to delay the freedom that you promised?

MENAECHMUS I:

Brother, what he asks is very fair and fine. Please do it for me.

MENAECHMUS II:

> *(to* MESSENIO, *the formula)*

"Be thou free."

MENAECHMUS I:

> The fact you're free now makes me glad,
> > Messenio.

MESSENIO:

> *(broadly hinting for some cash reward)*

Actually, I need more facts, *supporting* facts to keep   1149–
> > me free.   1150

MENAECHMUS II:

> *(ignoring* MESSENIO, *to his brother)*

Since our dreams have come about exactly as we wished,
> > dear Brother,

Let us both return to our homeland.
MENAECHMUS I:

> Brother, as you wish.

I can hold an auction and sell off whatever I have here.
Meanwhile, let's go in.
MENAECHMUS II:

> That's fine.

MESSENIO:

> (to MENAECHMUS I)   May I request a favor of
> you?

MENAECHMUS I:
What?
MESSENIO:

Please make me do the auctioneering.
MENAECHMUS I:

> Done.

MESSENIO:

> All right.
> Then please inform me: 1155

When should I announce the auction for?
MENAECHMUS I:

> Let's say—a week
> from now.

> *(The brothers go into* MENAECHMUS' *house,*
> *leaving* MESSENIO *alone on stage.)*

MESSENIO:

> *(announcing)*

In the morning in a week from now we'll have Menaechmus'
> auction.
Slaves and goods, his farm and city house, his everything will
> go.
Name your prices, if you've got the cash in hand, it all will
> go.
Yes, and if there's any bidder for the thing—his wife will go. 1160
Maybe the entire auction will enrich us—who can tell?
For the moment, dear spectators, clap with vigor. Fare ye
> well!

The Haunted House

(Mostellaria)

for Mason Hammond

virtute id factum tua et magisterio tuo.
(line 32)

About the Play

The virtues of the *Mostellaria*[1] cannot be overstated. Scintillating, polished, witty and lyrical, it is Plautus' masterpiece.[2] Every single character is a singular characterization. The theme—trickery—is Plautus' favorite. The clever slave himself announces that this is one of the great bamboozlements in all comedy,[3] and he may well be correct. The plot involves no great variation on a theme, but it is the verve which accompanies the familiar theme that distinguishes the *Mostellaria* from a run-of-the-mill New Comedy situation in which the father has gone abroad (on business, of course) while the son stays home and lives it up.

Under the tutelage of Tranio his slave,[4] young Philolaches has forsaken outdoor for indoor sports (lines 30ff.). He has fallen in love with Philematium, a pretty young thing, all the more attractive because her name means "kiss-me-darling."[5] The young man has purchased his beloved on borrowed cash, and proceeds to run up a

---

1. The Latin title means "little ghost story."
2. The play is not absolutely flawless. Certainly the "toilette scene" (lines 157–292) is overlong, and the charm of the dialogue is worn out by repetition. But then a wise director would trim this for performance, as I have little doubt Plautus himself did during rehearsal.
3. Cf. lines 1149ff. Tranio advises Theopropides to recount his misfortunes to a comic playwright, thus providing "the perfect trickery plots," *optumas frustrationes . . . in comoediis* (line 1152).
4. I have used the word "tutelage" to suggest, as I believe Plautus does, some perversion or inversion of the Roman ideal. The young man specifically places himself in the "custody" of his slave (line 406). Grumio argues that Tranio has wrought a change in the youth as a result of the slave's *magisterium* and *virtus* (line 32). This latter term in particular, as scholars have emphasized of late, has particularly Roman connotations.
5. Φιλημάτιον = Philematium = (literally) "my teeny-weeny kiss."

huge catering bill on borrowed time. As is standard procedure in plots of this sort, Father arrives just at the wrong time. If he should discover the results of his son's riotous ways, all would be lost—especially Tranio's life. And so a bamboozlement is in order. Not one, in fact, but a crescendoing series of dodges, deft parries to the old man's pragmatic thrusts: Where is my son? Where is my money? What's going on?

Tranio outfaces the returning patriarch brilliantly. After moving the son and his party guests into the house and locking it up tight,[6] he then convinces old Theopropides, whose name ironically suggests omniscience,[7] that his domicile is haunted. Tranio's fantastic tale, concocted on the spot and subject to constant revision and elaboration, is the high point in the play. No sooner does he convince the old fellow that his house has been abandoned because of a vengeful ghost that haunts it (the "specter"'s speech surprisingly resembles that of Hamlet's father!),[8] than he must then account for the presence and persistence of a monomaniacal moneylender—who also must be staved off by a flurry of fabrications. Tranio sprints from one side of the stage to the other, inventing on the run. He must work each new and unwelcome arrival into his impromptu scenario. To ward off present disaster, he claims that he and his young master have purchased the house next door, hence the cash owed to the moneylender. But then the owner of the next-door house appears! Now he too must be dealt with, or rather, double-dealt with. Tranio's fount of fictions seems inexhaustible. Though forever on the move, he never reaches his wits' end.

From start to finish, the *Mostellaria* presents a parade of richly drawn characters. First, there is the puritanical slave Grumio, whose boisterous bickering with Tranio begins the play and tosses out exposition in a far more lively manner than any prologue could.[9]

---

6. Plautus repeats the verb *occludere* again and again, to indicate how very "shut up tight" the house is.

7. Theopropides is derived from Θεοπροπέω, "to prophesy."

8. Compare Tranio's account of the sacrilegious assault on the guest-ghost who then went to the next world "unfuneraled," *insepultum* (line 502), with the plaint of Hamlet's father that he was murdered, "unhous'led, disappointed, unanel'd" (I, v, 77). That Shakespeare read the *Mostellaria* is beyond doubt. I leave the reader to speculate on the significance of this similarity.

9. Ben Jonson used this scene as a model for the opening of his *Alchemist*, which also shows several other influences of the *Mostellaria*. In *Taming of the Shrew* Shakespeare names two servants Tranio and Grumio, but here the similarity seems to end.

Then there is the dilapidated lover Philolaches; for once, a Plautine youth has a distinguishable personality, even if it be, as the youth himself says, that of a broken-down building (lines 84ff.). An interesting simile, by the way, since the comedy is all about houses. His beloved Philematium remains a one-man woman despite the corrupting counsel of her bawdy maid Scapha, who voices some of the earthy pragmatism Shakespeare's nurse will later urge upon Juliet. The old father Theopropides is among the most colorful of Plautus' dupes (the color is usually red—for embarrassment or rage); he is credulous, superstitious and money-hungry, qualities which make him an ideal victim for bamboozlement.[10] The moneylender Misargyrides is one of the great skinflints in Plautus' gallery of misers. Here is an obsessive caricature worthy of Molière. As usual, Tranio himself provides the aptest comment:

MISARGYRIDES:

My interest now, my interest, interest; pay me interest!
Will you please pay my interest to me right away?
I want my interest!

TRANIO:

"Interest" here and "interest" there.
The only interest this man has in life is "interest."

(lines 603–606)

This fellow is so stingy he will not even "expend" the energy to leave and return later for his promised payment. Hence he stays around—to further confound matters for Tranio.

Even a secondary figure like old Simo, the next-door neighbor, is a vivid characterization. Simo belongs to the "friendly old codger" family of Plautine oldsters, along with Periplectomenus in *The Braggart Soldier*. Interestingly enough in this "house play," while at one side of the stage the boys and girls are reveling and making love, Simo is fleeing his own home to avoid his unattractive wife's embraces (line 690ff.), and sings a song which concludes: "Better work in the forum than bed her at home" (lines 706–707). Thus, as

---

10. Significantly enough, these happen to be character traits shared by the Romans of this period.

in the other two comedies in this volume, we find one house on stage standing for complete indulgence, the other for abstinence.[11]

However bright these other stars may glow, they are still only satellites to the shining Tranio. He is the ultimate in clever slaves, the finest portrait of Plautus' favorite character. Tranio is bouncy, brazen, bold and brainy. His powers of improvisation are never on better display than in his haunted-house narrative, where at every cul-de-sac he reaches once again into his bag of tricks. We can be no less extravagant in our praise of him than he is for himself:

They saw Kings Alexander and Agathocles
Were two who did big things. Now would you say *I'm* third—
Who solo does so many memorable things?

(lines 775–777)

This exultant role is sung again and again by brilliant servants like Jonson's Mosca, Molière's Scapin and Beaumarchais's Figaro. In fact, Tranio voices a rather democratic notion which would later be celebrated as Figaro's philosophy:

If a man has talent, it's no different if he's a slave or master!

(line 407)

Tranio embodies the spirit of comedy. When warned by a fellow slave that his roguery may bring him punishment very soon, he retorts:

I have my "now," let "very soon" come when it comes.

(line 71)

And even his "now" is something very special. With Saturnalian audacity, Tranio faces up to all the mischief he has done, and even boasts of his exploits right before his outraged master. When surrounded by whippers, with but temporary refuge on a holy altar,[12] Tranio is unregenerate, cheeky and proud. The slave always remains master of the situation, defying his antagonists and deifying himself.[13] This is the supreme topsy-turvydom of Plautine comedy.

---

11. Cf. Introduction to *The Brothers Menaechmus*, p 118.
12. The altar onto which Tranio leaps for sanctuary seems to have been part of the traditional Roman theater "set," perhaps used for a ceremony preceding the performance. The onstage altar is also referred to in *Aulularia*, line 606.
13. Cf. line 1104. On "the divinity of the clever slave," see my *Roman Laughter*, chapter IV, especially pp. 131ff.

On any ordinary occasion, a Roman Tranio would suffer a whipping—or even the gallows—for his rogueries. Today is different: tomorrow is another story, as Tranio himself admits (line 1178). For the moment, this creature of a single day, the figment of the "now" imagination, is "permitted the outrage, but spared the consequences."[14] The rules—and the audience—relax. Indeed, the latter testify to their complicity in Tranio's un-Roman rogueries[15] but two lines later—with their applause.

14. This paraphrase of Freud's theory of comedy is Eric Bentley's definition of the appeal of farce, which then continues: "Chaplin's delicacy of style is actually part of the pattern: he parades an air of nonchalance while acting in a manner that, in real life, would land him in Bellevue or Sing Sing." From "The Psychology of Farce," in *Let's Get a Divorce and Other Plays*, edited by Eric Bentley, New York, 1958, p. xiii. This essay has enjoyed many reprintings in various anthologies.

15. The anti-Roman "in" jokes which spice this comedy are too numerous to recount in full. Some are mentioned in the notes, for example, the joke in line 828, a gibe at the Romans' bland eating habits. Tranio's irreverent behavior toward his elders is, of course, as un-Roman as anything imaginable.

Dramatis Personae

TRANIO, slave to Philolaches
GRUMIO, a slave
PHILOLACHES, a young man
PHILEMATIUM, a girl of joy
SCAPHA, her maid, an old hag
CALLIDAMATES, a young man
DELPHIUM, a girl of joy to Callidamates
THEOPROPIDES, an old man, father to Philolaches
MISARGYRIDES, a moneylender
SIMO, an old man, neighbor to Theopropides
SLAVES
WHIPPERS in the employ of Theopropides

The scene is a street in Athens.
There are two houses on stage,
with an alley between them.
One house belongs to THEOPROPIDES,
the other to SIMO.
The latter has an altar before it.

(Enter GRUMIO,
a puritanical slave from one of THEOPROPIDES' *farms.*
In a huff, he storms up to the door of THEOPROPIDES' *house,*
and shouts inside.)

GRUMIO:

Come out here from the kitchen, will you, Whipping Post?
You show such cleverness amidst the pots and pans.
Come out here, come outside, you master's ruination!
I'll get revenge on you some day, out at the farm.
Come out, you kitchen stink-up; don't you hide from me!   5

(From inside the house saunters TRANIO.*)*

TRANIO:

(smiling and calm)

Why all this shouting here outside the house, you wretch?
You think you're in the country? Go away from here.
Go to the country, go to hell—but go away.

(throws a flurry of punches)

Do you want *this*?

GRUMIO:

(cringing)   Oh no! Why beat *me* up?   9–10

TRANIO:

Because you live.

209

GRUMIO:

       All right. If our old master comes—

(melodramatically, to heaven)

Oh, let him come back safe, the man you're eating up!

TRANIO:

Your symbols and your similes are terrible.
How can a person eat a person who's not here?

GRUMIO:

Terrific city wit! The people love your jokes.   15
You mock my country ways, but you wait, Tranio.
I'll see you there, and very soon—chained to the mill.
Know what awaits you in a while or two, my boy?
Irons on the fire for you, in the country.
Now, while you still can do it, booze and bankrupt us,   20
And keep corrupting Master's wonderful young son.
Keep drinking day and night, and Greek-it-up† like mad!
Buy mistresses and free 'em, feed your flatterers,
Buy groceries as if you all were caterers!
Did Master bid you do this when he went abroad?   25
Did he expect to come back finding things like this?
And did you think this is the way good slaves behave—
By ruining Master's wealth and Master's son as well?
For ruined he is, to judge by his behavior now.
That boy, who out of all the boys in Attica   30
Was once so chaste, so frugal, once so well behaved,
Now takes the prizes in completely different sports,
Thanks to all your tutoring and all your talent.

TRANIO:

Why do you give a damn for me? Why do you care?
Can't you go find some country cows to care for?   35
It's fun to drink, to love, to have a lot of whores.
I'm risking my own back, you know, not risking yours.

GRUMIO:

How bold he talks! *(to* TRANIO*)* Well, "foo" to you!

TRANIO:

                            By Jupiter

---

†*Greek-it-up* . . . The Latin verb *pergraecari*, also used in lines 64 and 960. See
Introduction, p. xiv. (Horace uses the verb *graecari* in *Satires* 2.2.11.)

And all the gods, the hell with you—you reek of garlic!
Of homemade country mud, of goats and pigs combined—   40
All scum and scatologic.

GRUMIO:

                   Well, what do you want?
Not all of us can smell of fancy foreign perfumes,
Or have the place of honor at a banquet table,
Or live as high and mighty off the hog as you do.   44–45
You keep your doves, the fancy fish and fancy birds,
And let me live my life the way I like—with garlic.
Right now you're very high, I'm very low. I'll wait.
As long as in the end we end up in reverse.   49–50

TRANIO:

Why, Grumio, it seems to me you're acting jealous!
But things are best when best for me and worst for you;
For I was made for wooing—you were made for . . .
                        mooing.
Thus I live very high and you, of course, live low.

GRUMIO:

Oh, torture-target—which I know you'll soon become,   55
When whippers prod you manacled right through the streets
With goads—*(reverently)* if ever our old master does return.

TRANIO:

Can you be sure your turn won't come before my own?

GRUMIO:

I've not deserved it. *You* deserve it, always have.

TRANIO:

Oh, save your efforts, save your words as well,   60
Unless you'd like a lot of lashing for yourself.

GRUMIO:

               (to business)

Look, are you going to give me feed to feed the cows?
Unless you eat *that,* too. Go on and gallivant
The way you've started, drink and Greek-it-up like mad,
Eat on and stuff yourselves, destroy the fatted calf.   65

TRANIO:

Shut up, back to the sticks! I'm off to the Piraeus†

—————————
†*the Piraeus* . . . principal port of Athens. Plautus is wont to make a gallimaufry of Greek
and Roman geography. Across the stage from the (Athenian) Piraeus is the (Roman) forum.

To buy myself a little fish for this night's dinner.
I'll have someone deliver you the feed tomorrow.

(starts to go off, notices GRUMIO *glaring at him)*

What's up? What is it now you want, you gallows bird?

GRUMIO:

I think *you'll* be the gallows bird—and very soon.   70

TRANIO:

I have my "now," let "very soon" come when it comes.

GRUMIO:

Oh, yes? Remember this one thing: "What comes in life
Is not so much what you would like, but what you don't."

TRANIO:

Right now you bother me. Go back to farming, move!
By Hercules, I want no more delays from you!   75

*(*TRANIO *skips offstage.)*

GRUMIO:

Well, has he gone and treated my words just as straws?

(fervently, to heaven)

O ye immortal gods, I call on you and pray,
Do let our senior master come back home to us—
Although he's gone three years. And let him come before
It all is lost, the house and holdings. If not now,   80
In little time, there'll only be remains remaining.
I'm for the farm. *(notices offstage)* But look—here comes our
                                                                 junior master.
Behold—a most corrupted youth—once oh so fine.

*(*GRUMIO *walks sadly offstage,
in the opposite direction to that in which* TRANIO *left,
whence now young* PHILOLACHES *enters.
This lad is typical of Plautus' young men,
wide-eyed and handsome, but not very bright.
In fact,* PHILOLACHES *is rather an imbecile.
When he reaches center stage,*
PHILOLACHES *sings a doleful lament.†)*

---

†*a doleful lament* . . . I have rendered Philolaches' famous "Man Is a House" song
rather freely, keeping the sense and making a mish-mash of the meter. This is the first
"lyric" in the play. There will be four more: at 313ff.; 690ff.; 783ff.; 858ff.

PHILOLACHES:

I've been pounding my head a lot, pondering.
Deep in me, words have been wandering.   85
Things roll around in my mind—if I do have a mind—
And I've thought and I've sought many answers to find.

(a breath)

What is a man when he's born?
I mean, what is he like?
After looking around, here's the answer I've found: 90

(a breath, then a profound conclusion)

Like a house. Like a newly built house.
That's a man when he's born, and it's true.
Perhaps you don't quite see the likeness,
                                    I'll see that you do.
And my words will confirm and convince you.
I'm sure when you hear what I say,
You will see things my way.
So hark to my argument, folks, and you'll be
Just as smart in this matter as . . . me.   100

A house when it's steady and ready, all straight with no
                                                tilt,
A house when it's perfectly built,
Both the building and builder are praised; the approval's im-
                                                mense.
People all want the same sort of house; they won't spare the
                                                expense.

But then—suppose some lax and lazy lout moves in   105
And brings a filthy laggard group along. Your cares begin.
For even one mistake can make a good house . . . break.
You know what also happens often? Storms.
    Tiles and gutters shatter,
Then suffer from the lazy man's neglect.   110
    Rain blows right through and flows right through the
                                                walls.
    The timber goes. A good construction job is wrecked.
    It grows still worse with wear, as you'd expect.

Of course it's not the builder's fault at all.
Repairs are costly, people are so cheap.   115
  The less they spend, the more they have to keep.
They wait till it must be rebuilt completely, all is in a heap.

So far I've talked of houses. Now I shall proceed
To state why men are similar to houses—till you've all agreed.

Now, first of all, a parent is a builder of a child.   120
He lays the groundwork, as it were, sees that he's styled.
He brings him up, prepares him to grow tall and straight,
In hopes that what he builds may someday serve the state—
Or stand alone at least. In all events,
They spare no pains, and they spare no expense.   125
Then it's lots of schooling: arts and letters, legal lore to build
                                                        his brain.
Expensive. Parents strain
To raise a son who'll show the level others might attain.
Then it's off to the army, prepared he is sent
To serve as some relative's reinforcement.   130
It's goodbye to the builders, he's out of their hands,
And now people see if the building still stands!

  Speaking now for myself, I used to be one of the top,
A genuine model—at least while I stayed in the shop.
But when left to my own sweet devices at last,   135
The builder's whole structure began to slip fast.
  Laziness came like a storm.
  There was raining and hailing.
  The next thing I knew all my virtues were failing.
  A sudden unroofing caught me unaware,   140
  Unroofing I was a bit slow to repair.
Then in place of the rain a swift new storm would start:
For then *love* billowed in, and it drenched my whole heart.

Then, all at once, my name, my fame, my fortune, all that
                                                once was fair
Had fled the camp. Now day by day, it grows still worse with
                                                wear.   145
My roof, it leaks, and it so creaks
My house can't be repaired now, it's a total wreck for good.

The whole foundation's finished. Nothing helps—and nothing
                                                    could.
What pain to see me now, and know what once I used to be:
There never was a cleaner-living youth than me.   150
No greater athlete in the arts gymnastic,
In throwing, riding, running, fighting—I was just fantastic.
It nourished me with joy
To be a model of restraint and ruggedness to every boy.
All the noblest people looked to me for discipline,   155
But now, it's all my fault, I'm nothing—see the awful shape
                                                    I'm in.

> *(After his song,* PHILOLACHES *hears the sounds
> of someone approaching from the back
> [the women's quarters] of his house.
> He steps to the side of the stage to observe,
> as* PHILEMATIUM *and* SCAPHA *enter.
> The first is a dazzling young girl of joy,
> recently freed by* PHILOLACHES,
> the second a wise and wizened ex-whore,
> now serving as* PHILEMATIUM's *personal maid.*
> SCAPHA *carries a sort of make-up table and a stool
> on which her mistress can sit to perform her toilette.†*
> PHILEMATIUM *and* SCAPHA *converse,
> as young* PHILOLACHES *observes from the sidelines,
> and comments.)*

PHILEMATIUM:

By Castor, it's a while since I have had a fresher bath,
Or a better one, dear Scapha. Why, I feel all scrubbed and
                                                    polished.

SCAPHA:

> *(the hard pragmatist)*
Well, time will tell. You know, just like the recent harvest
                                                    stored away.‡

---

†*perform her toilette* . . . Because the conventional city-street set made it impossible to
show interiors, the authors had to bring the "inside" outside.
‡*harvest stored away* . . . A puzzling allusion. Is it some sort of proverb? Or is it a
reference to the Roman harvest, the occasion at which the play may have been
presented? The latter seems more likely. Call it an "in" joke, whose precise connotations are lost to us.

PHILEMATIUM:

What does the recent harvest have to do with my own
                                                bathing?   160

SCAPHA:

As much as your own bathing has to do with it.

PHILOLACHES:

                            (aside, ecstatic)   O queen of
                                                      Venus!

(to the audience, pointing at the girl)

Look, there's my storm, the one that unroofed all my repu-
                                                tation.
I used to have a roof, but Love and Cupid showered on me.
Love soaked right through my heart, and it's beyond repair.
My walls are oozing and my house is losing its whole struc-
                                                ture.   165

PHILEMATIUM:

Do look me over, Scapha. Is my costume nice enough?
I long to please my darling benefactor Philolaches.

SCAPHA:

No need for lovely ornaments when you yourself can glitter.
The lovers don't love women's clothes; *(with a leer)* they
                            love what's stuffed inside them.

PHILOLACHES:

(aside)

By all the gods, that Scapha's charming; she knows all the
                                                tricks!   170
How charmingly she speaks of love affairs and lovers'
                                                thoughts!

PHILEMATIUM:
    And now?
SCAPHA:
            My dear?
PHILEMATIUM:
                Please look me over. Am I nice enough?
SCAPHA:
    You're beautiful inside and so you beautify your clothes.

PHILOLACHES:

(aside)

For that nice thought, dear Scapha, you shall get a gift today.
You won't have complimented my sweet love without reward.   175

PHILEMATIUM:

I don't want simply flattery.

SCAPHA:

                You're such a silly girl.
I think you'd rather have false criticism than true praise.
By Pollux, I myself would much prefer false flattery.
Who wants true criticism? People laughing at my looks?   180

PHILEMATIUM:

Not I. I much prefer the truth. I can't abide a liar.

SCAPHA:

I swear, by Philolaches' love for you, you're simply lovely.

PHILOLACHES:

(aside)

What's that you swear, you bitch? By all my love for her?
But what of hers for me? You left that out. Forget the gift.
You're finished, fully finished, now that gift has flown away.   185

SCAPHA:

And yet I'm quite amazed. I thought that you were shrewd
                        and wise.
You're being foolish foolishly.

PHILEMATIUM:

                What's this? Have I done
                wrong?

SCAPHA:

By Castor, yes. You're wrong to put your hopes in just one
                      lover,
To be so dutiful† to him, rejecting other men.
Fidelity's for wives, but not for mistresses.   190

PHILOLACHES:

(aside)

By Jupiter, what sort of evil earthquake shakes my house?
May all the gods and goddesses destroy me with distress

---

†*To be so dutiful* . . . The Latin is *morem gerere*, which connotes the devotion of an ideal (Roman) *wife*.

If I don't kill that hag with hunger, thirst and freezing cold!

PHILEMATIUM:

But, Scapha, I don't want to learn such wicked things.

SCAPHA:

You're foolish
To think that man will always be your friend and benefactor.   195
I warn you, someday he'll be jaded—you'll be faded—then
he'll leave.

PHILEMATIUM:

I *hope* not.

SCAPHA:

"Things unhoped-for come more often than things
hoped."
Well, I suppose I never will convince you with my words,
But learn from my example, what I am and what I was:
For once I was a charming beauty just as you are now   200
And, loved as you are now, was dutiful to just one man.   200a
He loved me, yes, by Pollux, till with time my hair turned
gray,
Then left me in the lurch. *(a sigh)* I know the same will come
to you.

PHILOLACHES:

(aside, furious)

I'm barely in control, I'd fly right at the evil bitch's eyes.

PHILEMATIUM:

He freed me—spent such sums to be my single swain.
I only think it's right I stay . . . monogamous† to him.   205

PHILOLACHES:

(aside)

By the immortal gods, a lovely girl—and ladylike.
By Hercules, it's worth it to be bankrupt all for her.

SCAPHA:

By Castor, as you so unshrewd?

---

†*monogamous* . . . What I have rendered "monogamous" is *obsequens*, "compliant,"
in the Latin. *Obsequentia* was a particularly Roman wifely virtue, a quality frequently
lauded on memorial inscriptions.

PHILEMATIUM:

But why?

SCAPHA:

To care for him,
To hope he really loves you.

PHILEMATIUM:

Why should I *not* care?

SCAPHA:

You're
free.
You've got what you desired now. If he won't love you still,   210
He really would be suffering a loss from his investment.

PHILOLACHES:

(aside)

I'm dead, by Hercules, if I don't chop that bitch to bits!
That vicious, ill-advising villainess corrupts my love!

PHILEMATIUM:

How can I ever show my gratitude for what he's done?
Don't ever bid me love him less, stop all this trying.   215

SCAPHA:

I will, but do remember this: if you serve one man now
While you're in full bloom, then when you're old, you'll *look*
for men.

PHILOLACHES:

(aside)

I wish I could transform into a rope to choke that poisoner,
By winding round her evil, ill-advising throat—and kill her.

PHILEMATIUM:

But since I have my freedom, I should show the same af-
fection,   220
And be as lovey-dovey to him as I was before.

PHILOLACHES:

(aside)

Whatever heaven does, now that I've heard those little words,
I'd free you ten times over—and kill Scapha twice as dead.

SCAPHA:

If you feel that your contract spells eternal love,
And he's to be your only lover for your whole life long,   225
Then honor and obey—put on a wifely hairdo.†

PHILEMATIUM:

Your reputation gets you what you earn in life.
If I preserve my reputation, then the cash will come.

PHILOLACHES:

(aside)

Why, if I had to sell my father, I would rather sell him‡
Than let this lovely girl lack anything while I'm alive.   230

SCAPHA:

But what of other men who love you?

PHILEMATIUM:

Well, they'll love me
more
To see how I show gratitude in paying back a kindness.

PHILOLACHES:

(berserk with joy)

Oh, someone bring the news right now—the news my
father's dead!
I'll disinherit myself, and make *her* heir to all my
goods!

SCAPHA:

His cash will soon be gone, through dining, drinking day and
night.   235
He never saves a single thing. It's clear-cut gluttonizing.

PHILOLACHES:

(aside)

By Hercules, for you I'll change my style and start to save.
I won't give *you* a thing to eat or drink for ten whole days!

---

†*a wifely hairdo* . . . You could tell by her coiffure if a Roman lady was married. Cf.
Braggart Soldier, lines 791ff.
‡*rather sell him* . . . To be sold into slavery was, for a Roman, a fate worse than death.
Roman fathers, who had the power to execute their sons, could *not* sell them into
slavery. Moreover, the Romans' reverence for their elders cannot be overemphasized.
Hence, to behold Philolaches' impious desire to sell his father, not to mention his
wishing the old man dead (line 233), would be especially shocking (and gratifying?) for
the Roman audience.

PHILEMATIUM:

> If you have anything that's nice to say of him, then say it.
> But if you keep abusing him . . . I'll beat you up.   240

PHILOLACHES:

> *(aside)*

> If I had used that cash to sacrifice to Jove supreme
> Instead of buying her, I couldn't be more blessed than now.
> Look how she loves me—deep, in depth. Oh, what a lucky
> man I am!
> I freed a girl protector; she defends me masterfully.

SCAPHA:

> Although I see you spurn all other men for Philolaches,   245
> I won't be beaten up because of him. I'll say he's nice,
> If you're so assured your contract is eternal with him.

PHILEMATIUM:

> Quickly, Scapha, now my mirror, and my box of jewelry.†
> I must be completely dressed before my darling Philo comes.

SCAPHA:

> Mirrors are for women who have doubts and need a glass
> to cling to.‡   250
> *You* don't need a glass; why, you're a really first-rate
> glass yourself.

PHILOLACHES:

> *(aside)*

> Lovely words, dear Scapha—and they won't be unrewarded
> either.

---

†*box of jewelry* . . . The meter changes from iambic to trochaic.
‡*a glass to cling to* . . . In Scapha's speech here, and in the conversation that follows, there is a crescendo of sexual puns, with special emphasis on the similarity between *speculum*, "mirror," and *peculium*, which can mean penis. We know that at times the *s* in *speculum* was not strongly pronounced. Surely the bawdy Scapha would be carefree with her *s*'s, accentuating the positive, as it were. Once the low tone of innuendo is established, almost every word can assume sexual overtones. *Speculum* is not unlike the word *specus*, which can refer to a woman's genital area. Thus by the time the conversation reaches line 271 and we encounter a phrase like ". . . *in mentem venit de speculo*," we can no longer naïvely think that Plautus means "it came into her mind about the mirror." No, into our minds come the words *mentula* and *specus*, male and female sex organs. The result is that when Philematium calls for a little table, *mensula* (line 308), the word is denuded of its ordinary innocence. We can be quite sure that the Roman audience felt the courtesan was calling for her boyfriend's *mentula*.

I'll be sure and give a little bonus thing to—Philematium.†

PHILEMATIUM:

Everything in order? How's my hairdo, coiffed with quality?

SCAPHA:

You have quality, my dear, and so how could your coif be
otherwise?   255

PHILOLACHES:

What on earth could be more awful than that wicked woman
there?

Now she's full of compliments, when she was all complaints
before.

PHILEMATIUM:

Powder, please.

SCAPHA:

But why on earth do you need powder?

PHILEMATIUM:

For
my cheeks, of course.

SCAPHA:

That would be like white-on-white; no need to gild the lily,
dear.

PHILOLACHES:

(aside)

Very nicely put, the gilding and the lily, Scapha, good!   260

PHILEMATIUM:

All right, pass the rouge to me.

SCAPHA:

I won't. You know, you're
not too bright.

Do you want to overpaint an absolutely perfect picture?
Blooming girls like you should never ever use false coloring.
Never rouge, or cream from Melos, never any paint at all.

---

†*thing to—Philematium* . . . This kind of joke is called a *para prosdokian* (Greek for
"counter to expectation"), what we would call a "twist." We expected him to be
offering the gift to Scapha, but no—everything for his sweetheart. As for the nature of
his potential gift, see the previous note.

PHILEMATIUM:

> *(pleased, looks at herself, kisses the mirror,*
> *hands it to* SCAPHA*)*

Take the mirror then.

PHILOLACHES:

> She kissed it! Oh, my god, she kissed
> the glass!   265
Oh, I want a rock; I want to knock a piece of glass right off!

SCAPHA:

Here's a towel; better wipe your hands off very well.

PHILEMATIUM:

> But why?

SCAPHA:

> *(ironically)*

You've just held the mirror—and your hands might smell of
silver now.†
Philolaches might suspect you've taken silver from a man.

PHILOLACHES:

I don't think I've ever seen a shrewder bitch than that old
bag!   270
What a neat and clever thing—to prick her mind about the
glass.

PHILEMATIUM:

Do you think perfuming with some perfumes might be—?

SCAPHA:

> Not at all.

PHILEMATIUM:

Why?

SCAPHA:

> The perfect women smell of absolutely nothing, dear.
Only hags try renovation, perfuming themselves with perfume,
Youthless, toothless hags who try to hide their faults with
false aromas.   275

---

†*smell of silver now . . .* We must infer that the mirror is made of silver. Scapha is
being extra-ironic about Philematium's fidelity.

Ah, but when their body sweat at last commingles with the
                                                     perfume—
What a smell, just like those soups in which the cooks put
                                                     everything!
What you're smelling there's no telling, you just know they
                                              smell like hell!

PHILOLACHES:

What a woman, worldly-wise in everything. Who could be
                                                     wiser?
And she speaks the truth, as many people in this theater
                                              know.†   280

(to audience, grinning)

Haven't you got smelly wives whose only perfume is their
                                                     dowry?

PHILEMATIUM:

Scapha, please inspect my dress and jewels. Are they nice
                                              enough?

SCAPHA:

I can't answer that.

PHILEMATIUM:

                  Who can?

SCAPHA:

                        Philolaches, of course.
After all, would he have bought you jewels he didn't like
                                              himself?   285
And besides, he doesn't need displays of what he doesn't
                                                     want.   287
Pretty girls are prettier without their clothes—however lush.   289
Any dress is overdressing for a beauty.

PHILOLACHES:

                              I can't wait!   292

(dancing out to meet his beloved)

---

†*people in this theater know* . . . Plautus frequently has his characters address the
audience directly, although this practice was no innovation even when Aristophanes did
it. Yet the allusion here is especially Roman: then (as now) greed often inspired
marriages of convenience, which ultimately proved inconvenient. Cf. Simo's song, lines
690ff. For similar Plautine jokes on the pains which accompany dowried wives, see
Menaechmi, line 766, *Braggart Soldier*, lines 680–681.

Hi, what are you doing?
PHILEMATIUM:

> Dressing up to please you.

PHILOLACHES:

> > Don't dress
> > more.

(to SCAPHA*)*

You be off and take those trinkets with you. *(to* PHILEMA-
TIUM) You, my joy,
Philematium darling, I would love to booze it up with you.   295
PHILEMATIUM:

I would like to do so with *you*; everything you love, I love.
Darling—
PHILOLACHES:

> Ah, that single word is cheaply bought at twenty
> minae.†

PHILEMATIUM:

Give me ten, my darling. For my love I give a lovely discount.
PHILOLACHES:

Fine. You're holding ten—and yet the price for you was
thirty minae.

(leaning over to kiss her)

Balance my account.
PHILEMATIUM:

> Oh, why assail me with those thirty
> minae?   300

PHILOLACHES:

I assail my very self about those thirty minae, love.
That's the best investment deal I ever made in my whole life.
PHILEMATIUM:

Where could I have found a better place to place my loving
in?

PHILOLACHES:

Look at our accounts: income and outgo balance perfectly.

---

†*twenty minae . . .* How much is a mina worth in dollars? Sixty minae make a talent.
Simo's house is worth more than six talents (see line 913). Ergo, a mina is worth ⅟₃₆₀ of
the price of a house on Main Street.

You love me and I love you. Our two appraisals are the
same. 305

PHILEMATIUM:

Come and lie beside me. *(calls inside)* Water! Put a cock-tail
table here.

Bring the dice! *(to* PHILOLACHES) Sweet perfume, dear?

PHILOLACHES:

(puts his arm around her) No, I've got sweetness right
beside me.

(looks offstage)

Say—isn't that my pal right there—approaching with his
lovely mistress? 310

Yes—Callidamates with his mistress! Goody! *(calling)* Darling
boy!

Soldiers are assembling,† seeking shares in all the beauty
booty.

(Enter young CALLIDAMATES, *incredibly drunk.*
He is leaning heavily on his mistress, DELPHIUM.
A SLAVE *follows behind them.)*

CALLIDAMATES:

(singing)

Philolaches told me to meet him here,
Told me to meet him on time.

(to SLAVE)

Listen, I've given you orders.

(SLAVE goes.)

I'm here, I'm on time.
I fled from the party I was at before.
315
I didn't have fun there,
It was a big bore.

---

†*Soldiers are assembling* . . . The soldiers Tranio refers to are Roman *manuplares*,
companies of 120 men, 30 of which composed a legion. No doubt this pleased the
military men in Plautus' audience. And, since everybody was a soldier, it pleased
everybody. Cf. *Braggart Soldier*, line 815.

With Philolaches, I'll have a great revel,
He'll welcome me then, and we'll both raise the devil
And spirits will soar.   316

(to DELPHIUM*)*

Do I seem to be—*(eyes her bosom)* titititit-tipsy to you?†

DELPHIUM:

(smiling)

Always . . . always . . . always.   320
And always delays. Here's the place we should go.

CALLIDAMATES:

Wanna hug and embrace you all over the place. You wanna
                                        hug too?

DELPHIUM:

If it will make you glad—

CALLIDAMATES:

(drunkenly embracing her)
                It'll make me and make me!
Now take me to them.   *(His knees buckle.)*

DELPHIUM:

(holding him up)

        Oh, don't fall, baby, stand.

CALLIDAMATES:

Dadadadadadada-darling, my honey,   325
I'm yours—to lead by the hand.   325a

DELPHIUM:

Oh, baby, don't fall in the street—
We can lie by and by where the mattress is sweet.

CALLIDAMATES:

Let me fall. I like falling and falling and falling. . . .

DELPHIUM:

If you fall, I fall with you—

CALLIDAMATES:

"It's falling that binds you—till somebody finds you."   330

---

†*titititit-tipsy to you* . . . "Titititit-tipsy" seemed a justifiable rendering of *mamma-madere*. *Madere* means "to be drunk," and *mamma* means "breast."

DELPHIUM:

(to the audience)

He's tipsy.

CALLIDAMATES:

(gazing at her bosom again)

I'm tititit-tipsy, you say?

DELPHIUM:

Do give me your hand, don't get hurt on the way.

CALLIDAMATES:

(operatically)

Take my hand!

DELPHIUM:

Come along.

CALLIDAMATES:

Where we going?

DELPHIUM:

Where do you
think?

CALLIDAMATES:

Oh, now I recall—going home for a drink.

DELPHIUM:

Well, you're on the right track.

CALLIDAMATES:

Yes, it's all coming back!   335

(They stagger along a bit.
PHILOLACHES, *who has been watching all this with amusement,*
now turns to PHILEMATIUM.)

PHILOLACHES:

Shall I meet them and greet them, my darling?
He's my best pal of all, and our friendship is strong.

(stands up to go)

I'll be back in a jiffy.

PHILEMATIUM:

A jiffy's too long.

CALLIDAMATES:
Hey, anyone home?

PHILOLACHES:
                Me.

CALLIDAMATES:
                     Philo! *(to* DELPHIUM*)* It's Philo, it's
                                  Philo!
That marvelest, wonderf'lest, friendliest fellow!   340

PHILOLACHES:
Hello!

CALLIDAMATES:
    Hello!

DELPHIUM:
         Hello!

PHILEMATIUM:
         Hello!
Where do you come from?

CALLIDAMATES:
                    Where roses are red—and the
                          rose wine is mellow.

PHILEMATIUM:
Sit down, dear Delphium, let's all drink deep.

CALLIDAMATES:
         (suddenly collapsing)   I'm going to sleep.

PHILOLACHES:

          (smiling)

It's not something new. . . .   345

DELPHIUM:
But what should we do?

PHILEMATIUM:
              Let him get forty winks,
While meanwhile the rest of the party has—drinks!

       (Music. Laughter.
       They revel for at least a few seconds.
       TRANIO *runs onstage, in a great panic.)*

TRANIO:
Jupiter supreme with his supremest might and mighty main

Surely wants to kill me and my master Philolaches, too.
Hope is absolutely gone—we have no refuge we can trust in.   350
Safety couldn't save us if she wanted—safety's unsafe, too!
Terrors and titanic tides of troubles have just touched the
                                                        harbor—
And I saw them. Master's back from foreign fields—and now
                                        I'm finished!
Anybody in the audience would like to make a little money?
All you have to do today is take my place—for crucifixion.   355
Come, speak up, you whip-resisters, iron glad-men, raise your
                                                        hands.
Where are you—you men who'd storm a city wall for next to
                                                        nothing?†
And get paid with ten or twenty . . . javelins, right in the gut.
You can have a talent if you win the race to bear my cross.
Nailing down your fee as soon as arms and legs are nailed
                                        down twice.   360

                    (smiles)

After crucifixion, then present yourself—and I'll pay up.

                    (then reflects)

Am I not a tragic fool? I should be sprinting home with speed!

            (At this moment, PHILOLACHES *notices that*
                    TRANIO *has appeared.)*

PHILOLACHES:
    Ah, he's back from shopping. Look—there's Tranio, back
                                        from the harbor.

            (TRANIO *now runs up to his master.)*

TRANIO:
    Philolaches—!
PHILOLACHES:
                Hi!

_____

†*next to nothing* . . . This is probably a reference from the Greek original, composed at
a time (late 4th–early 3rd century) when mercenaries were replacing Greek citizen
armies.

TRANIO:

          Both you and me—

PHILOLACHES:

                    Both you and me?

TRANIO:

                            We're
                            finished!

PHILOLACHES:
  What?
TRANIO:

      Your father's here!
PHILOLACHES:

                 What's that you say?

TRANIO:

                       I say we're
                    both destroyed!   365

  Father's here, your father's here!
PHILOLACHES:

                    He's where?

TRANIO:

                    He's here, ar-
                        rived!

PHILOLACHES:
  What? Who says so? Who has seen him?
TRANIO:

                    I myself.

PHILOLACHES:

                    Oh, woe is
                      me!

  Gad—I'm lost—where am I now?
TRANIO:

                You're lying down, that's
                    where you are.

PHILOLACHES:
  Did you really see him?
TRANIO:

             Yes.

PHILOLACHES:

             For sure?

TRANIO:

For sure.

PHILOLACHES:

For sure—I'm
dead!

Dead—if what you say is true.

TRANIO:

But why on earth would I tell
lies?   370

PHILOLACHES:

Tell me what to do—what should I do?

TRANIO:

(pointing to the party stuff)   Have this mess
cleaned up.

Who's the guy asleep?

PHILOLACHES:

Callidamates. *(to DELPHIUM)* Delphie,
wake him up.

DELPHIUM:

(shaking CALLIDAMATES)

Dear Callidamates, do wake up.

CALLIDAMATES:

(drunkenly)   I am awake. *(quickly)* I want
a drink.

DELPHIUM:

Do wake up now—Philolaches' father's back!

CALLIDAMATES:

(toasting drunkenly)   Welcome, Father!

PHILOLACHES:

Welcome Father, goodbye me!

CALLIDAMATES:

(drunkenly, half hearing)   Who'd buy me? Buy me? What
for?   375

PHILOLACHES:

Please, by Pollux, do stand up—my father's here!

CALLIDAMATES:

(drunkenly)   Your father's
here?

Tell him to go off again. Why did he have to come back here?

PHILOLACHES:

(terribly upset)

What can I do now, when Father comes and finds me drunk
like this,
Finds his house is overflowing full of girls and party guests?
What a thing—to start to dig a well when you're already
thirsty.   380
That's my problem—what to do. My father's here and I'm
in trouble.

TRANIO:

(indicating CALLIDAMATES*)*

Look, your friend has fallen off asleep again. Do shake him
up.

PHILOLACHES:
Hey—wake up, my father's come back home.

CALLIDAMATES:

What's that?
Your father?
Get my sandals and my weapons, then I'll go and kill your
father!†

PHILOLACHES:
You'll destroy us!

DELPHIUM:

Do be quiet.

PHILOLACHES:

(to slaves)   Carry this guy in at once.   385

CALLIDAMATES:

(drunkenly, to one of the slaves carrying him inside)

Hey—are you a chamber pot? You will be in another second.

(They carry CALLIDAMATES *inside.)*

---

†*kill your father . . .* Another parricidal utterance, no less shocking to the Romans than
Philolaches' unspeakable thoughts spoken in lines 229 and 233. See note on *Brothers
Menaechmus,* line 870, p. 177.

PHILOLACHES:

Oh, we're dead!

TRANIO:

Be brave. I'll medicate your misery . . . with
                                                    wit.

PHILOLACHES:

Oh, I'm finished.

TRANIO:

Quiet, will you? I'll dream up some remedy.
Look—will it suffice you if I see your now-arriving father
Doesn't set foot in this house and even rushes far from it?   390
For the moment, go inside and clear the party stuff away.

PHILOLACHES:

Where will I be?

TRANIO:

Where you like it best: with her. And Cal
                                                    with Del

DELPHIUM:

Wouldn't it be better if we left?

TRANIO:

Don't even budge, my dear.
If you stay inside, you can drink up no less than right out
                                                    here.

PHILOLACHES:

Oh, ye gods, what will your sweet words bring? *I'm* drunk
                                            with fear!   395

TRANIO:

Look—can you keep calm and follow all my orders?

PHILOLACHES:

Yes, I
                                                    think.

TRANIO:

First and foremost, girls, I want the two of you to go inside.

DELPHIUM:

Both of us will be most dutiful to you.†

        (*The girls slink off into the house.*)

_____

†*dutiful to you* . . . The girls offer to be *morigerae*, i.e., loyal as wives. Cf. line 189.

TRANIO:

Jove make it so.

(playing commander in chief, to PHILOLACHES*)*

All right, pay attention now; I'll tell you what I want from
you:
First and foremost, have the house completely closed and
locked up tight.†   400
Be on guard inside; don't let a single person mumble—

PHILOLACHES:

(nods) Yes.

TRANIO:

Make it look like no one really lives here.

PHILOLACHES:

(repeating) "No one lives here."

TRANIO:

Right.
When the old man knocks, nobody answers. Not a living soul.

PHILOLACHES:

Yes, what else?

TRANIO:

The front door key, that locks you in from
here outside,
Get it to me, then I'll lock the house and close it up completely.   405

PHILOLACHES:

(getting emotional)

Tranio, it's in your hands—my welfare and my wealth as
well.

(He goes into the house.)

TRANIO:

(much bravado)

If a man has talent, it's no different if he's a slave or master.   407–
408

---

†*locked up tight* . . . In all that follows, the verb *occludere,* "to lock up tight," is used
over and over, almost giving a characterization to the house itself.

*(TRANIO goes to the front of the stage
to address the audience.)*

The man who has no bit of boldness in his breast,
It doesn't matter if he's high or low in life,   410
He fails as fast as anyone—if he's a failure.
And yet you have to seek out someone super-smart
To take a bungled business that is in hot water
And see that everything calms down, no damage done,
While he himself is not ashamed of anything.   415
Now *that's* what *I* intend! I'll take our sea of troubles
And soothe them down to absolute tranquillity,
No single bit of pain produced for anyone.

(At this moment, a BOY SLAVE *steps out of the house,
carrying a huge key.)*

TRANIO:

But why have you come out here, Sphaerio? *(sees key)* Ah,
                                                        good!
You fully followed my instructions.

BOY:

(carefully repeating a message)

                              Master orders—   420
And begs you please—to chase his father off somehow.
Don't let him come inside.

TRANIO:

                        You tell our master this:
His dad will feel such terror just to *see* the house
He'll flee completely panicked, with a shrouded head.
I'll take the key. Go in and lock the doors up tight.   425
I'll also lock them up out here. *(Boy exits.)* We're ready for
                                                        him.
The games we hold today, while this old man's alive,
Will far outmatch whatever games he'll get when dead.†

---

†*games he'll get when dead* . . . The Latin word *ludus* means not only a "game" or
"show" but a "deception" as well. What will be a deception for Theopropides will be
a show for everyone else. Tranio also alludes to the practice of holding funeral games
for distinguished persons (Terence's *Adelphoe* was presented on one such occasion).
But in so doing he is wishing his master dead. Still another parricidal utterance!

I'll leave the door and set a lookout post up here.

(He skips to a corner of the stage, peers off.)

And when the old man comes, I'll fill him full of it.†   430

(A pause [musical interlude?].
Finally, enter old THEOPROPIDES,
dressed in his traveling clothes.)

THEOPROPIDES:

O Neptune, what a debt of gratitude I owe thee!
For thou allowed me, half alive, to reach my home.
Indeed, if after this you learn I've gone to sea,
Or set a single foot upon a wave, proceed
To do me in the way you almost did me now.   435
Away with you, away, away forevermore!
I've trusted you with everything I'll ever trust.

TRANIO:

(aside)

By Pollux, Neptune, thou hast really blundered badly:
For thou allowed the perfect chance to slip right by.

THEOPROPIDES:

I'm coming home from Egypt after three long years.   440
My people surely are most anxious to receive me.

TRANIO:

(aside)

The man your people are most anxious to receive
Is someone who would bring them news that you were dead!

*(*THEOPROPIDES *has gone up to his house.)*

THEOPROPIDES:

I say, what's this? The doors are all locked up in daytime?
I'll knock. *(He knocks.)* Hello—is someone home? Hey—open
                                                                  up!   445

TRANIO:

(revealing himself to THEOPROPIDES, *melodramatically)*

What man is this who now approaches our front door?

---

†*fill him full of it . . .* This may sound anachronistic, but the Latin is *sarcinam
imponere*, "to load him up." See note on *Braggart Soldier*, line 768 (p. 59).

THEOPROPIDES:

It's Tranio, my slave!

TRANIO:

O Theopropides!

Dear master, greetings! Great to see you safe and sound.
Have you been well?

THEOPROPIDES:

As well as now.

TRANIO:

(a bit uneasy)   That's nice to hear.

THEOPROPIDES:

And you—are you unwell?

TRANIO:

Unwell?

THEOPROPIDES:

Well, look at you—   450

You stroll while not a living soul stays in the house.
No guard, no janitor, no one to open up.
I nearly broke both doors from knocking on and on.

TRANIO:

(in mock shock)

What's that—you touched the house???

THEOPROPIDES:

You have to touch to 454–
knock.   455

TRANIO:

You touched it?

THEOPROPIDES:

Yes, I knocked it too.

TRANIO:

Oh, god!

THEOPROPIDES:

What's wrong?

TRANIO:

A dirty deed.

THEOPROPIDES:

What's going on?

TRANIO:

                                Impossible
To say how horrible, horrendous—also bad.

THEOPROPIDES:

But what?

TRANIO:

                Just flee! Flee far from this most foul front door!   460
Flee hither, flee to me. *(THEOPROPIDES approaches
                        TRANIO.)* Sir, did you really touch?

THEOPROPIDES:

You tell me how to knock and still not touch a door.

TRANIO:

By Hercules, you killed—

THEOPROPIDES:

                (quivering)   I killed?

TRANIO:

                                        Your near and dear ones.

THEOPROPIDES:

Oh, what an omen—gods and goddesses forbid!

TRANIO:

I tremble . . . Can you purify yourself and kin?   465

THEOPROPIDES:

But why? What is this unexpected shock you bring?

        (Two of THEOPROPIDES' PORTERS *now come onstage,
        to deliver the old man's baggage to his house.*
        TRANIO *watches them approach with trepidation.)*

TRANIO:

Oh no, hey, hey! *(to* THEOPROPIDES*)* Please tell those two
                                        to both retreat.

THEOPROPIDES:

You two—retreat!

TRANIO:

                                (to PORTERS*)*

        Don't touch the house—oh no!
Go quickly—touch the ground!

THEOPROPIDES:

                        But tell me what's so wrong
                                with touching?

(TRANIO *sighs a deep sigh, as if to say, "This is it."*)

TRANIO:

It's seven months now since we haven't gone in there.   470
It's seven months since we have all moved out.

THEOPROPIDES:

But why? Speak up!

TRANIO:

First look around for other people.
Does someone try to catch our conversation?

THEOPROPIDES:

(*Looks high and low. Sees nothing.*)   All clear.

TRANIO:

(*stalling for time—to dream up a story*)

Uh—look around again.

THEOPROPIDES:

(*looks high and low*)

There's no one. Speak up, will you?

TRANIO:

The sin . . . was murder.

THEOPROPIDES:

Huh? I don't quite understand.   475

TRANIO:

A sin committed long ago in ancient times.

THEOPROPIDES:

In ancient times?

TRANIO:

We just found out in modern times.

THEOPROPIDES:

What sort of sin? And who committed it? Tell, tell!

TRANIO:

A guest was taken unawares by a host—and slaughtered.
I think it was the man who sold the house to you.   480

THEOPROPIDES:

S-slaughtered?

TRANIO:

Yes. And robbed his own guest's gold, and
then—

He buried his own guest right in this house of yours.

THEOPROPIDES:

(trembling)

But how—how did you know of it—did you suspect?

TRANIO:

I'll tell you. Listen carefully: he had dined out—
Your son, that is—and after dinner he came home.   485
We went to bed. We all of us were sleeping tight.
By chance, I had forgotten to put the lantern out.
And suddenly he screamed. An awful scream he screamed!

THEOPROPIDES:

Who screamed? My son?

TRANIO:

Be quiet, will you? Listen closely.
He told me that the corpse came to him in a dream.   490

THEOPROPIDES:

So it was in a dream?

TRANIO:

It was, but listen closely.
He told me that the corpse addressed him in this manner—

THEOPROPIDES:

Within a dream?

TRANIO:

How could he talk to him awake?
The man was murdered over sixty years ago!
At times you can be rather silly, sir. . . .   495

THEOPROPIDES:

(chastened)

I'll shut my mouth.

TRANIO:

And then within the dream, he spake:
"My name's Transoceanus from . . . across the sea.†
I'm housèd in this house where I must house myself—

---

†*across the sea* . . . The name Tranio has invented is Diapontius, which is straightfor-
ward Greek, meaning "from across the sea." The actor's hesitation before coming out
with place of birth as "across the sea" would show the audience that Tranio was
improvising on the spot—and stalling for time.

The King of Hades has refused to let me in
Because I died . . . too early. And I was deceived   500
By someone's word of honor: my host slaughtered me,
And buried me in secret—here—unfuneraled.
A sin. A sin for gold. Now, boy, move out of here!
The house is full of sin, the habitation cursed.''

(to THEOPROPIDES*)*

I'd need at least a year to tell you all the horrors, sir.   505

(Suddenly, noise filters out from the closed house.)

TRANIO:

            (whispering loudly to those within)   Sh, sh!

THEOPROPIDES:

By Hercules, what's happened now?

TRANIO:

                                    The door has creaked.
It's *he* who tapped.

THEOPROPIDES:

    (in terror)   I haven't got a drop of blood left!
The dead can carry me alive right down to Hades!

TRANIO:

                    (to himself)

I'm lost! Those guys inside perturb my perfect story!   510
I greatly fear he'll catch me in the act of lying!

THEOPROPIDES:

What are you saying to yourself?

TRANIO:

    (stirring up panic again)   Retreat, retreat!
And flee, by Hercules!

THEOPROPIDES:

                    Flee where? Why don't *you* flee?

TRANIO:

I have no fear. I've made my peace with all the dead.

(From inside the house, young PHILOLACHES' *voice)*

PHILOLACHES:

Hey, Tranio!

TRANIO:

> *(whispering through the door)*
>
> > Wise up—don't call me by my name!   515
>
> *(now aloud, a statement to ''the ghost'')*

I'm wholly blameless. *I've* not tapped these sinful walls.   516

THEOPROPIDES:

Who *are* you talking to?

TRANIO:

> *(to* THEOPROPIDES, *pretending surprise)*
>
> > Oh, was that you who called?   519

Dear gods above, I thought it was the dead man speaking,
Perhaps to ask me why you dared to touch the door.
But why do you still stand there? What of my advice?

THEOPROPIDES:

What should I do?

TRANIO:

> > Flee! Don't look back—and shroud your
> > > head!

THEOPROPIDES:

And you don't flee?

TRANIO:

> > I told you, I'm at peace with them.

THEOPROPIDES:

But just a while ago you were in fear and trembling.   525

TRANIO:

Don't worry, please, I'll look out for myself.
But you go on—go flee and fly with utmost speed.
And call ''Sweet Hercules!''

THEOPROPIDES:

> *(obeys completely, starts running)*
>
> > I call ''Sweet Hercules!''
>
> *(He scurries offstage.)*

TRANIO:

I'll call on him as well—to give you awful trouble.

Immortal gods above, I bid you all draw near 530
To see the splendid trouble I've created here!

> (TRANIO *ecstatically skips off—to the back of*
> *the "haunted" house.*†

> *From the exit nearer the forum,*
> *enter* MISARGYRIDES, *the moneylender, a miser-of-misers.*
> *As he begins to address the audience,*
> TRANIO *re-enters from inside the house.)*

MISARGYRIDES:

It's been a cursed year for lending cash at interest.
I've never seen a season worse than this has been.
I'm in the forum all day long from dawn till dusk
Unable to find customers to lend a bit. 535

TRANIO:

> (*noticing* MISARGYRIDES, *aside*)

Oh, now we're fully finished off forevermore!
The broker's here, who lent us cash on interest
To buy the girl and pay for our expensive parties.
We're caught red-handed if I don't do something fast
To keep this from our senior master. I'll go meet him.

> (*And now enter* THEOPROPIDES *as well!*
> TRANIO *sees the old man and is struck by yet another blow.)*

What's this? What brings *that* fellow back so soon?
I tremble—has he got a hint of what we've done?
I'd better greet him too! Am I in awful shape!·
There's nothing worse than *knowing* that you've done a
                                                      wrong.
And do I know! But since I've stirred things up already, 545
I'll go on stirring. That's the order of the day.

> (*He goes to* THEOPROPIDES.)

What a surprise!

---

†*the "haunted" house* . . . When this play is being acted, this would seem the ideal
spot for an intermission. There were, it seems, no breaks in Plautus' day.

THEOPROPIDES:

I met the chap I bought the house from.

TRANIO:

(taken aback)

Uh—did you mention anything—of what I told you?

THEOPROPIDES:

By Hercules, I told him everything!

TRANIO:

(aside)   Oh no!

I tremble—all my tricks have permanently perished!   550

THEOPROPIDES:

(to TRANIO*)*

What are you mumbling?

TRANIO:

Nothing, nothing. Tell me this:

What did you say?

THEOPROPIDES:

Why, everything from start to finish.

TRANIO:

Did he confess about his guest?

THEOPROPIDES:

No, he denied it.   554

(a new topic)

What's your advice for now?

TRANIO:

You're asking my advice?   556

By Hercules, I'd take the thing to arbitration.

(aside)   But get a judge who'd swallow anything I say.

You'd win as easily as foxes eat a pear.†

MISARGYRIDES:

But look—there's Philolaches' slave man Tranini.‡

Those fellows never pay me principal or interest.

---

†*as foxes eat a pear* . . . Perhaps an allusion to a then-current proverb, now lost to us.
‡*Tranini* . . . The moneylender calls Tranio *Tranius,* which may be a diminutive, or pet name of some sort.

*(TRANIO starts toward MISARGYRIDES,
who is on one side of the stage,
while THEOPROPIDES stands at the opposite end.)*

THEOPROPIDES:

(to TRANIO)

But where're you going?

TRANIO:

(to himself)   Nowhere. I'm in no condition.
Oh, am I cursed, born under inauspicious stars.
The man will dun me while my master's here. It's tragic.
On either side of me an awful time awaits.   565
I'll seize the situation.

MISARGYRIDES:

He approaches. All is saved.
There's hope for money yet.

TRANIO:

(aside)   He's happy—but he's wrong.

(calling)

Hello, Misargyrides, hope you're feeling well.

MISARGYRIDES:

Well, what about my money?

TRANIO:

Do behave yourself.
The minute I arrive, you throw your javelins.   570

MISARGYRIDES:

A worthless man!

TRANIO:

(ironically)   Now there's a truthful prophecy.

MISARGYRIDES:

Don't start some dodge with me.

TRANIO:

Then speak—what's on your
mind?

MISARGYRIDES:

Where's Philolaches?

TRANIO:

> *(too, too friendly)*

>> Ah, dear friend, you couldn't have
Arrived more opportunely than you've just arrived.

MISARGYRIDES:

How come?

TRANIO:

> Come over here . . .

> *(beckons* MISARGYRIDES *to a quiet corner)*

MISARGYRIDES:

> *(loudly)*   When do I get my interest?   575

TRANIO:

I know you've got a healthy voice; please don't shout.

MISARGYRIDES:

By Hercules, why not?

TRANIO:

> Do me a little favor.

MISARGYRIDES:

What sort of little favor?

TRANIO:

> Won't you please . . . go home?

MISARGYRIDES:

Go home?

TRANIO:

> Come back here sometime after midday, please.

MISARGYRIDES:

But will I get my interest then?

TRANIO:

> You will. Now go.   580

MISARGYRIDES:

> *("adding" things up in his miserly mind)*

But why expend the effort and exhaust myself?
I think I'll wait around right here till midday.

TRANIO:

Oh no, go home. By Hercules, it's better home.   583

MISARGYRIDES:

Why don't I get my interest? Why these jokes with me?   585

TRANIO:

By Hercules, I wish you would . . . go home for now.

MISARGYRIDES:

By Hercules, I'll call my client—

TRANIO:

(ironically)   Loud, I'm sure!
Your greatest joy is loudness.

MISARGYRIDES:

I just want what's mine.
For days and days you've held me off with tricks like this.
If I annoy you, pay me, then I'll go away.   590
The single phrase "I'll pay" will end all complications.

TRANIO:

(a sudden thought—to faze MISARGYRIDES*)*

Well—take your principal.

MISARGYRIDES:

I want my interest first!

TRANIO:

What's that? You lowest, basest, vilest man on earth!
You're practicing extortion? No, go do your worst.
He owes you zero.

MISARGYRIDES:

(flabbergasted)

Owes me zero?

TRANIO:

Now you won't get   595
A single spot of dust from us. Are you afraid
He'll leave the city, just to dodge your interest?
He's offering the principal.

MISARGYRIDES:

But I don't want it!
I first and foremost want to get some interest paid me.   599–600

TRANIO:

Look, don't annoy us. Nothing you can do will help.
You think that you're the only moneylender here?

MISARGYRIDES:

(starting to foam at the mouth)

My interest now, my interest, interest; pay me interest!
Will you please pay my interest to me right away?

I want my interest!

TRANIO:

          "Interest" here and "interest" there,   605
The only interest this man has in life is "interest."
Do go away. I think in all my years on earth
I've never seen a fouler, viler beast than you.

MISARGYRIDES:

By Pollux, you don't scare me with those words of yours!

(Across the stage,
old THEOPROPIDES *has been waiting quasi-patiently.)*

THEOPROPIDES:

Hot talk! Why, even over here I feel the heat.   609a

(a bit louder)

I wonder what that interest is the man is after.   610

TRANIO:

(to MISARGYRIDES, *indicating* THEOPROPIDES*)*

Look, there's his father, just returned from overseas.
He'll give you back your principal and interest too,
So stop your bearing down and shady practices.
That man won't make you wait.

MISARGYRIDES:

                 I'll take what I can get.

THEOPROPIDES:

(to TRANIO*)*

Hey, Tranio!

TRANIO:

      Yes, sir?

(dashes over to THEOPROPIDES*)*

THEOPROPIDES:

           Who's that? What is he claiming?   615
Why does he seem to mention my son Philolaches?
Why does he make this sort of hue and cry to you?
What's owed the man?

TRANIO:

By Hercules, give orders, sir,
To smash this rotten fellow's face with all his cash.

THEOPROPIDES:
Give orders?

TRANIO:

Yes—to knock his block off with hard currency. 620

MISARGYRIDES:
I'd gladly suffer any knocks for blocks of cash. 621

TRANIO:
Did you hear that? The perfect moneylender speaks. 625
A moneylender—vilest, foulest breed there is.

THEOPROPIDES:
Don't tell me what he is; I don't care where he's from.
I really want to know and long to be informed. 628
What is this sum that Philolaches owes this man? 622

TRANIO:
A teeny bit.

THEOPROPIDES:
How teeny?

TRANIO:

Forty thousand drachmae.
That isn't very much.

THEOPROPIDES:
(ironically)   Oh no, it's tiny. 624
I hear there's interest due as well. So what's the total? 629

TRANIO:
Our total debt to him is—*(quickly)* forty-four thousand
drachmae. 630
Just say you'll pay—and send him off.

THEOPROPIDES:

Just say I'll pay??? 633

TRANIO:
Just say you'll pay.

THEOPROPIDES:
Myself?

TRANIO:

In person. Listen, sir,

Go on and say it, I command you.
TRANIO:

THEOPROPIDES:

                                   Tell me this: 635
That money—what'd you do with it?
TRANIO:

                                   It's solid.

THEOPROPIDES:

                                   Solid?
Then pay him back yourself, if that's the case.
TRANIO:

(comes up with a big idea, makes a big announcement)

                                   Your son—
Has bought a house.
THEOPROPIDES:

                    A house?

TRANIO:

                    A house.

THEOPROPIDES:

                    (ecstatic)   Oh, goody, goody!
His father's son he is,† he is, he's going into business!
A house, you say?
TRANIO:

          (nods)   A house. And do you know what kind?   640
THEOPROPIDES:

How could I know?
TRANIO:

                    Oh, boy!

THEOPROPIDES:

                              What kind?

TRANIO:

                                   Don't even ask!

THEOPROPIDES:

Oh, tell!
TRANIO:

          A splendiddifferiffic, brilliant building!

---

†*His father's son he is* . . . The Latin verb is *patrissare*, from a similar Greek coinage,
meaning ''fatherizing.''

THEOPROPIDES:

    By Hercules, well done! What did he pay for it?

TRANIO:

    Two silver talents. One plus one—like you and me.

    He gave as cash deposit forty thousand drachmae.   645

THEOPROPIDES:

    By Hercules, well done!

MISARGYRIDES:

          (to himself)   The day is fast collecting noon.

TRANIO:

                (to THEOPROPIDES*)*

    Let's rid ourselves of him—before he pukes on us.

THEOPROPIDES:

                (to MISARGYRIDES*)*

    Young man, you'll deal with me.

MISARGYRIDES:

        (to THEOPROPIDES)   So I collect from you?

THEOPROPIDES:

    Collect tomorrow.

MISARGYRIDES:

             Good. Tomorrow. Good, good, good.

    (Rubbing his greedy hands in anticipation,

        MISARGYRIDES *shuffles off.)*

TRANIO:

        (at MISARGYRIDES. *as he goes)*

    May all the gods and goddesses give trouble to you!   655

    You missed destroying all my plans by half-a-hair's breadth.

             (to audience)

    By Pollux, you won't find a fouler class of men

    Or men less lawful than the moneylending breed!

THEOPROPIDES:

    What sort of neighborhood did my boy buy this house in?

TRANIO:

             (aside)

    I'm lost again!

THEOPROPIDES:

          Speak up, I asked you something.   660

TRANIO:

I can't—I just forgot the former owner's name.

THEOPROPIDES:

Come on, just use your wits, my lad.

TRANIO:

        (aside) What can I do?
Unless I choose our neighbor's house . . .
And claim this is the house his son just bought. I've heard
That lies taste best when served up piping hot. All right,   665
Whatever hodgepodge heaven hints, I'll hand to him.   667

THEOPROPIDES:

Well, have you thought it out?

TRANIO:

     (to THEOPROPIDES*)*   That goddamned owner, sir—

     (aside)

My goddamned master! *(aloud)* Sir . . . it is your neighbor's
                         house.

     (indicating SIMO*'s home)*

Your son just bought this house.

THEOPROPIDES:

     (wide-eyed with joy)   I can't believe it's true!   670

TRANIO:

Well, if you pay whatever cash is due, it's true.
If you don't pay the cash, then what I'm saying isn't true.

THEOPROPIDES:

And not just in a goodly part of town—

TRANIO:

     (feeding his enthusiasm)   The very best!

THEOPROPIDES:

By Hercules, I'd love to look inside. Please knock.
Yes, Tranio. Go summon someone from inside.   675

TRANIO:

     (aside)

I'm lost again—I really don't know what to say!
Another time the tide has turned me on the rocks!

THEOPROPIDES:
    What now?
TRANIO:

                        (aside)

    By Hercules, I don't know what to do.
    I'm caught red-handed.
THEOPROPIDES:
                            Call somebody out at once.
    I want a tour.
TRANIO:
    (nervously)   But, sir . . . there are the women, sir.   680
    We ought to ask permission—if they are presentable.
THEOPROPIDES:
    The proper thing to do. You go ahead and ask.
    And while you do, I'll wait outside right here.
TRANIO:

                (aside to the audience)

    May all the gods and goddesses destroy this oldster—
    For giving all my plans attacks from every side!   685

*(At this very moment, the door of the "new" house opens,
        and out comes* SIMO, *a chubby old man,
        who is slightly wined-up from dinner.)*

TRANIO:
    What luck! The owner of the house is stepping out.
    Old Simo in the flesh. I'll step aside to watch,
    And call a senate assembly inside my interior soul.
    I'll broach the man as soon as I think up a plan.
            (As TRANIO *slinks into the alley to eavesdrop,*
            SIMO *steps downstage to sing a solo.)*
SIMO:

                (singing)

    That was the best meal of the year.   690
    Never have I eaten better.
    What a fine dinner prepared by my wife.
    But after she wanted to "sleep" and I wouldn't let
                                            her.

That old hag made a dinner better than usual,   695
Simply a plot to get me to bed.
"Sleep isn't good after dinner," I said.
Secretly, quietly, I have slipped out.
Wife will be wild at me, I have no doubt.

TRANIO:

(aside)

What a bad evening's preparing for that old duffer.   700
In sleep and at supper he'll suffer.

SIMO:

The more I reflect, as I think very deep,
I see wedding a hag for some gold in a bag
Means you won't oversleep.
The bedroom is torture, so I'd rather roam.   705
Better work in the forum than bed her at home.   706–707

(winks at the audience)

By Pollux, I don't know of your wives—are their
                                                ways diverse?
I know my case is bad and it's bound to get worse.   709–710

TRANIO:

(aside)

It's your own ways, old man, that have made your
                                                life worsen.
Blame no god in the sky, blame your own very   712–
                                                person.   713
But it's time now for me to deceive that old man.
For I've just had a thought and I've just found a
                                                plan,   715
A ruse that will fend off a bruise just as far as I
                                                can.
I'll approach him and broach him. Hi, Simo—the gods
                                                make you glad.

SIMO:

Ah, Tranio!

TRANIO:

How have you been?

SIMO:

Not too bad.

(They shake hands warmly.)

Doing what?

TRANIO:

Shaking hands with a wonderful guy.

SIMO:

(smiles)   Thank
you, lad.

I would like to requite those nice words you just gave:

(with a smile)

I am now shaking hands with a wonderful . . . rogue of a
slave.   720

THEOPROPIDES:

(calling from across the stage)

Hey, you whipping post, come over here.

TRANIO:

(calling over, nervously)   One minute, one
minute!   721a

SIMO:

(to TRANIO, *confidentially)*

How's the house?

TRANIO:

Sir?

SIMO:

The house. What is now going on in it?

I approve! Life is short.   725

We must live every minute!

TRANIO:

Uh, sir? Beg your pardon?

I scarcely can grasp what you're saying.

SIMO:

I'm saying—keep playing. Live life as a song—

Keep wining and dining, keep rolling in clover—

TRANIO:

>> (*confidentially, to* SIMO) That 729–
>> life is . . . all over.   730

SIMO:

What?

TRANIO:

> All of us, one great big fall of us, Simo.

SIMO:

It was all going well for you.

TRANIO:

>> I can't deny that's a fact.   735
> We lived it, we loved it, there's nothing we lacked.
> But, Simo, a storm came, our good ship is racked.

SIMO:

But your ship was so sound, pulled right up on dry
>> ground.

TRANIO:

But another ship rammed. Now we're damned—and we're
>> drowned!   740

SIMO:

I'm on your side, but what's the problem? Tell me, please.

TRANIO:

Master—back from overseas.

> (*End of musical moment. A pause.*
>   SIMO *gets the picture.*)

SIMO:

> (*to* TRANIO, *with a wry smile*)

For you a slight *ironic* twist. You're in a kind of cruci—fix?

TRANIO:

I beg you, please don't tell my master.

SIMO:

>> He won't get a thing 744–
>> from me.   745

TRANIO:

Thank you, you're my patron.

SIMO:

>> I don't need your kind of client,
>> thank you.

TRANIO:

But now the reason Master sent me here to you—

SIMO:

No, first you answer something I would like to ask:
How much of your affairs does he already know?

TRANIO:

Why—not a thing.

SIMO:

He hasn't shouted at his son?   750

TRANIO:

His sky is blue and calm and balmy. All is clear.
But now he's asked me to convey a strong request.
He'd like to take a look around inside your house.

SIMO:

It's not for sale.

TRANIO:

I know, of course. But the old man
Is anxious to build women's quarters in his own house,   755
And baths and paths and porticoes, a big construction.

SIMO:

Whatever made him dream of doing this?

TRANIO:

I'll tell you, sir.

He's very anxious that his son now take a wife
As soon as possible. And so—the women's quarters.
He said he heard some architect, I don't know who,   760
Discuss your house design. The man was mad with praise.
And so he'd like to copy from it, do you mind?
The special thing he wants to copy from your house is this:
He's heard you have terrific shade, all summer through,
And all day long, and even if it's awfully bright.   765

SIMO:

(surprised)

But listen here—when shadows fall all over town
There's *never* shade in here. It's sunny all day long.
The sun just stays—as if it were a bill collector.
The only shade I have at all is down my well.

TRANIO:

(with a weak laugh)

Well . . . shady things are shady,† sun is . . . nice and bright.   770

SIMO:

Look, don't annoy me. Things are as I've just explained.

TRANIO:

But still, he'd like to look around.

SIMO:

Well, let him look!
If he sees anything he likes and wants to copy,
Why, let him build it.

TRANIO:

Can I call him?

SIMO:

Go and call him.

(TRANIO *struts across the stage
and shares his satisfaction with the audience.*)

TRANIO:

They say Kings Alexander and Agathocles‡   775
Were two who did big things. Now would you say *I'm* third—
Who solo does so many memorable things?
I've saddled up both oldsters like a pair of mules.
This latest ploy I've started isn't bad at all!
For just as muleteers have saddled mules to ride,   780
I've got two saddled men to act as mules for me.
They're loaded up—and what a load they're carrying!

(Music begins.)
(singing)

---

†*shady things are shady* . . . Plautus is playing on the word *umbra*, "shadow," and the town of Sarsina in Umbria. Most scholars believe Sarsina was the birthplace of Plautus. This translator believes that Plautus never could resist a pun, so why not *umbra* and *Umbria*? Cf. his pun on Animula, a town in Apulia, in *Braggart Soldier*, line 648.

‡*Alexander and Agathocles* . . . Alexander is, of course, the Great, a conqueror whose exploits were much admired by the Romans. Agathocles of Syracuse (361–289 B.C.) fought some brilliant campaigns against the Carthaginians. In 304 B.C., he crowned himself *King* of Syracuse, and was at this time the only ruler among the Western Greeks to own this title. It was most likely Plautus who linked Alexander and Agathocles. The soldierly Romans would know both these names well. The clever slave comparing himself to a heroic general is a distinctive feature of Plautine comedy.

Now I must talk to him, walk up and talk to him.
Hey, Theo, hey!

THEOPROPIDES:

              Who's calling, I say?

TRANIO:

Your multi-faithful servant.

THEOPROPIDES:

                      Say, where have you been?   785

TRANIO:

Your mission, sir, is, sir, accomplished. You now can begin.

THEOPROPIDES:

But what on earth caused such a delay?

TRANIO:

The man was engaged in some business, so I had to wait.

THEOPROPIDES:

I know you—the slow you—you've always been late.

TRANIO:

The ancient proverb, sir, still bears repeating: 790
"No one can whistle the same time he's eating."
I couldn't be with you right here—and also be there too.

THEOPROPIDES:

What now?

TRANIO:

           You can visit his house just as long as you care to.

THEOPROPIDES:

Go on, lead the way.

TRANIO:

                Am I causing delay?

THEOPROPIDES:

                          Lead the way.

TRANIO:

(confidentially to THEOPROPIDES)

Look at the old boy just standing there—sad to behold it,   795
He's very unhappy—regrets having sold it.

THEOPROPIDES:

Why so?

TRANIO:

      He's been constantly begging, pursuing

And pleading to cancel the sale.

THEOPROPIDES:

(the tough businessman)   Nothing doing!

"A man sows his crop, and the man must then reap it."   800

If *we* were complaining, he'd force us to keep it.

No, "All sales are final," "What's been done, don't undo,"

"Pity's a luxury," "Eat what you chew."

TRANIO:

Your words of wisdom slow me down. Please follow me.

THEOPROPIDES:

That's what I'll do.

Faithfully I'll follow you.

(They cross the stage to SIMO.*)*

TRANIO:

(to THEOPROPIDES*)*   Look—there's the oldster. *(to* SIMO*)*

Here's your man . . .

SIMO:

Greetings, Theopropides, I'm glad you're back both safe and

sound.   805

THEOPROPIDES:

Greetings.

SIMO:

Your man told me that you'd like to look around.

THEOPROPIDES:

If you wouldn't mind.

SIMO:

I wouldn't mind. Go in and look around.

THEOPROPIDES:

But of course, the women—

SIMO:

Women? Don't you care a hoot

for them!

Stroll around in any room you'd like; pretend the house is

yours.

THEOPROPIDES:

(whispers to TRANIO*)*

What—"pretend"?

TRANIO:

(whispers back) Oh, let's not put the gentleman through
                                    further pain,   810
Throwing up the fact you've bought his place. You see how
                                    sad he looks.

THEOPROPIDES:

Yes, I see.

TRANIO:

Well, let's not make it worse by making fun of him.
Let's not mention that you've bought it any more.

THEOPROPIDES:

I see your
point.
Well advised. I think that's very sensitive of you, my boy.†
Now what, Simo?

SIMO:

Go inside, just take your time and look
around.   815

THEOPROPIDES:

Very nice, considerate. I thank you kindly.

SIMO:

You're quite wel-
come.

(TRANIO further "sells" his master on
the qualities of the house.)

TRANIO:

Look at what a vestibule it has; observe the wonderful front
path.

THEOPROPIDES:

Splendid, splendid, oh, by Pollux—

TRANIO:

Take a good look at those
pillars.

---

†sensitive of you, my boy . . . Theopropides thinks Tranio is being humanus. This is the
only time Plautus employs the adjective to connote anything like "humane," in the
manner of Terence's famous homo sum: humani nil a me alienum puto (Heauton
Timorumenos, line 77), "I am a man: I consider nothing human alien to me."

*(ironically gestures to the audience that he means
the two oldsters)*

Solid, strong, and oh so thick. Oh yes, dear Master, oh so
thick!

THEOPROPIDES:

Never have I seen more pretty pillars.

SIMO:

And the price I paid— 820
Pretty penny, even long ago.

TRANIO:

(to THEOPROPIDES*)*   You hear that "long ago"?
He can scarcely keep from weeping.

THEOPROPIDES:

(to SIMO*)*   How much did you pay
for them?

SIMO:

Paid three hundred drachmae for them both; delivery was
extra, too.

THEOPROPIDES:

(examining more closely)

Hercules! I see they're not as good as what I first believed.

TRANIO:

Why?

THEOPROPIDES:

Because, by Pollux, they've got termite trouble, both
of them.   825

TRANIO:

(again, ironically to the audience, suggesting the oldsters)

Past their prime is what I'd say's the major trouble with them
both.
Still and all, they'd do quite well, if we'd just throw some
tar on them.
They're well built. No pasta-eating *foreign* workmen† did the
job.

---

†*pasta-eating* foreign *workmen* . . . There is a double (and doubly ironic) Roman
reference here. What I have rendered as *pasta* is, in the Latin, *puls,* a kind of bland
porridge which was the Romans' staple food. "Foreign" translates Plautus' *barbarus,*

Also, sir, observe the door joint.

THEOPROPIDES:

Yes, I see.

TRANIO:

Terrific dolts!

THEOPROPIDES:

Dolts, what dolts?

TRANIO:

Excuse me, sir, I meant "terrific bolts,"
of course.   830

Seen enough?

THEOPROPIDES:

The more I see, the more I really like the house!

TRANIO:

(to mock them still further, points above the doorway)

See the picture painted there—the crow who's mocking two
old vultures?

THEOPROPIDES:

I don't see a thing.

TRANIO:

But *I* do. I can see the crow is standing
Right between the vultures and by turns he twits at each of
them.

Look at me, just look at me, and tell me if you see the crow.   835

(THEOPROPIDES *turns.*)

See the crow?

THEOPROPIDES:

(confused)   Why, no, I see no crow of any kind at all.

TRANIO:

Look in your direction, then, although the crow's not in your
sight.

Maybe if you glance about, you'll catch a glimpse of those
two vultures.

"barbarian," which is how the Greeks were wont to refer to the Romans, to the
latters' displeasure. This bit of self-mockery, then, has Plautus saying—to Romans—
"no lousy Roman workman made this!" Cf. note on *Braggart Soldier*, line 211,
p. 20.

THEOPROPIDES:

(frustrated)

Stop this, will you, I can't see a painted bird of any sort!

TRANIO:

Well, forget it, I forgive you. At your age, it's tough to spot.   840

THEOPROPIDES:

What I can see I adore, I'll tell you that. I just adore it!

SIMO:

Look some more; you'll find it worth the effort.

THEOPROPIDES:

Pollux, good
advice!

SIMO:

(calling to a slave inside his house)

Boy, come here and take this fellow round the house and all
the bedrooms.

(to THEOPROPIDES*)*

Can't take you around myself. I've got some business in the
forum.

THEOPROPIDES:

(feeling very smart)

Never mind a runaround from anyone; I need no leading.   845
When it comes to being taken in, I'm taken in by no one.   846–

SIMO: 847

Even into houses?

THEOPROPIDES:

(smiles)   No one ever takes me in.

SIMO:

Then go!

THEOPROPIDES:

In I go.

TRANIO:

But wait—beware the dog!

THEOPROPIDES:

(unbrave)   Y-you beware for me!

TRANIO:

(now an impromptu dog act)

Dog! Hey, dog! Go 'way! Go kill yourself! Go right to hell!   850
Dog, go, dog! *(to* THEOPROPIDES) The dog won't go. *(to*
                                           "dog") Go, dog!

SIMO:

                              That little thing can't hurt you.†
She's as harmless as all other pregnant pooches. Go, be brave!
Forum for myself for now. Farewell.

                    (He walks off.)

THEOPROPIDES:

          (calling after SIMO)   Farewell—and many
                                             thanks.

Tranio, be good enough to get someone to take that dog off.
Even though she isn't . . . fearsome.

TRANIO:

(peeking at the "dog" again) Look at her—so sweetly
                                           sleeping.   855
You don't want to have the people think you're frightened.

THEOPROPIDES:

          (halfheartedly)   No—you're right.
Follow me inside now.

TRANIO:

(grandiloquent)   Sir, there's nothing can deter me from
                                             you.

          (They both enter SIMO's *house.*
          After a pause [musical interlude?],
       enter PHANISCUS, *slave to young* CALLIDAMATES.
       He sings of the joys of good slave behavior.)

PHANISCUS:

It's the slaves who are fault-free and *still* fear the whips
   Who serve masters best.
The slaves who fear nothing, they earn themselves some-
                                           thing.   860
   They'll pay for their folly—they'll soon be distressed.
All they're doing is training for sprinting. They run. When
                                     they're caught,

---

†*can't hurt you* . . . The translator does not know whether it was a stuffed dog, a
painted dog, a real dog, or an imaginary one. Perhaps the last guess is best (and least
troublesome for the producer).

They see it's a nest egg† of torture they've bought.
   For the sake of my skin is how I always act.   868
   So I keep it intact.
If my hand is commanded, my roof will stay strong.   870
Let it rain in on others, let others do wrong.
For however the slaves treat their master, that treatment they
                         see:
He's good if they're good; if they're bad, bad he'll be.
Our own slaves at home are the worst on this earth;
Their "goods" are expended, bad treatment is all that they're
                       worth.   875
   Just now we were commanded to meet Master here,
   But not one volunteer!
They all mocked me for going, the duties I'm showing,
   I've gone out and my goodness will pay:
I'm the one single slave to fetch Master today,   880
   So that breakfast for them will be cowhide to eat.

          (smiles)

   I am one slave who's too good to be beat.
I don't really care about *their* backs, I just care for mine.
They'll be drawn and quartered, *I'll* do what I'm ordered . . .
              and be fine.

(Another slave, PINACIUM, *rushes in after* PHANISCUS.*)*

PINACIUM:
   Wait, Phaniscus!
   Stop a mite!
PHANISCUS:

        (haughtily)

   Don't annoy me!
PINACIUM:
   What a monkey!
   Won't you wait—you parasite?

---

†*nest egg* . . . In Latin, *peculium,* the private funds which slaves were urged to amass to buy their freedom. The better the slave, the larger his *peculium.* No need to say how bad a fellow with a *peculium* of trouble is. For another meaning of *peculium,* see the note on lines 250ff.

PHANISCUS:

I, a parasite?

PINACIUM:

(sarcastically)

Wherever you see food—you bite.

PHANISCUS:

Well, *I* enjoy it. You drop dead.

PINACIUM:

Talk tough—you share the master's bed!† 890

PHANISCUS:

You're blurring my eyes. Whenever you talk, there are fumes
that arise!

PINACIUM:

You're a maker of counterfeit coins and counterfeit groins.‡

PHANISCUS:

Nothing you do, boy, will make me lose tether.
Our master knows me.

PINACIUM:

But, of course! You've been sleeping 894—
together! 895

PHANISCUS:

Sober up, and don't curse me.

PINACIUM:

I know you can't bear me,
I feel quite the same about you.

PHANISCUS:

Kindly spare me.
Your lecture's a bore.

PINACIUM:

Well, I'll knock on the door.

(knocks at the ''haunted'' house, calls grandiloquently)

Is there a mortal to halt my great fistic assault on this portal? 899—
900

(to audience)

---

†*share the master's bed* . . . Yes. A homosexual joke.
‡Pierre Grimal of the Sorbonne suggests that this odd line was a joke—a pun in the
Greek original, whose innuendo is made clear in the lines that follow.

Not a soul at the door.
Suitable for disreputable people—they simply ignore.
But I'd better take care
Not to get myself singed in their flaming affair.

    (PINACIUM and PHANISCUS stand at the door,
       periodically knocking [in pantomime]
       while the next dialogue takes place.

    TRANIO *and* THEOPROPIDES *come out of* SIMO'S *house.*
       The slave is really baiting his master.)

TRANIO:
Tell me how the deal seems to you now.
THEOPROPIDES:

                    I'm overjoyed with it!

TRANIO:
Too expensive, do you think?
THEOPROPIDES:

              Expensive? Oh, by Pollux, never 905
Ever have I seen a house just tossed away!
TRANIO:

                    So then you're
                    pleased.

THEOPROPIDES:
"Pleased"? you ask me? Hercules, I'm more than that, I'm
                    super-pleased!
TRANIO:
How about the women's quarters? What a portico—
THEOPROPIDES:

                    Fantastic!
I don't think you'd find a public portico that's any bigger.
TRANIO:
Actually, your son and I, we personally toured the city, 910
Measuring the public porticoes.
THEOPROPIDES:

              You did?
TRANIO:

              And ours *is* biggest.

THEOPROPIDES:
What a luscious, lovely deal. By Hercules, if someone offered

Half a dozen silver talents, cash in hand, to buy this house
here,

I'd refuse it.

TRANIO:

Even if you tried to take it, *I'd* prevent you.

THEOPROPIDES:

I would say our capital is well invested in this deal.   915

TRANIO:

I don't blush to say how much I prompted and promoted this,
Forcing him to borrow cash on interest from the moneylender,
Giving it to Simo as deposit. . . .

THEOPROPIDES:

Lad, you saved the ship!
And we owe the moneylender eighty minae?

TRANIO:

Nothing more.

THEOPROPIDES:

He'll be paid today.

TRANIO:

You're smart. That way, there'll be no
complications.   920
Or—you could give me the cash, and I'll go pay the man
myself.

THEOPROPIDES:

(warily)

Give the cash to you? Some little trick is lurking in that
thought.

TRANIO:

(irony-clad protestation)

Would I ever dare to fool you for a fact—or even just for fun?

THEOPROPIDES:

Would I ever dare to *not* distrust you, or be *off* my guard?

TRANIO:

Since I've been your slave, have I bamboozled you in any
way?   925

THEOPROPIDES:

That's because I've been on guard. So thank me and my wits
for that.

Being on my guard with you is proof I'm smart.

TRANIO:

(aside)   I quite agree.

THEOPROPIDES:

(an order to TRANIO*)*

To the country now, and tell my son I'm back.†

TRANIO:

At your
command.

THEOPROPIDES:

Have him sprint with you back to the city—at full speed.

TRANIO:

Yessir.   930

*(*TRANIO *starts off, then stops to address the audience.)*

Now I'll join my fellow fighters by arriving through the rear
guard

To report the situation's calmed—and he's been beaten back.

*(*TRANIO *now skips down the alley between the two houses
to get into the "haunted" one through the back door.*

*Our attention now returns to the two slaves,
who have kept knocking at the "haunted" front door in pantomime
all during the* TRANIO-THEOPROPIDES *conversation.)*

PHANISCUS:

Not a sound of merrymaking, as there used to be.
I can't hear the singing of a musical girl—or anyone.

THEOPROPIDES:

(finally noticing the two servants)

Now what is this? Whatever do those people seek at my old
house?   935

Wonder what they want, what they are peeking at.

PINACIUM:

I'll knock
again.

---

†*tell my son I'm back* . . . Of course no one ever told Theopropides his son was in the
country—at least not in the text as we have it. Nobody in the audience would notice the
inconsistency.

Open up! Hey, Tranio, come loose the locks!

THEOPROPIDES:

                                   What farce is this?

PHANISCUS:

Open up—we've come to fetch our master, we were ordered
                                                    to.

THEOPROPIDES:

(calls over)

Hey, you boys, what are you doing, what's this beating on
                                          the house?

PINACIUM:

Hey, old man, why do you ask about what's no concern of
                                     yours?   940

THEOPROPIDES:

No concern of mine?

PINACIUM:

                   Unless you've just been made a new
                                            official,†
Authorized to make interrogations and to spy and eavesdrop.

THEOPROPIDES:

Where you stand is my own house.

PINACIUM:

                              Has Philolaches sold the
                                          place?

PHANISCUS:

(to PINACIUM*)*

Maybe that old geezer's simply trying to bamboozle us.

THEOPROPIDES:

(firmly)

Look, I speak the truth. Now tell me what's your business
                                             here.

PHANISCUS:

                                   It's this: 945

---

†*a new official* . . . There is no exact English equivalent for the Roman *praefectus,* a
kind of city administrator.

Here is where our master's boozing.

PHANISCUS: *(sic)* THEOPROPIDES:

                              Boozing here?

PHANISCUS:

                                    That's what
                                    I said.

THEOPROPIDES:
I don't like your cheekiness, my boy.

PHANISCUS:

                              We're here to pick him
                              up.

THEOPROPIDES:
Pick who up?

PINACIUM:

              Our master. Must we tell you all this twenty
                                        times?

THEOPROPIDES:

              (to PHANISCUS, *ignoring* PINACIUM*)*

Since you seem a decent chap, I'll tell you: no one lives here
                                        now.

PHANISCUS:
Doesn't that young Philolaches live right here inside this
                              house?   950

THEOPROPIDES:
Used to live here. He moved out of this house quite a while
                                        ago.

PHANISCUS:

              (whispers to PINACIUM*)*

This old geezer's mad for sure. *(to* THEOPROPIDES*)* You're
                              very wildly wrong, kind sir.
For, unless he moved last night—or earlier today—I'm certain
Philolaches lives here.

THEOPROPIDES:

              No one's lived here for six months.

PINACIUM:

                              You're dreaming.

THEOPROPIDES:
Dreaming?

PINACIUM:

Dreaming.

THEOPROPIDES:

(to PINACIUM*)* Don't butt in. Allow me to converse
with him. 955

(now to PHANISCUS*)*

No one lives here.

PHANISCUS:

Someone lives here now, and also yester-
day . . .
And the day before, the day before, the day before, et cetera.
Since his father went abroad, the party's been continuous.

THEOPROPIDES:

What is this?

PHANISCUS:

No intermission in the wining or the dining,
Or the wenching, Greeking-up, inviting women skilled in
music. 960

THEOPROPIDES:

Who's been doing this?

PHANISCUS:

Why, Philolaches, sir.

THEOPROPIDES:

What Philo-
laches, boy?

PHANISCUS:

Son of, I believe, one Theopropides.

THEOPROPIDES:

(aside) He's killing me!
If he tells the truth, he kills me. First I ought to follow further.

(to PHANISCUS*)*

So you say this person Philolaches has been boozing here—
With your master?

PHANISCUS:

Yessir.

THEOPROPIDES:

Boy, you're more a fool than you
first seemed. 965

Are you sure you didn't stop to have a little snack somewhere,
Having just a teeny-weeny bit too much to drink?

PHANISCUS:

                              Why so?

THEOPROPIDES:

Maybe it's an error and you chose the wrong house by
                                        mistake.

PHANISCUS:

Sir, I'm well aware of where I'm going, and the place I'm at.
Philolaches lives here—he's the son of Theopropides.   970
When his father went abroad on business, then the young
                                        man freed a

Music girl.

THEOPROPIDES:

              What? Philolaches?

PHANISCUS:

                        Philematium—the girl.

THEOPROPIDES:

              (almost afraid to ask)

How much?

PHANISCUS:

        Only thirty.

THEOPROPIDES:

                  Thirty talents?

PHANISCUS:

                        Thirty minae, sir.†

THEOPROPIDES:

              (in a state of shock)

So . . . he freed the girl . . .

PHANISCUS:

        (nodding)   For thirty minae, yes, indeed, sir.

---

†*thirty minae, sir* . . . Phaniscus' reply to the old man contains an exclamation to
Apollo in Greek. I thought it best to drop it entirely rather than confuse the issue by
using French—which is the standard practice of translators who render the occasional
Greek phrases which pop up in Plautus. His audience had at least a smattering of
(Sicilian) Greek.

THEOPROPIDES:

>   *(still in disbelief)*

Thirty minae . . . really . . . spent by Philolaches for a woman?

PHANISCUS:

Really.

THEOPROPIDES:

>   Then he freed her?

PHANISCUS:

>   Really.

THEOPROPIDES:

>   Following his father's faring   975
Forth for foreign fields, the fellow fell to full-time festive
>   boozing†
With your master?

PHANISCUS:

>   Really.

THEOPROPIDES:

>   *(almost too afraid to ask)*

>   Tell me, has he bought the house
>   next door?

PHANISCUS:

No, not really.

THEOPROPIDES:

>   Was there a down payment to the man who
>   lives there?

PHANISCUS:

No, not really.

THEOPROPIDES:

>   That's the finish!

PHANISCUS:

>   Yes—he finished his own
>   father.

THEOPROPIDES:

So—your tale is truth.

---

†*full-time festive boozing* . . . My fanfare of *f*'s suggests Plautus' fantastic fit of alliteration, all with the letter *p*, e.g.:

>   *Et postquam eius hinc pater*
>   *Sit profectus peregre, perpotasse* . . . etc. (lines 976–977)

All of this has an ironic echo in line 983, *perdidit patrem*, ''father's fully finished.''

PHANISCUS:

> Would it were fiction! You his father's
> friend?   980

THEOPROPIDES:

(nods "yes")

How do you foretell his father's fall in fortune?

PHANISCUS:

> That's not all.

Thirty minae is a straw compared to other wild expenses.

THEOPROPIDES:

(half aside)

Father's fully finished.

PHANISCUS:

> And from one slave, one unholy terror:

Tranio, a sinful rogue who'd even bankrupt Hercules!†
Oh, by Pollux, how I pity pitifully that boy's poor father.   985
When he finds this out, the fellow's little heart will fall apart!

THEOPROPIDES:

(agonized)

If the things you say are true—

PHANISCUS:

> What profit, sir, would lying
> get me?

PINACIUM:

(knocking)

Hey, will someone open up?

PHANISCUS:

(to PINACIUM)   Why are you knocking—no one's
> there!

I suppose they've moved the party to another place. Let's
> go . . .

---

†*bankrupt Hercules* . . . The Latin refers to *quaestus Herculis,* "the profits of Hercules."
The mythical strong man was also a god of gain, as he would be offered a tithe of any
great monies that might come a Roman's way. Thus, to bankrupt Hercules would be to
ruin the richest person in the universe.

(The two slaves start to exit.)

THEOPROPIDES:

(calling)

Boy—

PHANISCUS:

(to PINACIUM*)*

. . . and search some more for Master. Follow me.

PINACIUM:

I'll follow you. 990

THEOPROPIDES:

Boy—you can't just go.

PHANISCUS:

(going)   You have your freedom to protect your
back.†
I have no protection for my own . . . unless I serve my master.

(With this, PHANISCUS *and* PINACIUM *leave the stage.)*

THEOPROPIDES:

(in total consternation)

By Hercules, I'm finished. Why, from what I hear,
I haven't traveled back and forth from Egypt,
But through the vastest reaches, farthest beaches too.   995
I've circled so, I don't know where I am right now.

(looks offstage)

I'll soon find out, for here's the man who sold my son
The house. *(to* SIMO*)* How are you?

SIMO:

(entering)   Coming from the forum
home.

---

†*freedom to protect your back* . . . As already noted, all the nonclever slaves in Plautine comedy (i.e., those unlike Tranio and Palaestrio) are terribly worried about their backs' being whipped because they've disobeyed their masters (e.g., Sceledrus in *Braggart Soldier*, Messenio in *The Brothers Menaechmus*). The dichotomy between this class and the insouciant slave schemers is well drawn in the opening *agon* of this comedy, in the differing attitudes toward punishment of Grumio and Tranio.

THEOPROPIDES:

Did anything that's new transpire in the forum?

SIMO:

Why, yes.

THEOPROPIDES:

Well, what?

SIMO:

I saw a funeral.†

THEOPROPIDES:

And so?   1000

SIMO:

The corpse was new: he'd just transpired recently.
At least, that's how I heard it told.

THEOPROPIDES:

Oh, go to hell!

SIMO:

It's your own fault, you busybodied me for news.

THEOPROPIDES:

But look, I've just come back from overseas.

SIMO:

(sarcastically)   I'm sorry
I can't ask you to dinner. I'm invited out.‡   1005

THEOPROPIDES:

Look, I'm not hinting—

SIMO:

(jocular)   But tomorrow's dinner, then—
I'll let you ask me—if nobody else does first.

THEOPROPIDES:

Look, I'm not hinting for that, either. If you're free,
Please give me your attention now.

SIMO:

Of course, of course.

THEOPROPIDES:

From what I know, you've gotten forty minae from   1010

---

†*I saw a funeral* . . . Simo's "what's new" quip is rather grim. It may be merely a kind
of sick joke (uncharacteristic of Plautus), or else an oblique way of an old man saying,
"There's not much time left . . . for either of us." Since the play celebrates celebration,
i.e., living-it-up, this latter suggestion seems more likely.
‡*I'm invited out* . . . Evidently it was a custom (in Greece? Rome?) to invite a newly
arrived friend to dinner. Cf. line 1129, where Callidamates does indeed offer old
Theopropides a welcome-back meal.

My son.

SIMO:

From what *I* know, I've gotten no such thing.

THEOPROPIDES:

From Tranio, his slave?

SIMO:

That's *more* impossible.

THEOPROPIDES:

The first deposit that he gave to you?

SIMO:

You're dreaming!

THEOPROPIDES:

(now suspicious of SIMO's *motives)*

Oh no—you're dreaming if you hope this is the way
You'll cancel our negotiation by some masquerade.

SIMO:

I'd cancel what?

THEOPROPIDES:

The deal concluded with my son
While I was gone.

SIMO:

(surprised)   Negotiations with your son—
While you were gone? What were the terms? What was the
                                        date?   1020

THEOPROPIDES:

To start with, I still owe you eighty minae . . . cash.

SIMO:

Oh no, you don't—*(stops, thinks)* Well, if you say so, then
                              . . . pay up!
A deal's a deal, don't try to duck out with a dodge.

THEOPROPIDES:

I don't deny the debt at all. I'll gladly pay.
But you behave, and don't deny you got the forty.   1025

SIMO:

By Pollux, look me in the eye and tell me this:
What did they say you bought with all the cash?

THEOPROPIDES:

Your house.

[That's why I toured your portico and women's quarters.
SIMO:

Why, Tranio told me a wholly different story:]†
He said you were about to give your son a wife   1027
And wanted to add women's quarters to your house.
THEOPROPIDES:

I wanted to build . . . over *there*?
SIMO:

                              That's what he said.

THEOPROPIDES:

Oh no, I'm lost, I'm absolutely speechless.   1030
Oh, neighbor, I'm forever finished.
SIMO:

               (suspecting)   Tranio
Has started something?
THEOPROPIDES:

                    No, he's finished everything!
He flim-flammed me today in a disgraceful way.
SIMO:

What's this?
THEOPROPIDES:

          The situation can be summarized:
He flim-flammed me today for good, forevermore.   1035
But now, I beg you, Simo, aid me and abet me.
SIMO:

In what?
THEOPROPIDES:

          Please let me go with you back to your house.
SIMO:

I will.
THEOPROPIDES:

          Then give me several slaves and several whips.
SIMO:

They're yours.
THEOPROPIDES:

               And while you do I'll tell you everything—
The many-splendored ways he put me in a haze!   1040

---

†The bracketed lines are the translator's conjecture of an extremely fragmentary text.

(The two old men exit into SIMO'*s house.*

A pause [musical interlude?].
TRANIO *struts happily out of* THEOPROPIDES' *house.)*

TRANIO:

Any man who trembles in a crisis isn't worth a pittance.

(aside)

Actually I wonder what a "pittance" means—I'd love to
                                                    know.

(to the audience)

Anyway, when Master sent me countryward to get his son,
I sneaked off in secret down the alley to our own back   1044
                                                    garden, −1045
Flinging open wide the garden gate we have there in the
                                                    alley,
Leading out my whole entire legion, boy and girl divisions.
When I led my troops out of the siege conditions into safety,†
Then I thought it time to summon all my soldiers in a senate.
But no sooner summoned than the senate moved—to move   1050
                                                    me out!
Seeing how they planned to sell me out in my own forum,
                                                    quickly,
I reacted as men should whenever storms of trouble stir:
Stir the storm up even further. Not a thing could calm it now.
It's for certain there's no way to keep this all from my old 1054
                                                    master.
So I'll seek him out to sign a treaty. I delay myself!   1061
Wait, what's this? I hear the door creak in our neighbor's
                                                    neighborhood.
It's my master! I would like to drink in what he has to say.

*(*TRANIO *sneaks back toward the alley to eavesdrop.*
THEOPROPIDES *enters from* SIMO'*s house, giving instructions
        to the slave whippers he has enlisted.)*

----

†*siege conditions into safety* . . . We note once again the clever slave's predilection for
military language. Cf. the note on line 775.

THEOPROPIDES:

Stand inside the doorway there, all ready to be called to
action,
Then be quick to leap right out and manacle the man with
speed.   1065
I'll just linger here until my flim-flam man comes on the
scene,
Then I'll flim and flam his hide as sure as I'm alive today!

TRANIO:

(to audience)

All is out! Now, Tranio, think up a plan to save yourself!

THEOPROPIDES:

I'll be wise and wily if I want to catch him when he comes,
Won't show him my hook at once; I'll play him out with   1070
lots of line.†
I'll pretend I'm ignorant of everything.

TRANIO:

(sarcastically)   O tricky man!
No one in all Athens could be shrewder than that fellow is.
Fooling him's as hard a task as fooling some great—hunk of
stone.‡

Now I'll broach him and approach. . . .

THEOPROPIDES:

I just can't wait till
that man comes.

TRANIO:

Looking for me, sir? I'm present to present myself to you.   1075

THEOPROPIDES:

*(barely able to conceal his satisfaction
that the victim's here)*

Tranio—hel-*lo*! What's new?

---

†*with lots of line* . . . Theopropides compares himself to a fisherman, Tranio to a fish.
This has led at least one noted scholar to suggest the origin of Tranio's name in the
Greek *thranis*, or swordfish.
‡*hunk of stone* . . . For another ''stupid as a stone'' allusion, cf. *Braggart Soldier*, line
1024.

TRANIO:

> The hicks are coming from the
> sticks.†

Philolaches is en route.

THEOPROPIDES:

> *(still welcoming* TRANIO*)*

> By Pollux, what a nice arrival.‡

Say, our neighbor there is very bold and cunning, as I see it.

TRANIO:

Why?

THEOPROPIDES:

> Denies he ever dealt with you.

TRANIO:

> Denies?

THEOPROPIDES:

> And what is
> more—

Claims you never paid a thing.

TRANIO:

> Oh no, you're joking. He
> denies it?   1080

THEOPROPIDES:

Well?

TRANIO:

I know you're joking; it's not possible that he denies it.

THEOPROPIDES:

Still, he does deny it, and he claims he never sold the house.

TRANIO:

Unbelievable! And he denies we paid him cash for it?

THEOPROPIDES:

He'd be willing to go under oath, if I would like him to,
Swearing that he's never sold the house or gotten any cash.   1085
Still, I claimed he had.

TRANIO:

> What did he answer?

---

†*hicks . . . sticks . . . Veniunt ruri rustici.* Most likely a familiar expression, with a few
extra connotations now lost to us.
‡*what a nice arrival . . .* It is Theopropides who is being ironic here. He is happy over
the arrival of Tranio, his potential victim, not of his son, as he expects Tranio to understand.

THEOPROPIDES:

                              Offered all his
                                      slaves—

All of them to me for trial by torture.†
TRANIO:

                              Oh, he'll never give
                                        them.

THEOPROPIDES:

                    (portentously)

Yes, he will.
TRANIO:

            I'll go inside and look for him.

    (starts to exit)

THEOPROPIDES:

                              No—stay, stay,
                                        stay.

Let's investigate the matter.
TRANIO:
                    (stops)   Why not leave the man to me?   1090
THEOPROPIDES:
Let me get the slaves out here.
TRANIO:

                        You should have done that long
                                              ago.

Or at least have made a legal claim.
THEOPROPIDES:

                              What I want first of all is—

                    (heavy irony)

Trial by torture for the slaves.
TRANIO:

                        Indeed, by Pollux, good idea.

_____

†*trial by torture* . . . Getting at the truth by torturing a man's slaves was, alas, an actual
practice.

(leaps onto altar)†

While you do, I'll sit up on this altar.
THEOPROPIDES:

Why?

TRANIO:

Why, don't you
see?

While I'm here no other slave can flee for refuge from the
torture.   1095

THEOPROPIDES:

(extra sweetly)

Do get up.
TRANIO:

Oh no.

THEOPROPIDES:

Not on the altar, please.

TRANIO:

Why not?

THEOPROPIDES:

Actually . . . I'd *like* the slaves to flee for refuge on the altar.
Then I'll have a stronger case in court and win more money
too.

TRANIO:

Don't keep switching plans of action. Why sow seeds for
further trouble?   1100

After all, these legal things are very tricky, you know that.
THEOPROPIDES:

Do get up. Come over here. I'd like to ask for some advice.
TRANIO:

Here I'll be a fine adviser. Sitting down, I'm so much wiser.
Speaking from a holy spot, I can advise with greater strength.
THEOPROPIDES:

Do get up, no joking. Look at me.

---

†*leaps onto altar* . . . Fleeing to an altar for sanctuary was a familiar practice of slaves
in Greek comedy as well—not to mention Euripidean heroines. (Creusa in Euripides'
Ion is a fine example.) The holy altar meant immunity for the person who sat upon it.
Whether there was always an altar on the Roman stage, from the religious ceremony
which would precede the play, has been a subject of much discussion. Most evidence
suggests that there was indeed a permanent altar as part of the mise-en-scène.

TRANIO:

I'm looking.

THEOPROPIDES:

Do you see? 1105

TRANIO:

Well, I see if someone came between us, he would starve to
death.

THEOPROPIDES:

Why?

TRANIO:

(smiles)

We're both so tricky that we give no food for honest
thought.

(Now THEOPROPIDES *sees that* TRANIO *knows.
He drops his friendly pose.)*

THEOPROPIDES:

Go to hell!

TRANIO:

What's up?

THEOPROPIDES:

You tricked me!

TRANIO:

Did I?

THEOPROPIDES:

Oh, and what a
way you

Egged me on.

TRANIO:

(naïvely) Let's see your face: is any egg still on it now?

THEOPROPIDES:

No, of course not, since you egged me out of every brain
I had! 1110

Every evil deed of yours is now discovered—and in depth.

And from this discovery there's one recovery—in death!

TRANIO:

Well, you'll never get me up from where I sit.

THEOPROPIDES:

But I'll command
that
Fire and firewood be put around you, gallows bird. You'll
roast!

TRANIO:

Don't do that. I'm so much sweeter when I'm boiled, not
roasted up.   1115

THEOPROPIDES:

I'll make an example of you—

TRANIO:

(smiling)   Ah, so I'm exemplary.

THEOPROPIDES:

(angry)

Speak—when I went off abroad, what sort of son did I leave
here?

TRANIO:

Normal type—two eyes, two ears, two hands, two feet, et
cetera.

THEOPROPIDES:

That was not the question.

TRANIO:

Sorry, that was what I felt like
saying.

(peering offstage)

Look—I see your son's best friend, Callidamates, coming here.
Why not wait till he arrives and deal with me when he's at
hand?   1120

(Enter CALLIDAMATES, *now clearheaded and sober.)*

CALLIDAMATES:

(to audience)

After the effects of all my boozing were slept off and under,
Philolaches told me that his father's back from overseas,
Also how that slave had fooled his father as he just arrived.
Philo's too ashamed right now to step into his father's sight.   1125

So our little social circle chose me as ambassador to
Seek the sire and sue for peace. *(sees* THEOPROPIDES*)* But
        look who's here—how wonderful!
        (calls)
Greetings, Theopropides, I'm glad to see you safe and sound,
Back from overseas. Do come to dinner at our house tonight.

THEOPROPIDES:

Hail, Callidamates. Many thanks for dinner—I can't come. 1130

CALLIDAMATES:

Oh, why not?

TRANIO:

           (to THEOPROPIDES*)*

      Go on—or else I'll take the invitation for you.

THEOPROPIDES:

Whipping post—you mock me still?

TRANIO:

                Because I'd go to dinner
                    for you?

THEOPROPIDES:

Well, you won't. I'll see you go where you deserve—right
                    on a cross!

CALLIDAMATES:

           (to THEOPROPIDES*)*

Never mind all this; just say you'll come to dinner.

TRANIO:

                    Well,
                    speak up!

CALLIDAMATES:

           (to TRANIO*)*

Hey, why are you refugeeing on that altar—that's so stupid!† 1135

TRANIO:

        (indicating THEOPROPIDES*)*

---

†*that's so stupid* . . . Callidamates argues that Tranio's very flight to the altar is a
(stupid) confession of guilt. Line given entirely to Callidamates. Cf. Sonnenschein ad
loc.

His arrival frightened me. *(to* THEOPROPIDES) But tell me
                              what you claim I've done.
Now we have an arbitrator for us both, so state your case.

THEOPROPIDES:

I say you corrupted my young son.

TRANIO:

                              Now just a minute, please.
Yes, I will confess: he sinned while you were gone. He freed
                              a girl,
Drew a lot of cash on interest, threw the lot of cash away.   1140
Yet do other boys of noble families do otherwise?†

THEOPROPIDES:

Hercules, I must be careful of you; you're a tricky advocate.

CALLIDAMATES:

Let me be the judge. *(to* TRANIO) Get up, and I'll sit on
                              the altar now.

THEOPROPIDES:

Yes, that's good, get closer to the case.

TRANIO:

          (as CALLIDAMATES *sits next to him)*

                              I fear some trick in this.

          (to CALLIDAMATES)

If you want to sit in my position, take my fear from me.   1145

THEOPROPIDES:

All the rest I rate at nothing. I'm just angry at the way he
Made a fool of me.

TRANIO:

                  Well done it was, and I rejoice in it!
Oldsters with a hoary head should act their age in brains as
                              well.

THEOPROPIDES:

          (to CALLIDAMATES)

What do I do now?

---

†*noble families do otherwise . . .* This could very well be an allusion to aristocratic
youths in Plautus' Rome.

TRANIO:

> Well, if you're friendly with some comic
> author,†
> Go and tell him every way your slave bamboozled you today. 1150
> You'll provide the finest flim-flam plot for any comedy.

CALLIDAMATES:

> *(to* TRANIO*)*

> Quiet, will you? Let me talk a bit. *(to* THEOPROPIDES*)* Do
> listen, sir.

THEOPROPIDES:

> All right.

CALLIDAMATES:

> You know well that I'm the very closest friend your son has
> got.
> Since he's too ashamed to set a single foot in sight of you, 1155
> Knowing that you know all that's been done, he came and
> asked my help.
> Now I beg of you, forgive his youth and folly—he's your son.
> Boys are boys, you know, and when they're young, they play
> so playfully.
> What's been done, we did it both together, and we both
> were wrong.
> All the principal and interest, all the cash we paid to free the
> girl, 1160
> We'll both pay it back, we'll share the cost, and you won't
> pay a thing.

THEOPROPIDES:

> No more eloquent ambassador could come to me on his
> behalf.
> You succeed. I'm now not angry or annoyed at what he did.
> Even while I'm here let him drink up, make love, do what
> he'd like!

---

†*some comic author* . . . Plautus refers by name to the Greek New Comedy playwrights Diphilus and Philemon. There is no reason to believe that this name dropping was in the original on which Plautus based the *Mostellaria*. On the other hand, there is little to be gained from proving that Plautus himself added the references to these authors. What *is* significant, however, is that Tranio, like Pseudolus, another great Plautine clever slave, sees himself as a kind of comic playwright (cf. *Pseudolus*, line 401ff.).

If he feels ashamed at what he's done, that's punishment
                                        enough.   1165

CALLIDAMATES:
Very, very shamed he is.

TRANIO:
                        Now what about forgiving *me*?

THEOPROPIDES:
I'm for—giving you a thousand lashes.

TRANIO:
                        Even if I'm shamed?

THEOPROPIDES:
Hercules, I'll kill you if I live!

CALLIDAMATES:
                        Oh, can't you pardon *all*?
Let him go for my sake. Please forgive whatever wrong he's
                                        done.

THEOPROPIDES:
Anything but that—I would do *anything* for you but that!   1170
No—for every dirty deed, I'll make that dirty fellow bleed.

CALLIDAMATES:
Can't you let him go?

THEOPROPIDES:
                        But look how insolent he's posing there!

CALLIDAMATES:
Tranio, behave yourself.

THEOPROPIDES:

                        (*to* CALLIDAMATES)

                        And you behave—forget all this.
Don't annoy me, while I *beat* this fellow into deadly silence.

TRANIO:
Not a chance of that!

CALLIDAMATES:
                        Please don't take the trouble!   1175

THEOPROPIDES:
Please don't beg.

CALLIDAMATES:
                I beg.

THEOPROPIDES:

Don't beg me, please.

CALLIDAMATES:

Don't beg me
not to beg.
Just this once, I beg you, sir, forgive his wrong—at my
request?

TRANIO:

(to THEOPROPIDES*)*

Why persist? You *know* tomorrow I'll commit some fresh
new wrong.
Then you'll get revenge for both—for what I've done and
what I'll do.

CALLIDAMATES:
Please.

THEOPROPIDES:

(won over)

All right, no punishment. *(to* TRANIO*)* But you be
grateful to your friend.   1180

(turning to spectators)

Now I ask the audience to clap their hands. This is—the
end!

Pronunciation Guide

The following are intended merely to aid actors performing the plays. They are suggestions for easy speakability in English, not attempts to reconstruct the syllable sounds of 200 B.C.

THE BRAGGART SOLDIER

PYRGOPOLYNICES	purr-go-pol-uh-NYE-sees
ARTOTROGUS	ar-tow-TRO-guss
PALAESTRIO	pal-ESS-tree-oh
PERIPLECTOMENUS	perry-plek-TOW-men-uss
SCELEDRUS	SKELL-eh-druss
PLEUSICLES	PLOO-sih-klees
LURCIO†	LURE-kee-oh
PHILOCOMASIUM	FILL-oh-koh-MAY-see-um
ACROTELEUTIUM	AK-row-tell-OO-tee-um
MILPHIDIPPA	mil-fi-DIP-pa
CARIO	CAH-ree-oh

THE BROTHERS MENAECHMUS

PENICULUS	pen-IK-you-luss
MENAECHMUS	muh-NIKE-muss
MESSENIO	muh-SEEN-ee-oh
EROTIUM	eh-ROW-tee-um
CYLINDRUS	sil-IN-druss

---

†I have preferred spelling ''Lurcio'' as above, although there may be a case for ''Lucrio'' (LOO-kree-oh). The actor is welcome to choose.

THE HAUNTED HOUSE

TRANIO	TRAH-nee-oh
GRUMIO	GROO-mee-oh
PHILOLACHES	fill-oh-LOCK-ees
PHILEMATIUM	fill-eh-MAY-tee-um
SCAPHA	SKAH-fah
CALLIDAMATES	kah-LEE-dah-MAH-tees
DELPHIUM	DELL-fee-um
SPHAERIO	SFEAR-ee-oh
THEOPROPIDES	thee-oh-PROH-pih-dees
MISARGYRIDES	miss-AR-guh-REE-dees
SIMO	SY-moh
PHANISCUS	fan-ISS-cuss
PINACIUM	pin-ACE-ee-um

Selected Bibliography

The panoramic survey of all matters regarding Latin drama remains George E. Duckworth's *The Nature of Roman Comedy* (Princeton, 1952). Perhaps in a future edition some scholar will add an appendix dealing with the Menandrian plays discovered since Duckworth's otherwise complete study was published.

W. Beare, *The Roman Stage* (London, 3rd ed. rev., 1964), provides much information on the external aspects of play production in Rome.

F.H. Sandbach offers a succinct introduction to the subject in *The Comedy Theatre of Greece and Rome* (London, 1977).

John Wright's essay on Plautus in *Ancient Writers: Greece and Rome*, ed. T.J. Luce (New York, 1982), contains brief and illuminating discussions of all the extant comedies. By contrast, David Konstan focuses in more depth on only six Plautine plays (*Aulularia, Asinaria, Captivi, Cistellaria, Rudens,* and *Truculentus*) in *Roman Comedy* (New York, 1983).

An overall theory of Plautus' comedic art is presented in my own *Roman Laughter: The Comedy of Plautus* (Cambridge, Mass., 1968; rep. 1971).

Those seeking to undertake their own studies of Plautus should be aware of the useful bibliographies published by *Classical World:* "Scholarship on Plautus since 1950," by John A. Hanson, Parts I and II, *CW* 59 (1965–1966), 101ff., 141ff., and "Scholarship on Plautus 1965–1976," by Erich Segal, *CW* 75, (April–May 1981).

ABOUT THE TRANSLATOR

ERICH SEGAL, Adjunct Professor of Classics at Yale, has also taught at Princeton, Oxford, and the University of Munich. He has earned distinction as both literary scholar and novelist (*Love Story, The Class*).

In addition to these translations, he is the author of several studies of Plautus and other ancient poets, as well as the editor of the *Oxford Readings in Greek Tragedy* (published in America as *Greek Tragedy: Modern Essays in Criticism*).

He is currently completing a book on the history of ancient comedy.

Bantam Classics bring you the world's greatest literature—books that have stood the test of time—at specially low prices. These beautifully designed books will be proud additions to your bookshelf. You'll want all these time-tested classics for your own reading pleasure.

☐	21137	**PERSUASION** Jane Austen	$2.95
☐	21051	**DAVID COPPERFIELD** Charles Dickens	$2.50
☐	21148	**DRACULA** Bram Stoker	$1.95
☐	21044	**FRANKENSTEIN** Mary Shelley	$1.50
☐	21171	**ANNA KARENINA** Leo Tolstoy	$2.95
☐	21035	**THE DEATH OF IVAN ILYICH** Leo Tolstoy	$1.95
☐	21163	**THE BROTHERS KARAMAZOV** Fyodor Dostoevsky	$2.95
☐	21175	**CRIME AND PUNISHMENT** Fyodor Dostoevsky	$2.50
☐	21136	**THE IDIOT** Fyodor Dostoevsky	$3.50
☐	21166	**CANDIDE** Voltaire	$2.25
☐	21130	**THE COUNT OF MONTE CRISTO** Alexandre Dumas	$2.95
☐	21118	**CYRANO DE BERGERAC** Edmond Rostand	$1.75
☐	21048	**SILAS MARNER** George Eliot	$1.75
☐	21089	**FATHERS AND SONS** Ivan Turgenev	$1.95
☐	21032	**THE HUNCHBACK OF NOTRE DAME** Victor Hugo	$1.95
☐	21101	**MADAME BOVARY** Gustave Flaubert	$2.50
☐	21059	**THE TURN OF THE SCREW AND OTHER SHORT FICTION** Henry James	$1.95

Prices and availability subject to change without notice.

Buy them at your local bookstore or use this handy coupon for ordering:

Bantam Books, Inc., Dept. CL, 414 East Golf Road, Des Plaines, Ill. 60016
Please send me the books I have checked above. I am enclosing $_____
(please add $1.25 to cover postage and handling). Send check or money order
—no cash or C.O.D.'s please.

Mr/Mrs/Miss_____

Address_____

City_____ State/Zip_____

CL—12/84

Please allow four to six weeks for delivery. This offer expires 6/85.

SPECIAL MONEY SAVING OFFER

Now you can have an up-to-date listing of Bantam's hundreds of titles plus take advantage of our unique and exciting bonus book offer. A special offer which gives you the opportunity to purchase a Bantam book for only 50¢. Here's how!

By ordering any five books at the regular price per order, you can also choose any other single book listed (up to a $4.95 value) for just 50¢. Some restrictions do apply, but for further details why not send for Bantam's listing of titles today!

Just send us your name and address plus 50¢ to defray the postage and handling costs.